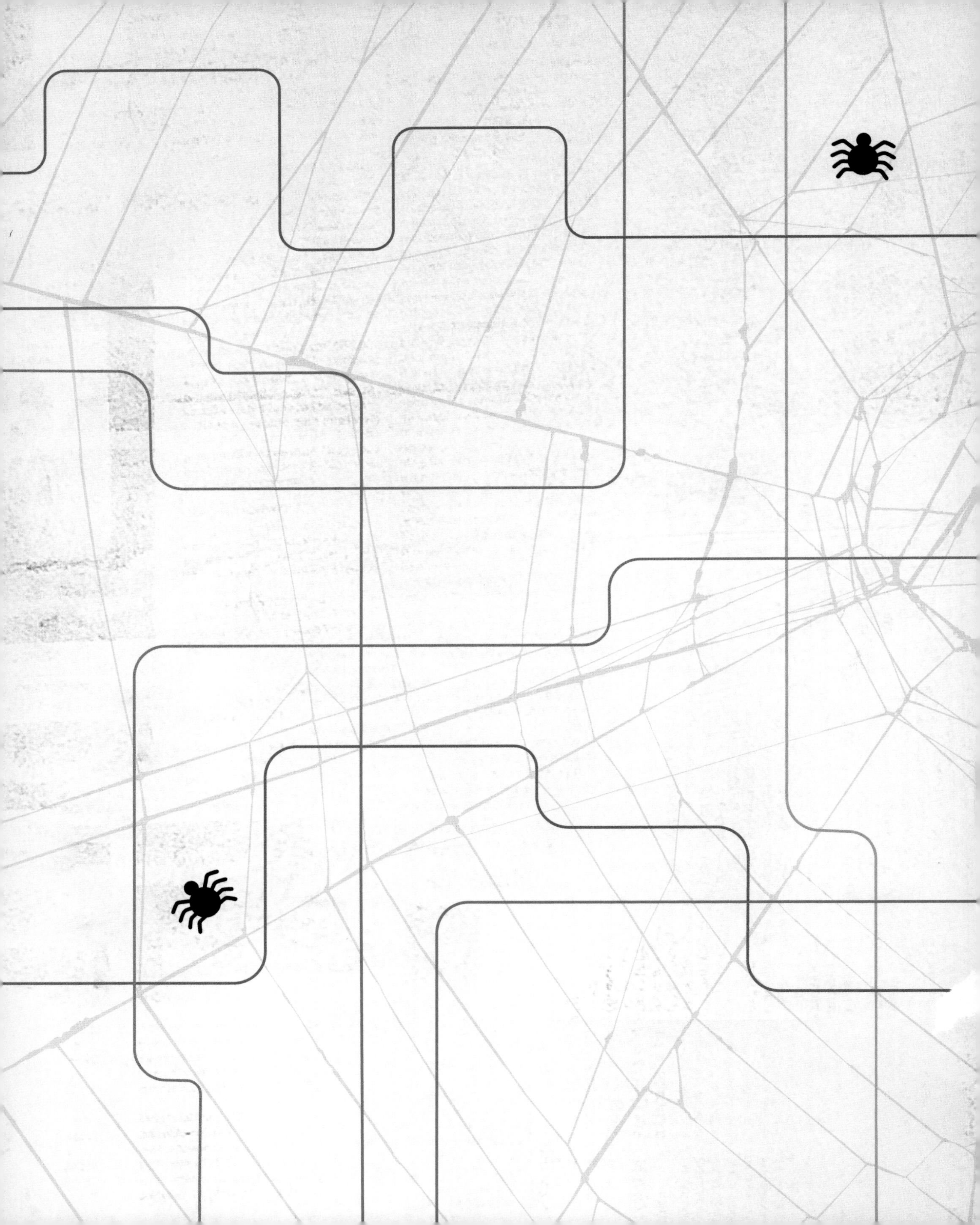

MARVEL

SPIDER-MAN

THE OFFICIAL

COOKBOOK

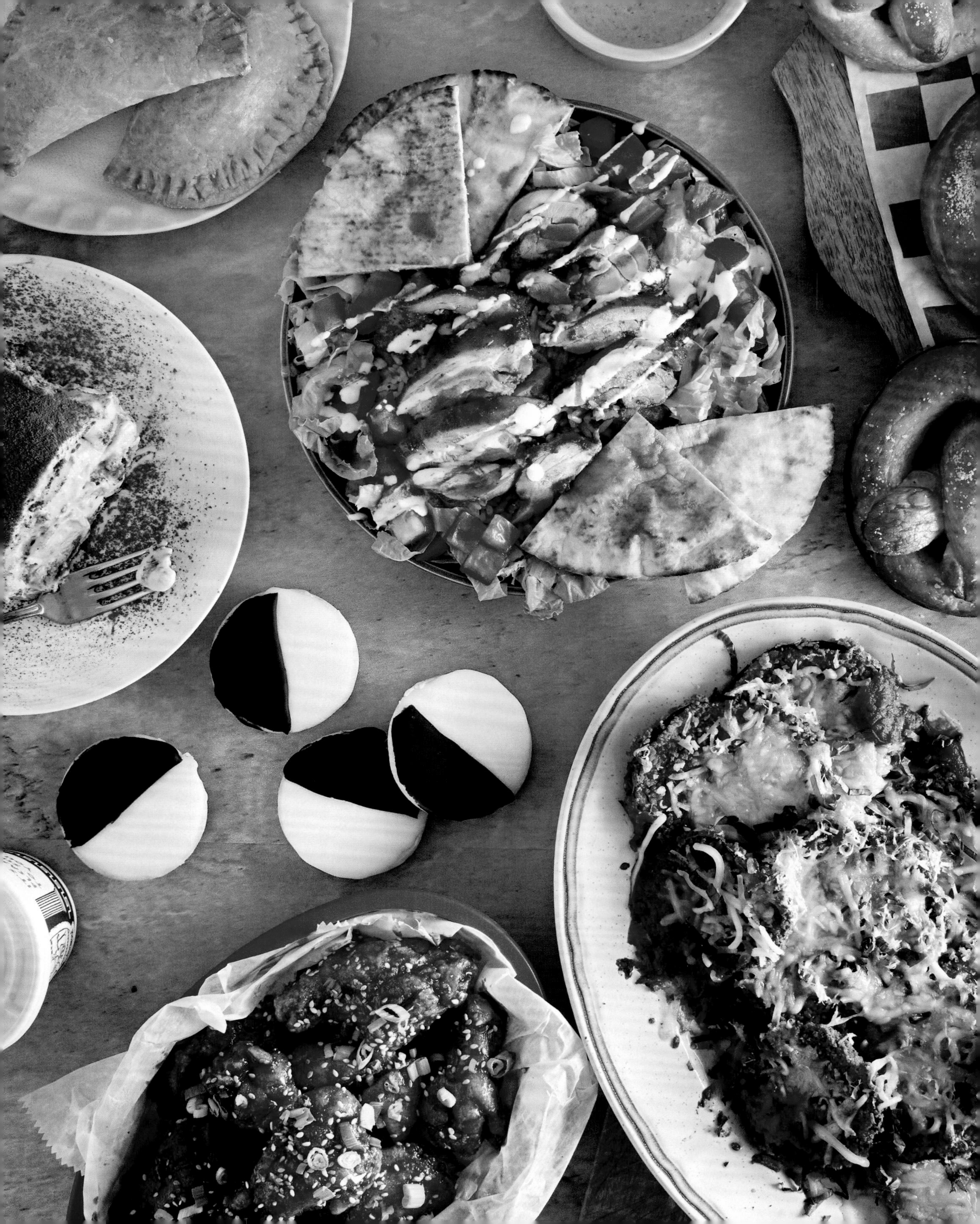

MARVEL

SPIDER-MAN

THE OFFICIAL COOKBOOK

YOUR FRIENDLY NEIGHBORHOOD GUIDE TO CUISINE FROM NEW YORK CITY, THE SPIDER-VERSE, AND BEYOND

Text by Jermaine McLaughlin
Recipes by Paul Eschbach
Contributing Recipes from Von Diaz

INSIGHT
EDITIONS

SAN RAFAEL · LOS ANGELES · LONDON

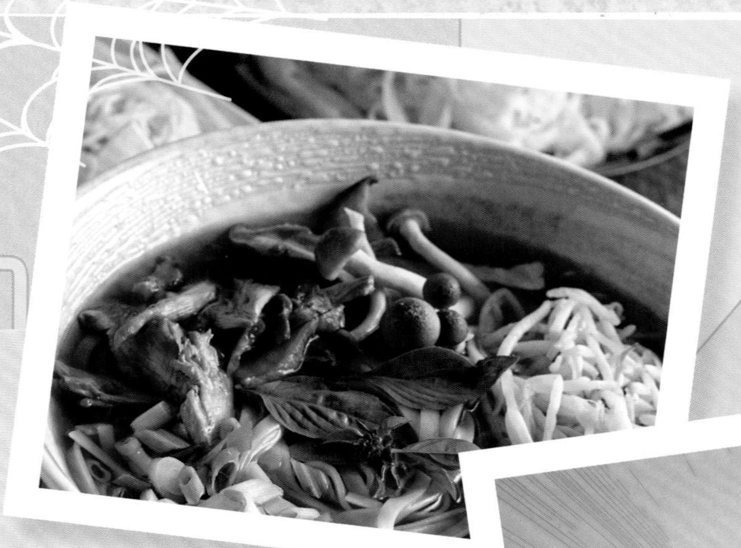

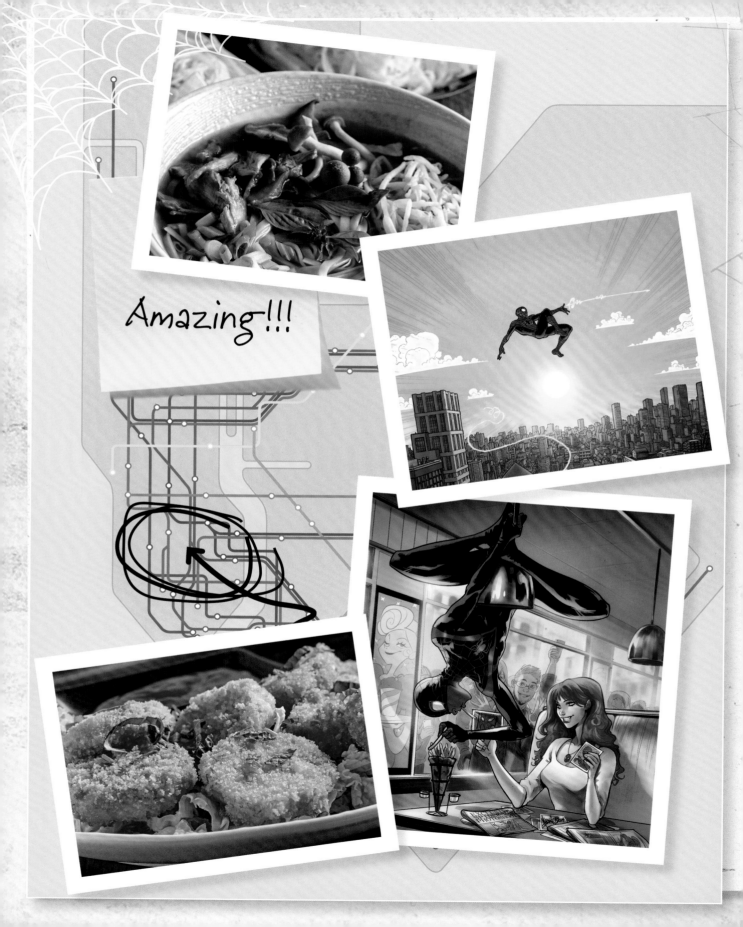

Amazing!!!

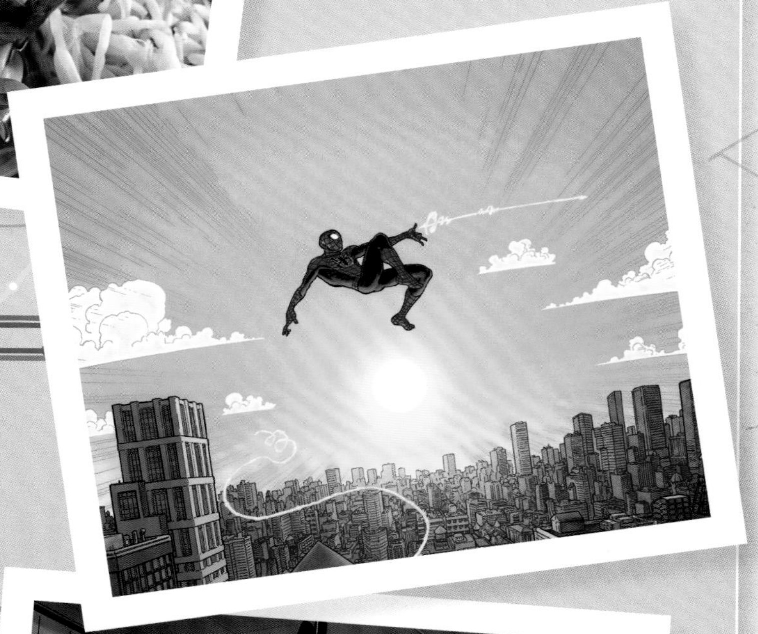

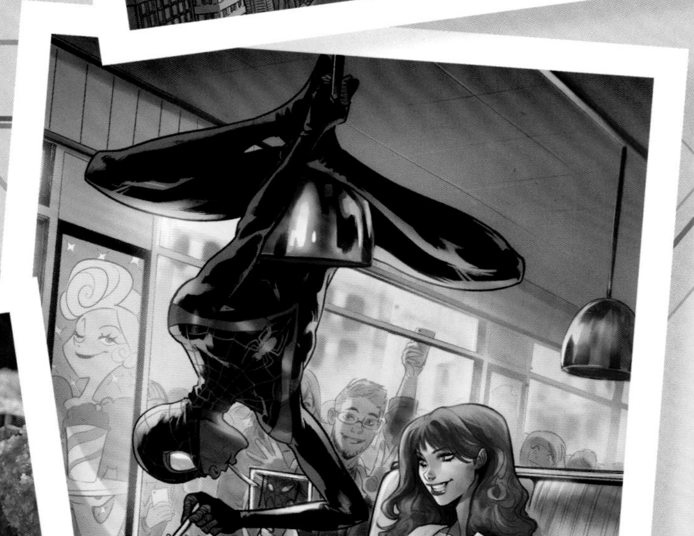

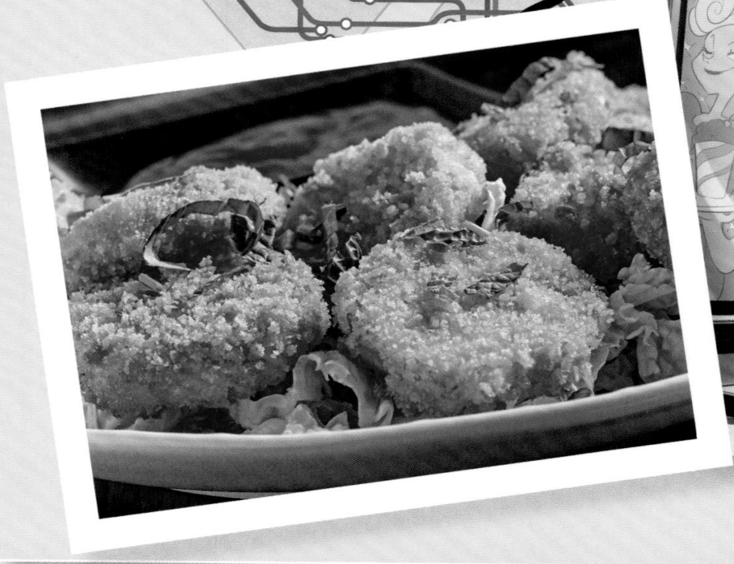

CONTENTS

Hi, your friendly neighborhood Spider-Man here.

As you know, a lot happens in New York. People come from all over to follow a dream or chase an adventure. And occasionally a super villain tries to launch a world-altering scheme. I hear this last bit has been the focus of the *Daily Bugle*'s coverage lately. I have to admit, the tenth time in a week I find myself dealing with the Sinister Six, I start seeing our city the same way. And agreeing with the *Bugle* is not a good look for me. On days like that, I know what I need to do: turn to friends, family, and, of course, food.

After all, New York is one of the great food capitals of the world. I should know. Some would say I'm as synonymous with this town as Central Park, the Empire State Building, and Midtown gridlock. That's why I've put together this cookbook as a guide to my New York and a reminder of what makes this place so special. It's also why I've asked for a little help from some friends. But more on that in a minute. Whether you're new in town, new to this whole super hero gig, or just in need of a fresh perspective (I'm looking at you, Logan), the pages that follow are written for you. You're welcome.

Call it dinner and a show, but I believe every meal comes with its own story. And over the years, I've picked up quite a few. I'll use my adventures through the city, from borough to borough, as way to highlight the food and the people that make NYC such a unique place to be a do-gooder. And it's not just me—I've reached out to friends, allies, and a literal Spider-army of web-spinners to help take you on this culinary journey. And yes, I do have a veritable multiverse of friends and alternate versions of me (for the record, the Multiverse is real, AND IT'S FILLED WITH ME. SO. MUCH. ME!!) who have also agreed to lend a recipe or two to this thing.

Now, some ground rules if you're reading this book: No pics, no DMs, no IMs, telepathic messages, astral projections, or old-school spy cyphers (looking at you, Fury!!) We're keeping our secret IDs secret as we write this, but even with that precaution, we are going as analog with this cookbook as possible. After all, there's a reason why you'll find a line around the block at every supposedly "under-the-radar" restaurant in town.

It goes without saying, but I'll say it anyway: I'm famously fun to work with. After all, I've put in time as an Avenger, as one of the Fantastic Four, running around with my Amazing Friends. Then there's the aforementioned Multiverse of me, and the times I've partnered up with most of you over the years. I know I'm no Spider-Island unto myself. And neither are our friends and neighbors here in New York. That's why I'm giving you all the okay to pass this book along to anyone you trust. Consider it a reminder that the "friendly" part of the job is just as important as the busting heads.

Most importantly, this is a love letter to New York City. Every borough, bridge, and tunnel. Every sleep-deprived citizen. Every unimpressed bodega cat. They're all unique, and they're all a part of this place. Sure, the sights and the sounds may reflect our city's personality, but it's the smells and tastes that capture its heart. This book is, at least for me, a culinary tour of this town we protect. Whether you're new here or have been fighting the good fight for years. So, let's dig in!

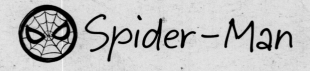

Spider-Man

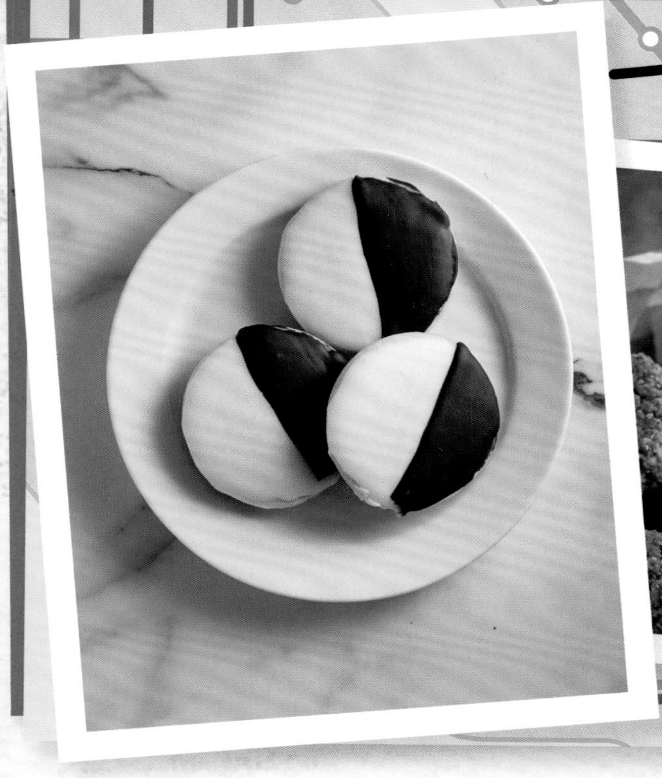

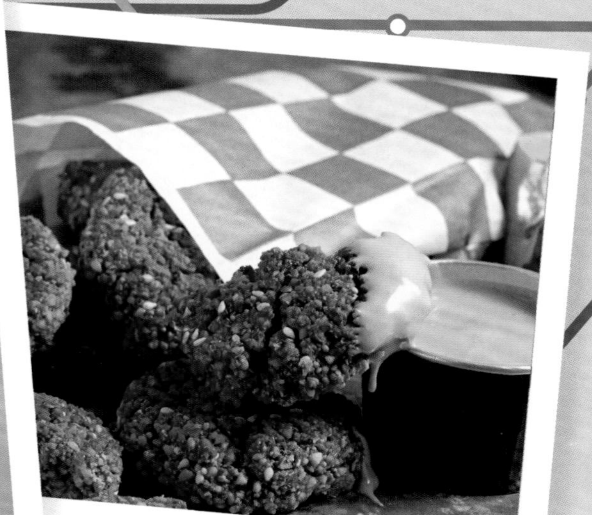

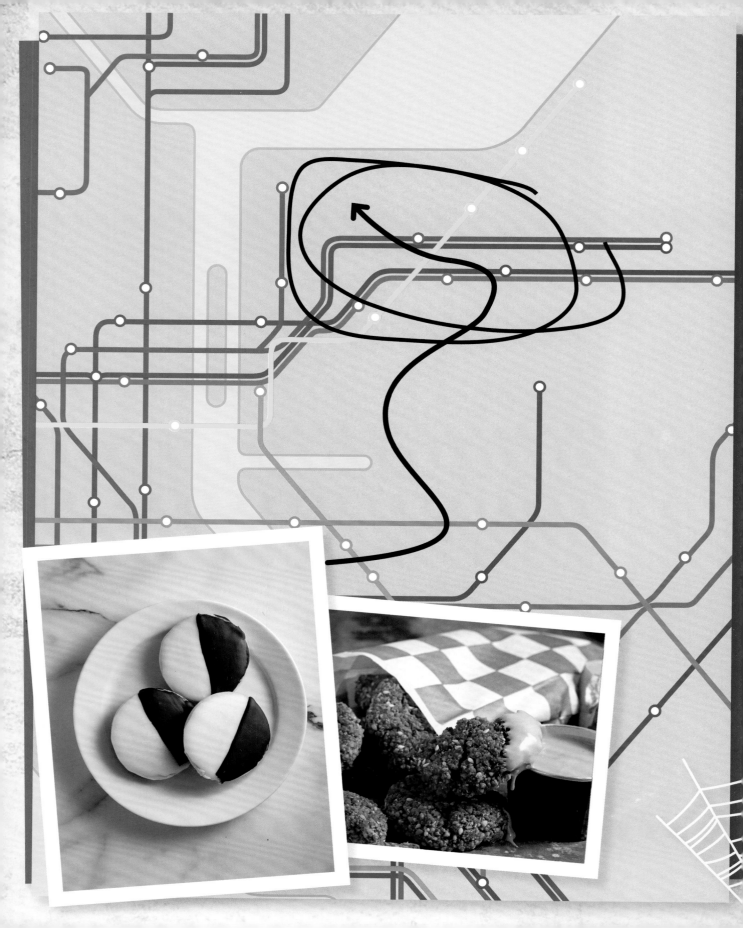

1 QUEENS

We're going to start with a borough near and dear to my early career.

I mean, how can I not get a warm fuzzy when I think about the first time the Vulture dropped me from a thousand feet in the air with no parachute, and how the Tinkerer nearly shocked me into oblivion with a souped-up Taser glove the first time I stormed his secret workshop in Corona Park? Yeah, yeah, those were good times. I did something to upset every well-established super villain in Queens back then. I was kind of persistent about it, so I guess I see where they were coming from.

Anyway, places like Flushing, Jackson Heights, and Forest Hills, especially, are where I initially spread my web wings. (Fun fact: Those wings, purely decorative. Couldn't fly or glide with them for the life of me . . . which would have helped when the Vulture put me in freefall back in the day . . . but again, I digress.)

So join me, if you will, as I take a trip back to the home of a baseball team that means well. There are some amazing residents in Queens who have helped me out in my early career against some of the biggest and baddest of my least favorite bad guys. They really helped this young spider learn to fly. (Again, figuratively. What was I thinking with those wings??)

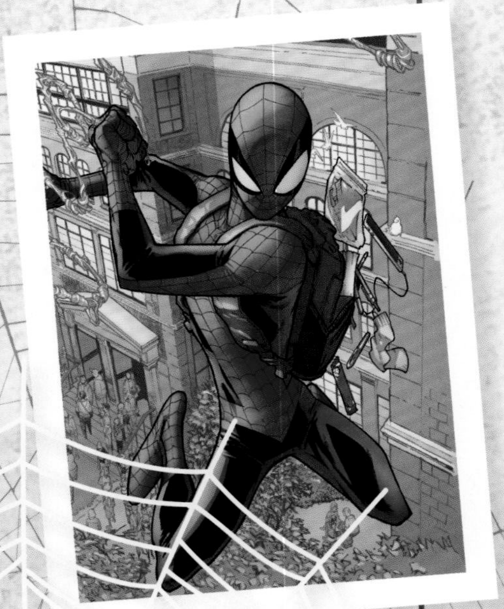

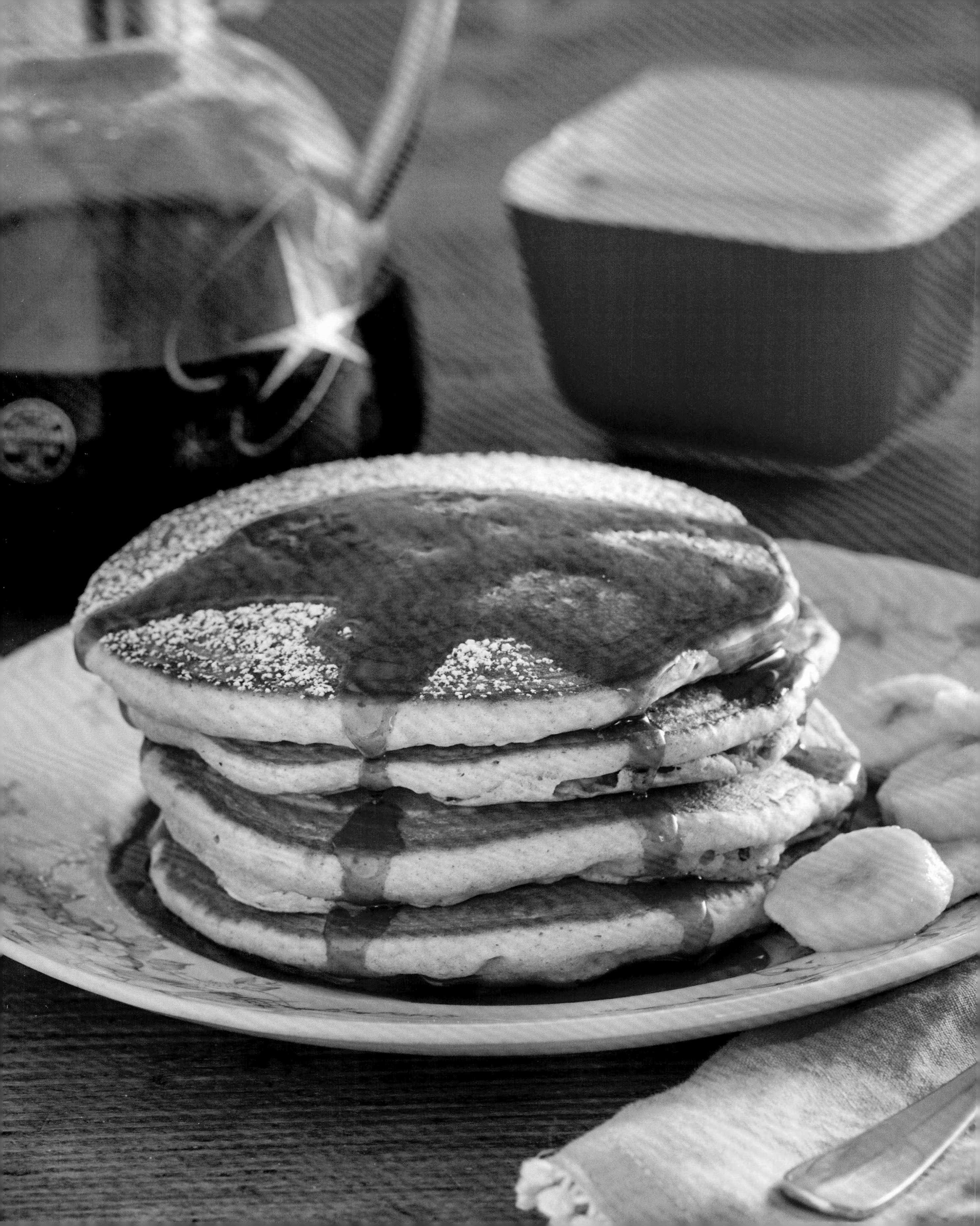

AUNT MAY'S WHEATCAKES

YIELD:
6 PANCAKES

PREP TIME:
10 MINUTES

The first recipe comes from my unofficial PR guy, Peter Parker. I only mention his full name as it's no secret he's developed a knack for being in the right spot to score pictures of me doing everything from catching stalled spaced capsules (I did that, that was me) to getting the tar pounded out of me by a trio of hench-trolls called the Enforcers. He always gets my good side as I'm getting my butt kicked. And his pictures have made the rounds over the years. They've been used by media mogul and all-around grumpy guy J. Jonah Jameson to turn me into public enemy number one aaaand why am I so friendly with this Parker guy? Anyway, he once mentioned this go-to meal that his aunt used to make (more on that delightful woman later). It kept him fueled up as he chased me all around Queens, and later Midtown (capturing my other good side.) He needed all the help he could get when he was starting out. Most of that early stuff was blurry and out of focus. Almost like he had his camera set on auto and had it hanging off a wall at odd angles.

¾ cup whole wheat flour

1 teaspoon baking soda

1 egg

1 cup buttermilk

4 tablespoons melted butter

2 teaspoons powdered sugar

1 banana, sliced

8 tablespoons maple syrup

1. In a medium-sized bowl, mix whole wheat flour with baking soda.

2. In a separate bowl, mix the egg with the buttermilk.

3. Using a spatula, add your egg mix into your flour mix. Be careful not to stir too much, it's okay if there are a few lumps.

4. Gently mix in the melted butter.

5. Place a seasoned or nonstick griddle on medium-high heat and ladle out the batter, a sixth at a time, into individual pancakes. When golden on the bottom side, flip to finish cooking, heating for approximately 3 minutes per side.

6. Shingle your wheatcakes and dust them with powdered sugar.

7. Serve three to a plate, with a side of sliced bananas and 4 tablespoons of maple syrup.

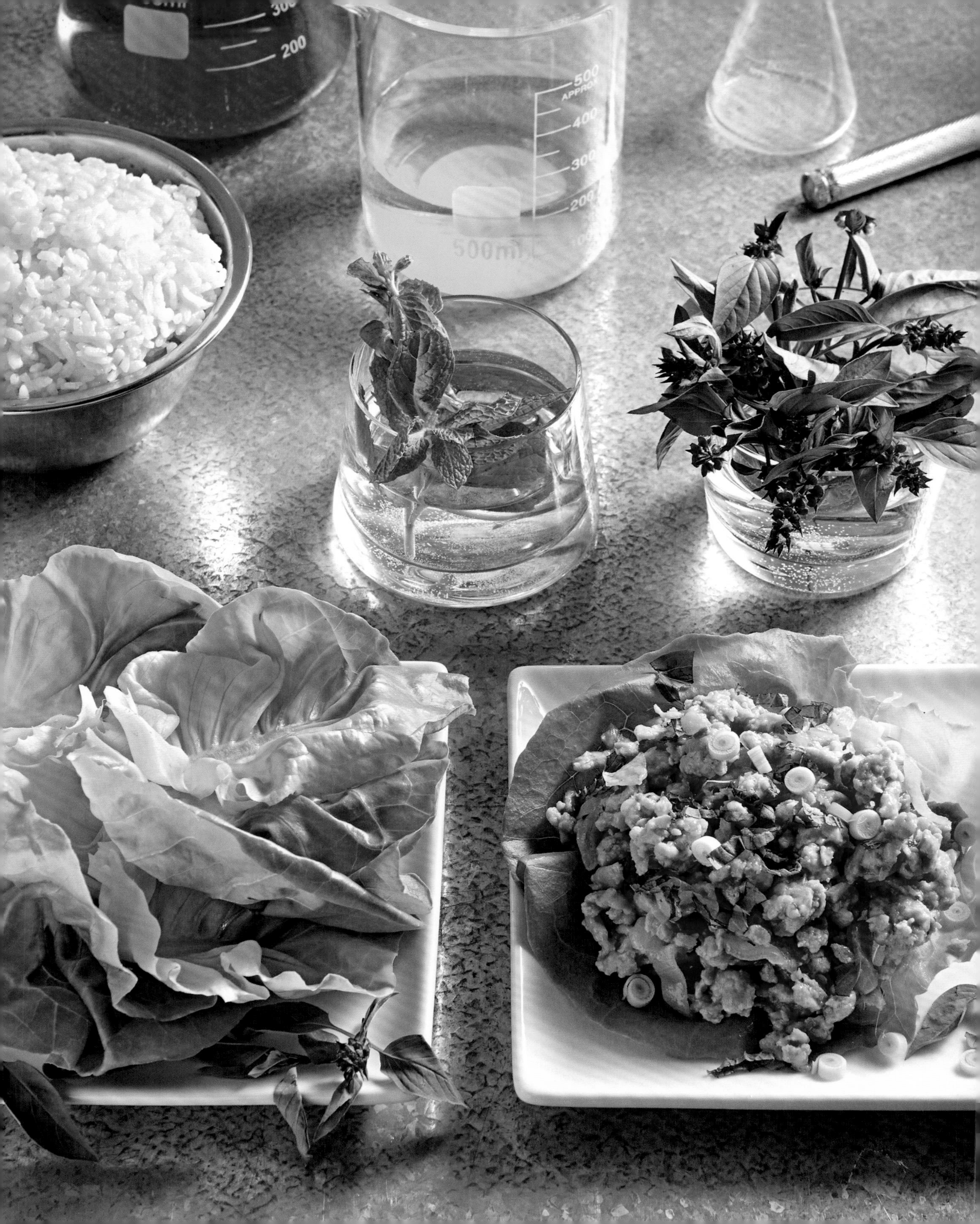
200
500
APPROX
400
300
500mL

CHICKEN LARB

🕷

YIELD:
2 SERVINGS
PREP TIME:
45 TO 60 MINUTES

I've had a, shall we say, *complicated* relationship with one of my most relentless foes, Otto Octavius, aka Doctor Octopus. "Complicated" culminating in that time not so long ago when he put his brain into *my* body and started a Spider-Militia to prove he could be a "Superior Spider-Man" to me. Yes, folks, this is my life. By the way, if I ever belittled, demeaned, out-and-out insulted, or just plain attacked you during that time, I'm sorry, I literally wasn't myself.

The thing about Otto is he's always been driven toward . . . innovation. That's the nice way of putting it. It showed with his work in nuclear physics, before those four extendo arms were grafted onto him. Apparently, his go-to brain food during late nights at the lab was Chicken Larb. This carried over into his megalomaniacal super villain phase. So much so, that during our early fights, the aroma of this crispy meat-and-rice combo always filled the air. I didn't realize until later, but it's become my post-fight meal whenever Doc Ock and I mix it up. We've got that in common, I guess. Though he absolutely wasn't willing to share *his* recipe for Chicken Larb. This one's my own.

4 tablespoons canola oil

¼ cup thinly sliced shallot

2 tablespoons minced fresh ginger

1 pound ground chicken

1 tablespoon fish sauce (gluten-free versions available, if preferred)

1 tablespoon sugar

2 limes, juiced

Salt

1 green bird chile, minced (or ½ teaspoon chile flakes)

½ bunch mint, stemmed and cut into chiffonade

½ bunch cilantro, stemmed and rough chopped

1 head hydroponic Bibb lettuce or green leaf lettuce

½ bunch Thai basil or basil, stemmed and rough chopped

OPTIONAL:

2 cups steamed jasmine rice

1 ounce lemongrass, minced

1. In a large nonstick pan heat the oil until almost smoking.

2. Add the shallot and ginger, as well as lemongrass if you're including it. Sauté until ingredients are very fragrant and almost golden.

3. Add the chicken and sauté, breaking up the chicken as you do until it starts to color.

4. Add the fish sauce, sugar, and lime juice. Season with salt and chile. Then remove from heat and toss in the chopped mint and cilantro.

5. On a large plate, place leaves of the lettuce of your choice and line them with basil. You want to choose leaves of lettuce that are suitable for cups. Arrange these on the plate so you can easily pick them up and fill with chicken.

6. To serve, spoon the chicken onto your plate or into a separate bowl, surrounded by your lettuce basil cups. Don't fill the cups before you serve, as they have a tendency to wilt if not eaten right away. If you'd like, serve with a side of jasmine rice.

KRAVING VEGGIE DUMPLINGS

I've got to hand it to Sergei Kravinoff. He's meticulous, he's cunning, he's driven—and the goatee! Yeah, there'd be a lot to admire about Kraven the Hunter if it weren't for the whole hunter part. Oh and the fact that I'm usually his prey. I mean the man wears a lion-themed ensemble, yet somehow this decidedly furless Spider jumps to the top of his list of big game? I'll put it to you this way. After the first time I tussled with Mr. Lion Pelt's nets, traps, and chiseled jawline, I swore off meat for a month. Fortunately, there was a spot in Astoria that made my favorite dumplings in a veggie variety. I became such a regular that they offered to let me pinch my own dumplings together before they cooked them for me. Note: I had them include detailed instructions on this technique, reproduced below. They offered to name the dumplings after me on the menu, but I thought the best revenge would be for them to name them after Kraven.

FOR THE DUMPLINGS:

3 tablespoons olive oil

1 tablespoon minced ginger

1 tablespoon minced scallion whites

1 teaspoon minced garlic

½ cup thinly sliced shiitake mushrooms

8 ounces tightly packed spinach

½ teaspoon sesame oil

2 teaspoons soy sauce

Salt and pepper

1 tablespoon cornstarch

1 pack of 16 white, round dumpling wrappers (look for eggless options to make vegan)

4 tablespoons water

FOR THE SAUCE:

2 tablespoons black vinegar

2 tablespoons soy sauce

1 tablespoon finely julienned ginger

1. In a medium nonstick pan heat 2 tablespoons of olive oil. Then add the minced ginger, scallion whites, and garlic. Sauté until fragrant and tender. Add the shiitake mushrooms and sauté until fully cooked.

2. Add the spinach; it will quickly wilt. Season with sesame oil and the soy sauce. Remove from heat, spread on a tray or plate, and place in the fridge or freezer to rapidly cool.

3. When the filling is cool, drain the excess liquid and put it in a food processor. Pulse until the filling is rough chopped and easily stays together when pressed. Season with salt and pepper.

4. To prepare your wrapping station, dust a tray with a bit of cornstarch to prevent the dumplings from sticking. Fill a bowl with a bit of water.

V

YIELD:
16 DUMPLINGS

PREP TIME:
1 HOUR

5. Start small, adding just a bit of filling in the center of your first wrapper. Wet the edges with your finger gently and close the wrapper around the filling, crimping as you go. The edges should meet in the center, creating the look of a pouch. Then go back around, pressing with two fingers at each fold to make sure it's fully sealed.
6. Alternative method: If you prefer a simpler approach, instead just fold over the wrapper and seal in a half-moon. You can start with a half-moon that has a couple of creases and add more as you make more dumplings and feel more confident.
7. Set aside on the dusted tray until ready to cook.
8. Once ready, place your dumplings in a nonstick pan evenly spaced with a tablespoon of oil and 4 tablespoons of water. Cover and cook on medium-high heat to steam until dumplings start to crisp up. Remove the lid and cook until golden on the underside. You can also boil water and drop the dumplings in and cook them until they float. Just be gentle and careful that you don't break them open. Do a test first in either case.
9. Combine the black vinegar, soy sauce, and ginger for the sauce and serve the dumplings on the side.

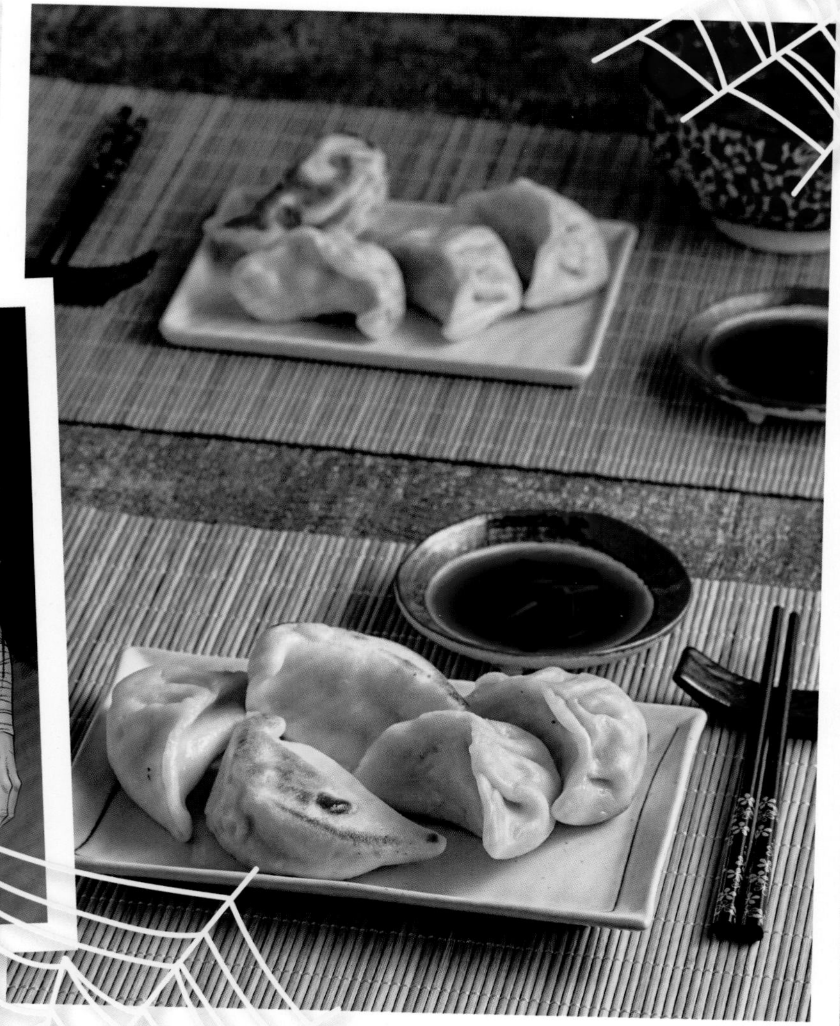

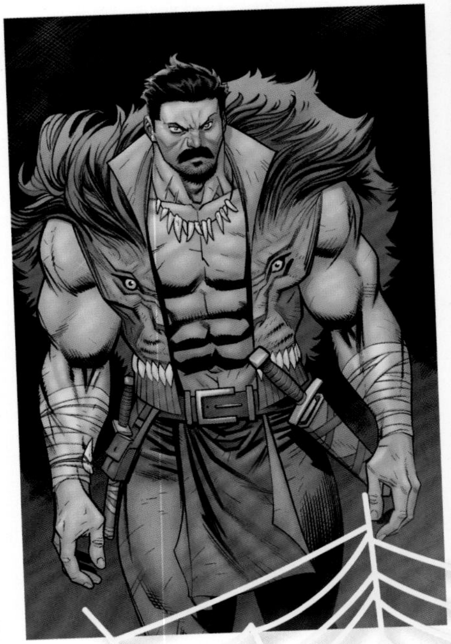

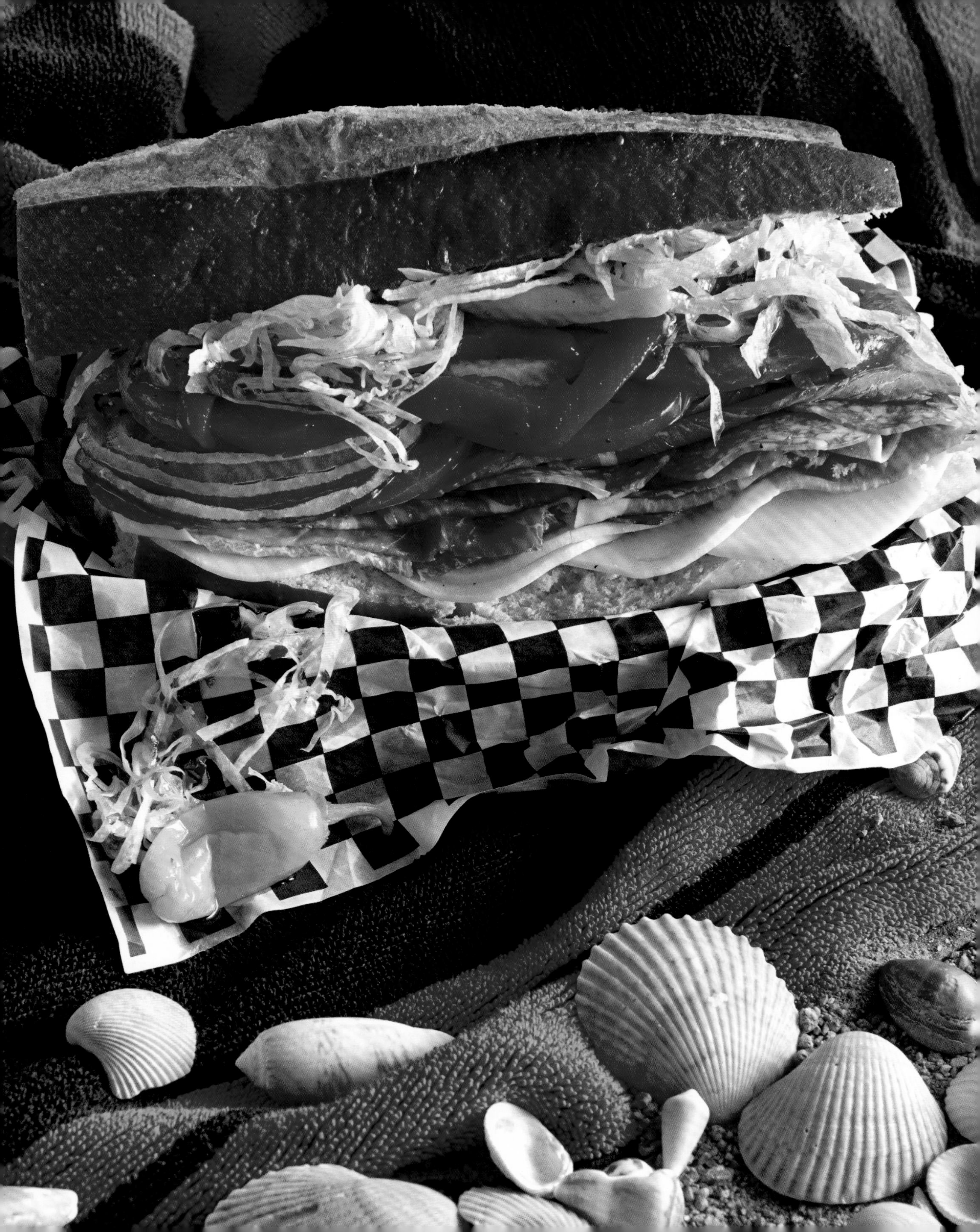

ITALIAN HERO

YIELD:
1 SANDWICH
PREP TIME:
20 MINUTES

This beachside staple became a favorite of mine after I was put through the Rockaway boardwalk storefront of a delicious hero shop owned by the wonderful Momma Allegra. Repeatedly. By the Sandman. Because he was the worst. Before he reformed and joined up with Silver Sable and her crew. But then went back to crime. And then reformed again. Hey, anybody reading this know if Sandy's a good or a bad guy this week? It's easy to lose track. Fighting Sandman at the beach comes with the bonus of finding grains of sand inside your costume for days afterward and being forced to wonder whether it's beach sand or Sandman sand. But aside from that gift that keeps on giving, I did walk away with a recipe from Momma Allegra to show there are no hard feelings. I just had to promise that I wouldn't bring any of my bad guys with me next time I visited. There's only one hero her customers look forward to seeing on the beach, and this sandwich has me beat every time.

FOR THE VINAIGRETTE:

¼ cup red wine vinegar

¼ cup olive oil

2 teaspoons oregano

1 teaspoon chile flakes

1 teaspoon cracked black pepper

½ teaspoon salt

FOR THE HERO:

One 8-inch bread roll

3½ ounces provolone

2 ounces prosciutto

2 ounces salami

1½ ounces sweet capicola

1 ounce pepperoni

½ cup thinly sliced tomato

1½ tablespoons thinly sliced red onion

⅓ cup sliced, roasted red bell peppers from a jar

2 tablespoons sliced black olive

4 leaves basil, cut in ¼-inch strips

3 tablespoons pepperoncini

2½ ounces iceberg lettuce, chopped thin

1. For the vinaigrette, combine red wine vinegar, olive oil, oregano, chile flakes, cracked black pepper, and salt in a mixing bowl. Set aside.

2. Split the bread roll lengthwise and wet the cut sides with 2 tablespoons of vinaigrette.

3. Begin to layer your cheese and meat evenly on the bottom halves of the rolls, starting with the provolone. Next, fold the prosciutto gently on itself as you layer, then top with the salami, sweet capicola, and pepperoni.

4. Add the tomato, red onion, red bell pepper, sliced black olives, basil, and pepperoncini.

5. Top with iceberg lettuce and season with another 1 to 2 tablespoons of vinaigrette. Top with the top bun, pressing down to lock everything in.

6. Cut with a serrated knife to the desired portion.

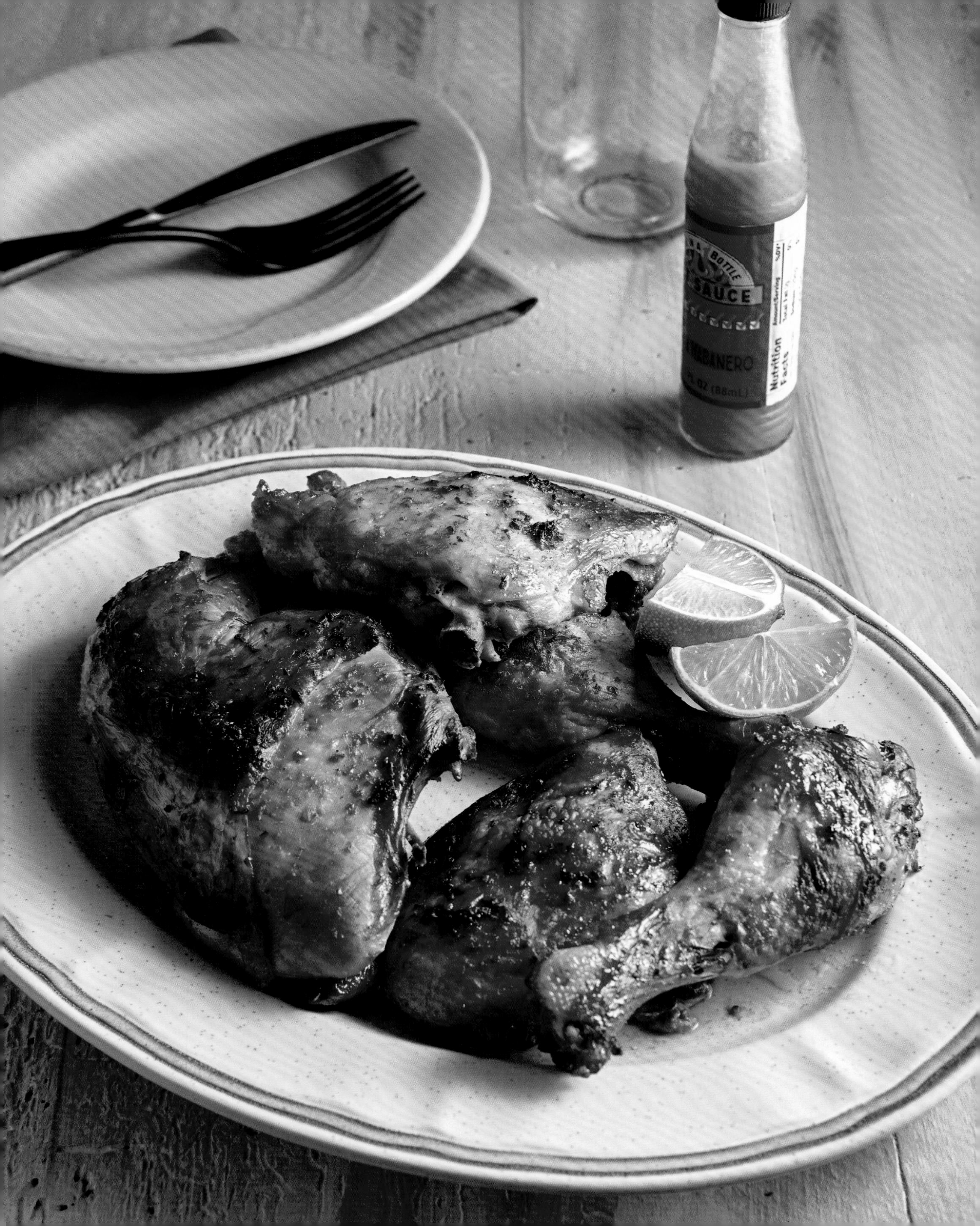
SAUCE
Nutrition Facts

JERK CHICKEN

GF

YIELD:
4 SERVINGS
PREP TIME:
OVERNIGHT, PLUS 50 MINUTES

Electro is the reason my spider-socks are insulated. And just like that I feel like I've overshared. Sorry. That said, one of my first few times tangling with my least favorite lightning rod ended with a stray bolt of his flying through the window of one Etta Baxter Clark. My heart dropped, thinking my fight with Sparky had destroyed her kitchen or, worse, had destroyed Etta! Imagine my surprise when I checked in on her and discovered his bolt had flash-cooked a serving of Jerk Chicken she was about to prepare. She gave me the recipe; said she wouldn't advise zapping the chicken with electricity. Yeah, that was probably a one-time thing.

6 ounces Jamaican jerk paste

½ cup soy sauce (gluten-free versions available, if preferred)

½ cup orange juice

2 shallots, peeled

2 ounces ginger, peeled

½ cup white wine vinegar

2 tablespoons light brown sugar

8 pieces chicken, cut into breast, legs, thighs, wings

1 lime, sliced into wedges

1. Combine everything but the chicken and lime in a food processor and blend until smooth.

2. Using a fork, stab the chicken all over *a lot*. You'll want to create tons of holes for the marinade to seep into.

3. Put chicken in a container, fully submerged in your seasoning, and let marinate overnight.

4. The next day, heat your grill. If possible, turn one side off so that you have a place with indirect heat to grill your chicken. Since this marinade is high in sugar and ingredients that tend to burn, it's a good idea to try to cook the chicken off the fire when you can. Alternatively, if you have wet smoking wood, you can create a platform to set the chicken on. Either way, remove excess marinade from the chicken before you start to grill.

5. Roast the chicken, turning after about 30 minutes.

6. Move the chicken around your grill and continue to turn it to control the browning. Keep at it until completely cooked and golden-brown delicious, approximately another 20 minutes.

7. Serve on a platter with lime wedges and enjoy!

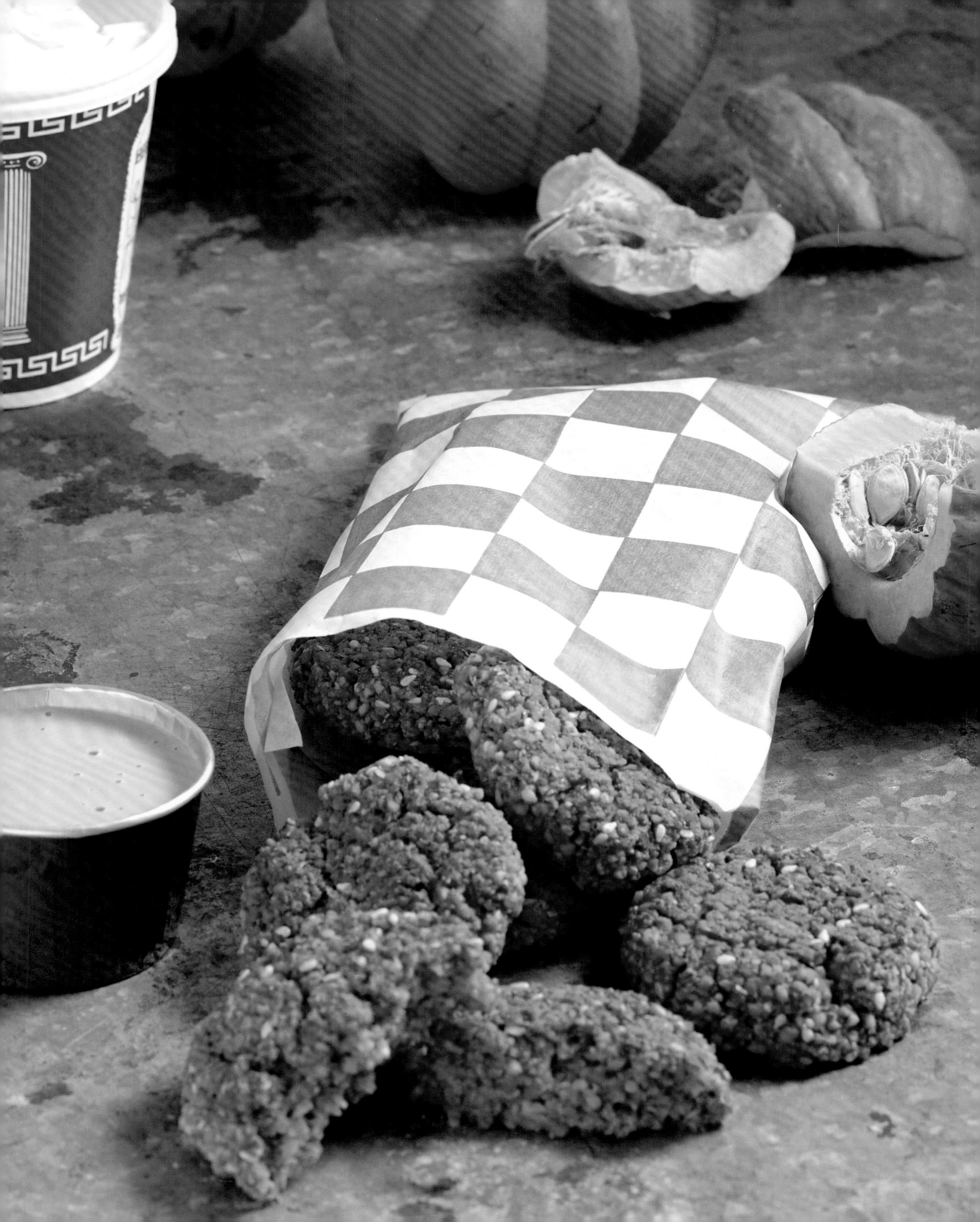

FALAFEL

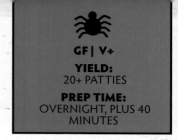
GF | V+
YIELD:
20+ PATTIES
PREP TIME:
OVERNIGHT, PLUS 40 MINUTES

Now, some will say that you find your best New York falafel in Midtown, during the lunch rush. I will tell you those poor unfortunate souls are misinformed. Don't worry, I take time out of my busy web-slinging day to correct them. It's just the kind of hero I am. One for the people. No mission too big or too small. I learned the truth from a true gentleman and scholar named Fadel. He goes to college locally during the day and mans the all-time best falafel cart at night for his father. We met on a warm summer night, during a tussle with one of my all-time worst baddies, the Green Goblin, who had me dangling behind him on his glider. He got a real kick out of that move back in the day. I really don't like this man. The Goblin dragged me over a food fair taking place in Corona Park, buzzing the gaggle of food trucks gathered below as he tried to turn me into spider-paste. On one low pass, the Goblin was pelted with a bottle of white sauce. Then a bottle of ketchup. By the time he had learned you don't mess with a group of chefs trying to earn a living, I had gotten free. The lead bottle pelter was Fadel, and I went back and thanked him once I was done with the Goblin. We've been friends ever since. This is his recipe. One that's been a comfort for me, personally, especially during those times my ears wouldn't stop ringing from taking a pumpkin bomb or six to the noggin.

2 cups dry chickpeas, soaked in water overnight

1 cup chopped sweet onion

2 cloves garlic, grated

½ cup chopped parsley

½ cup chopped cilantro

1 lemon, zested

1 teaspoon ground coriander

1 teaspoon ground cumin

2 teaspoons salt

½ teaspoon ground black pepper

1 teaspoon baking powder

6 tablespoons extra virgin olive oil

1 cup tahini

1. Soak the chickpeas overnight. The next day, rinse them well and spread them out on paper towels to dry.

2. In a food processor, combine onion, garlic, parsley, cilantro, and lemon zest and pulse.

3. Add chickpeas and blitz until the ingredients start to come together but are not yet a paste.

4. Add coriander, cumin, salt, pepper, baking powder, and 2 tablespoons of olive oil. Spin in processor until well mixed.

5. Preheat oven to 375°F and line a sheet tray with oiled parchment.

6. Form 1½-inch wide and ½-inch-thick patties and load the tray. Drizzle the remaining 4 tablespoons of olive oil all over the tops of the patties to help them crisp when baking.

7. Bake in the oven until golden and crispy, about 15 to 20 minutes.

8. Serve on a plate with tahini.

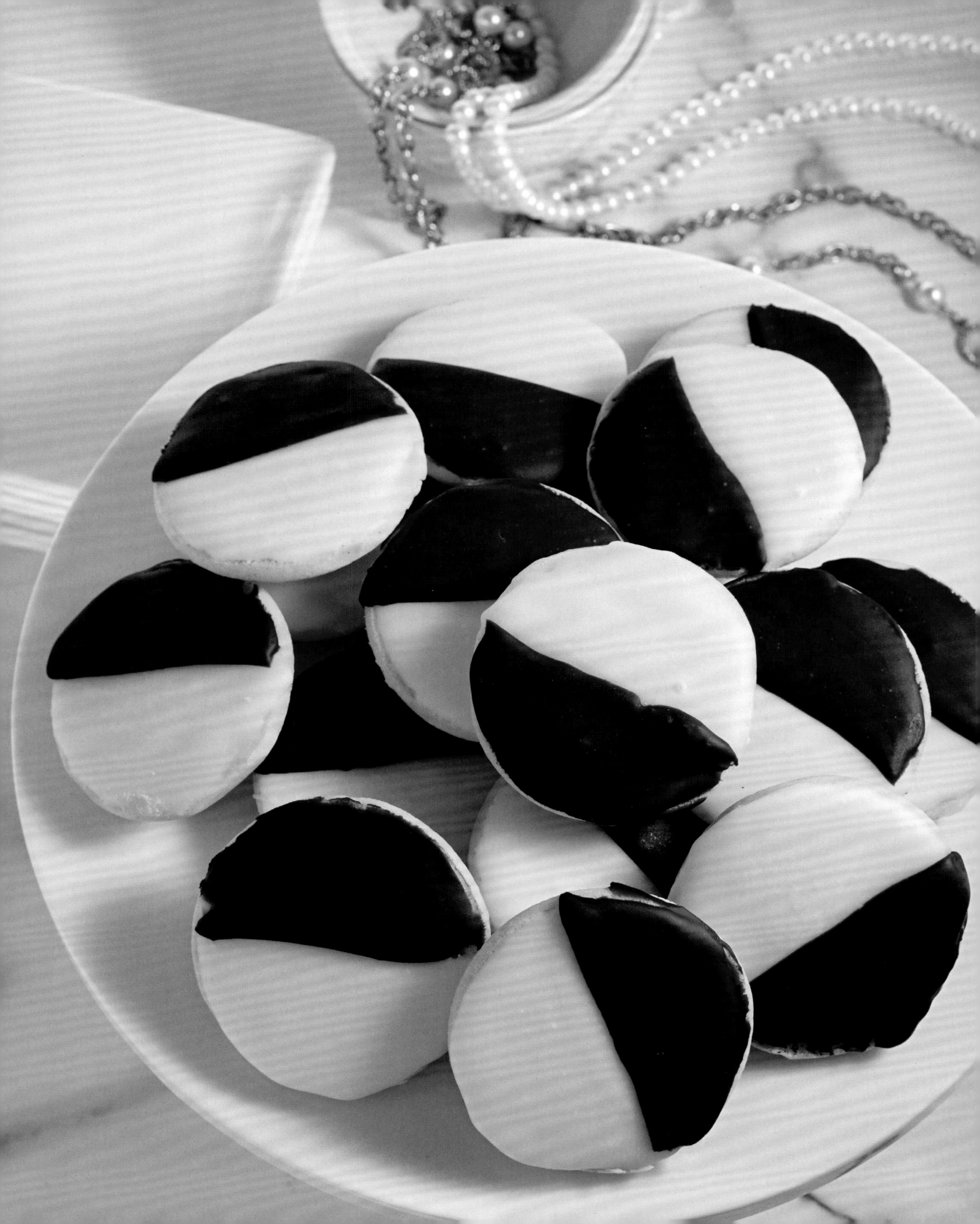

V

YIELD:
10 COOKIES

PREP TIME:
2 HOURS

BLACK-AND-WHITE COOKIES

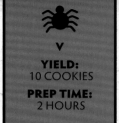

She calls me Spider, it's kind of awesome

Black Cat here, just jumping in very quickly to share my favorite dessert dish. When Spider told me he was putting this together, I was looking forward to helping. Then I realized, well, I'm not the cooking type. And after most of my heists (which of course are a thing of the past), my go-to celebratory dish is caviar, and it's always catered. However, Spider waxing poetic about the past inspired me to share a sweet memory from my days growing up here in Queens. I used to have this ritual with my father, a cat burglar extraordinaire in his own right. I knew at an early age what he was doing, but it didn't mean I didn't worry. So, we would bake these black-and-white cookies before he'd go off on a job. It was our private joke, because I was his little black cat and because these cookies were originally invented in Manhattan. The recipe was borrowed, of course. My father would say they may have started in Manhattan, but they were perfected by bakeries in Queens. He always made me swear we would wait to eat our latest batch together when he got home. I still bring them when I visit him in prison. I've yet to figure out how to bake a file into them, but I'm working on it. Kidding, Spider.

FOR THE COOKIES:

1¾ cups all-purpose (AP) flour
¼ teaspoon baking soda
1 teaspoon baking powder
¼ teaspoon salt
⅓ cup sour cream
2 teaspoons vanilla extract
1 teaspoon almond extract
¾ cup granulated sugar
2 eggs, room temperature
½ cup softened butter

FOR THE FROSTING:

5 tablespoons water
2 tablespoons corn syrup
4 cups confectioners' sugar
1 teaspoon vanilla extract
½ teaspoon salt
3 tablespoons Dutch cocoa powder

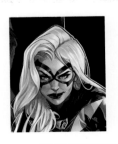

1. Preheat oven to 375°F.
2. Beginning with your cookie dough, mix the flour, baking soda, baking powder, and ¼ teaspoon of salt together in a bowl. Then, in a separate bowl, combine the sour cream, 2 teaspoons vanilla extract, and 1 teaspoon almond extract.
3. In a mixer, cream the granulated sugar, eggs, and butter until smooth and fluffy. Then fold in the flour and sour cream mixture in small portions, combining everything gently.
4. Scoop out 1½ inch balls onto a parchment lined or nonstick tray, with about 2 inches of space between them.
5. Bake, rotating the tray every 6 minutes until the cookies are only just firm. This should take approximately 12 to 18 minutes total.
6. Transfer to a rack and let cool.
7. While the cookies are cooling, make your frosting.
8. In a medium bowl, whisk 4 tablespoons of the water with the corn syrup and confectioners' sugar. Add 1 teaspoon of vanilla extract and ½ teaspoon of salt. Mix thoroughly so that the frosting is spreadable but not too runny.
9. Move half of the frosting into a separate bowl and mix in the cocoa powder, adding the last tablespoon of water if needed to maintain consistency.
10. Once the cookies are cooled, spread the vanilla frosting on half of all the cookies.
11. Wait for the vanilla frosting to dry and harden, then frost the chocolate on the opposite halves. Leave time for the chocolate-frosted side to set. Then serve and enjoy.

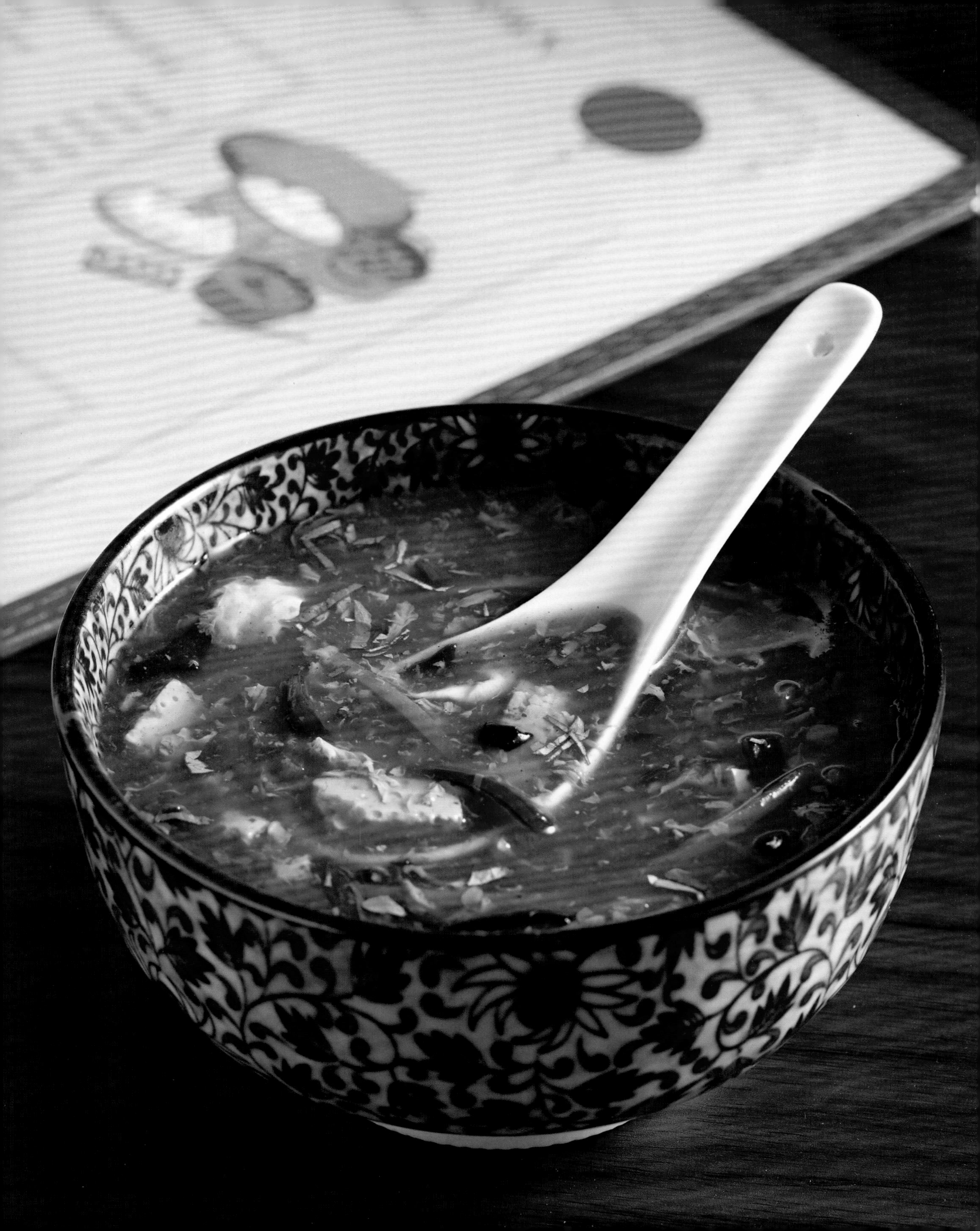

HOT AND SOUR SOUP

YIELD:
4 SERVINGS

PREP TIME:
45 MINUTES

First, let me clear something up. Old Iron Fist—nice guy, glowing fist, questionable collar choices. New Iron Fist—also nice. Also has a glowing fist on one hand. **AND AN ENERGY DAGGER** on the other. So much cooler. Objectively cooler. Sorry, old Iron Fist. Anyway, my teacher Shang-Chi (no, really, that's a thing, read on) put me in touch with the new Iron Fist while he was in town from Shanghai. The kid knew of a spot in Flushing where he and his fellow Agents of Atlas regularly hung out. And who am I to say no to a culinary adventure? Oh yeah, I'm a guy who doesn't carry money in his spidey-suit. That's who I am. Good thing the kid was buying.

2 tablespoons dried wood ear mushrooms, hydrated and sliced thin

6 cups vegetable stock

¾ cup julienned carrots

½ cup thinly sliced fresh shiitake mushrooms

¾ cup julienned bamboo shoots

8 ounces extra firm tofu, cut into ¼-inch-thick batons

3 eggs

1 tablespoon sesame oil

1 tablespoon chile oil

3 tablespoons soy sauce

8 tablespoons black vinegar

½ teaspoon ground white pepper

1 tablespoon kosher salt

1 teaspoon cornstarch

4 tablespoons cilantro chiffonade

1. Place the dried wood ear mushrooms in a heat safe bowl and cover with boiling water. Let hydrate for 10 minutes until soft and snappy.

1. Bring the vegetable stock and carrots to a simmer in a deep pot on medium-high heat.

2. After about 3 minutes, when the carrots are almost tender, add both varieties of mushrooms, plus the bamboo shoots and tofu. Return to a simmer for a few minutes.

3. In a separate bowl, crack and beat the eggs well. Then stream them into the simmering soup, stirring to pull the egg thinly through the broth.

4. In a separate bowl, mix the sesame oil, chile oil, soy sauce, black vinegar, white pepper, and kosher salt with the cornstarch. Stream this into your broth next, tasting as you go.

5. Serve and garnish with the cilantro.

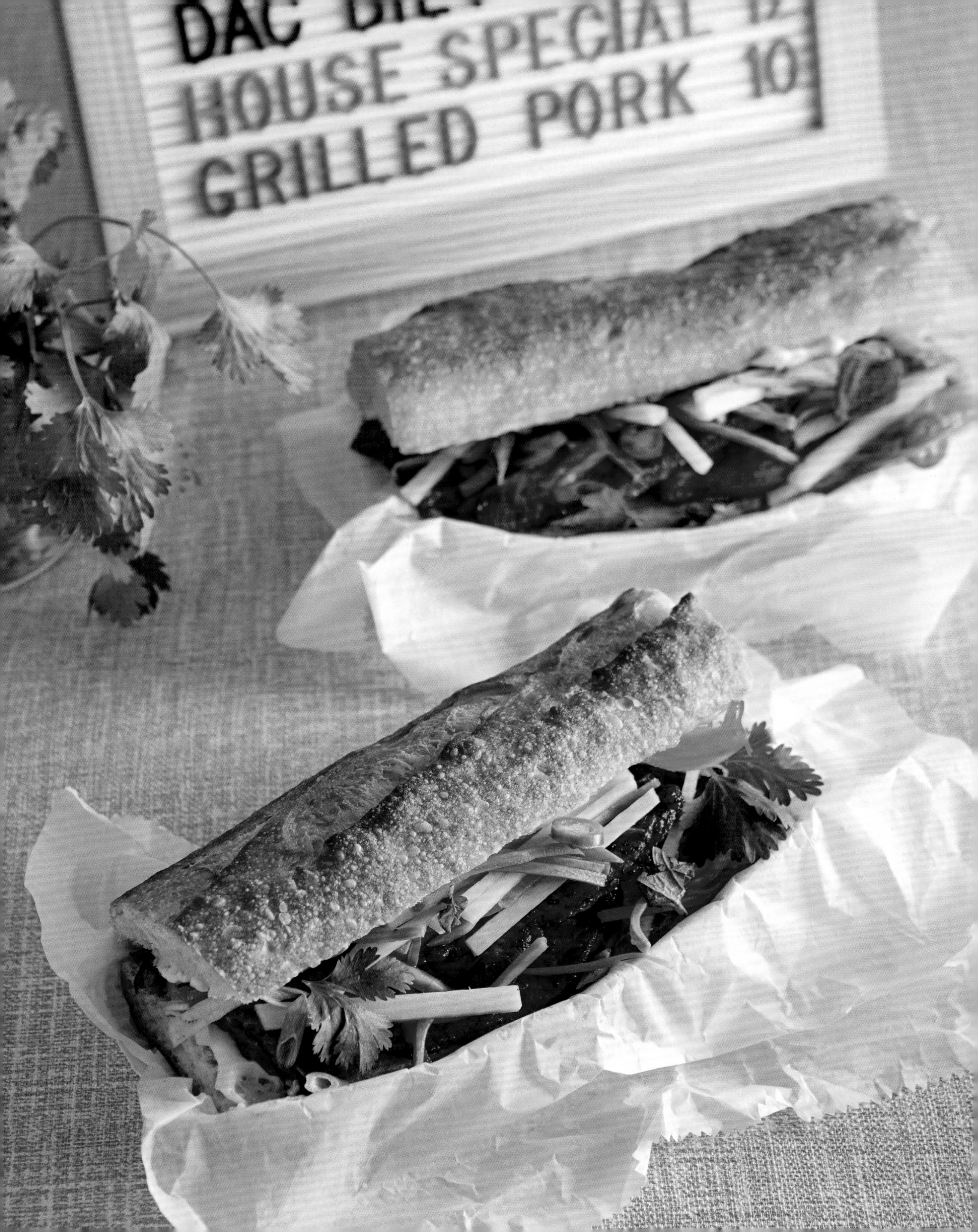
HOUSE SPECIAL
GRILLED PORK 10

BÁNH MÌ

YIELD:
2 SANDWICHES
PREP TIME:
OVERNIGHT, PLUS
1½ HOURS

Spider-Woman here. I'm a part of this ever-growing Spider family, but I come to web-slinging from a vastly different perspective than some of my cohort. And my web wings actually work (which I remind Spidey of constantly). For the purposes of this recipe, though, all you need to know is that for a good while I called San Francisco home. I was a private investigator out there, and bánh mì was my go-to stakeout dish. Since I moved back to New York, I've been searching high and low for somewhere that makes one as good as my West Coast connection. I'm glad I tracked down this recipe so I can share it with all of you. And to prove that my investigative skills are still sharp as ever. It took me making my way here to Queens to finally find my go-to East Coast version of my favorite comfort food.

FOR THE MARINADE:

2 ounces brown sugar

1 tablespoon fish sauce

2 tablespoons sweet soy sauce

3 shallots, sliced thin

2 cloves garlic, minced

2 lemongrass stalks, outer leaves removed, smashed and minced

1 teaspoon cracked black pepper

4 ounces extra virgin olive oil

16 ounces pork shoulder, sliced into ¼-inch strips across the grain

FOR PICKLING:

1 cup water

1 cup rice vinegar

1 teaspoon kosher salt

½ cup sugar

2 carrots, julienned

One 6-inch daikon, julienned

2 green finger chiles, sliced thin

FOR PLATING:

Two 8-inch baguettes

6 tablespoons mayonnaise

4 scallions, sliced thin

1 European cucumber, sliced into ribbons

8 sprigs cilantro, washed and patted dry

¼ bunch mint, stemmed

1. Marinade the pork the night before, or at least 2 hours before you begin cooking. Start by combining the brown sugar, fish sauce, sweet soy sauce, shallot, garlic, lemongrass, black pepper, and olive oil in bowl. Slather the mixture all over the pork slices and let sit, covered, in the fridge.

2. Start on your pickling next, which can be done the night before or at least 1 hour ahead of time. In a small pot, heat the water, vinegar, salt, and sugar for about 8 minutes, or until the sugar is melted. Then chill until room temperature.

3. After chilling, add the carrots, daikon, and chiles to your pot. Submerge everything to pickle.

4. The next day, or when you're ready to assemble and eat, preheat your broiler or grill to medium-high heat. Cook off the pork until well caramelized, about 15 to 20 minutes.

5. Partially split the rolls lengthwise, keeping them connected, and spread mayo all over the inside.

6. Lay the meat on the bottom of both rolls, followed by sliced scallions and the pickled carrots and daikon. Lay chile all over, depending on your heat preference.

7. Next top with ribbons of cucumber, as well as lots of cilantro sprigs and mint leaves. Close up and enjoy.

JAMAICAN BEEF PATTY

Mysterio played the hero role when we tussled for the first time, all the while using his gift for movie magic to kill the reputation of your favorite wall-crawler. It was Quentin Beck's version of tit for tat. I had inadvertently ruined his career in special effects when one of his stunts nearly wiped out an entire studio audience and I made the save. Beck never worked in the industry again and figured the appropriate response was to put a fishbowl over his head and try to squash yours truly, in the media and eventually in person. He used his gift for theatrics, stagecraft, and illusion to lure me to an abandoned movie studio, where I turned his fishbowl into a punch bowl. (Get it? Because I punched him. . . . I'm here all week.) I had worked up a heck of an appetite once I wrapped things up with Beck. Fortunately for me, there was a Jamaican bakery about a few miles away as the web flies. The chef took pity on a young Spider-Man who at the time had yet to figure out how to carry money in his spandex (wait—I still haven't) and gave me a sample of this killer beef patty, the recipe for which I'm passing on to you fine folks.

FOR THE DOUGH:

3½ cups all-purpose (AP) flour

2 teaspoons Jamaican curry powder

1 tablespoon turmeric powder

1 teaspoon kosher salt

1½ cups small-diced cold butter

1 tablespoon vinegar

¾ cup ice-cold water

FOR THE PATTIES:

4 tablespoons butter

1 cup minced sweet onion

1 pound ground beef

1 teaspoon fresh-picked thyme

1 teaspoon ginger powder

1½ tablespoons Jamaican curry powder

2 tablespoons soy sauce

½ cup beef broth

1 to 2 tablespoons Scotch bonnet hot sauce

½ cup panko or bread crumbs

Salt and pepper

2 eggs

1. Combine flour, Jamaican curry powder, turmeric powder, and salt, and mix well. Place everything in a food processor. Add the diced cold butter and blitz until pea-size pearls form.

2. Add the vinegar and ice-cold water, mixing until a dough forms. Remove the dough to a clean surface and knead until it forms a smooth, round ball.

3. Using a rolling pin, roll out your dough until it is about ⅛ inch thick. Using a 6-to-8-inch cutter, punch out approximately a dozen round pieces of dough and dust them gently with flour. Layer them on parchment or wax paper and set them aside in a cool place or even the fridge.

4. Begin on the patties. In large rondeau or sauté pan, melt the butter and sauté the minced onion on medium heat until the onion is translucent and tender.

5. Add the ground beef and cook on medium-high heat for around 10 minutes, using a spoon to fully break up the meat.

6. When the ground beef is fully rendered and browning, add the thyme, ginger powder, and Jamaican curry powder. Cook until fragrant, approximately 2 minutes.

7. Add the soy sauce, beef broth, and then the hot sauce to your liking. Once it's all combined, add panko just to bind and season with salt and pepper to taste.

8. Remove the pastry shells from the fridge and let temper while the beef filling is cooling. Preheat the oven to 350°F.

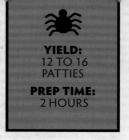

YIELD: 12 TO 16 PATTIES

PREP TIME: 2 HOURS

9. Once the beef filling has cooled and the pastry is at room temperature, spoon the filling onto the center of the pastry rounds. Fold over into crescents and seal the edges together with a fork.

10. In a small bowl, crack and mix the eggs well. Then brush the crescents with egg.

11. Bake in the oven on a nonstick baking tray, or a tray lined with parchment, to prevent sticking. Once the pastries are golden about and fully cooked, after about 25 minutes, remove from the oven and enjoy!

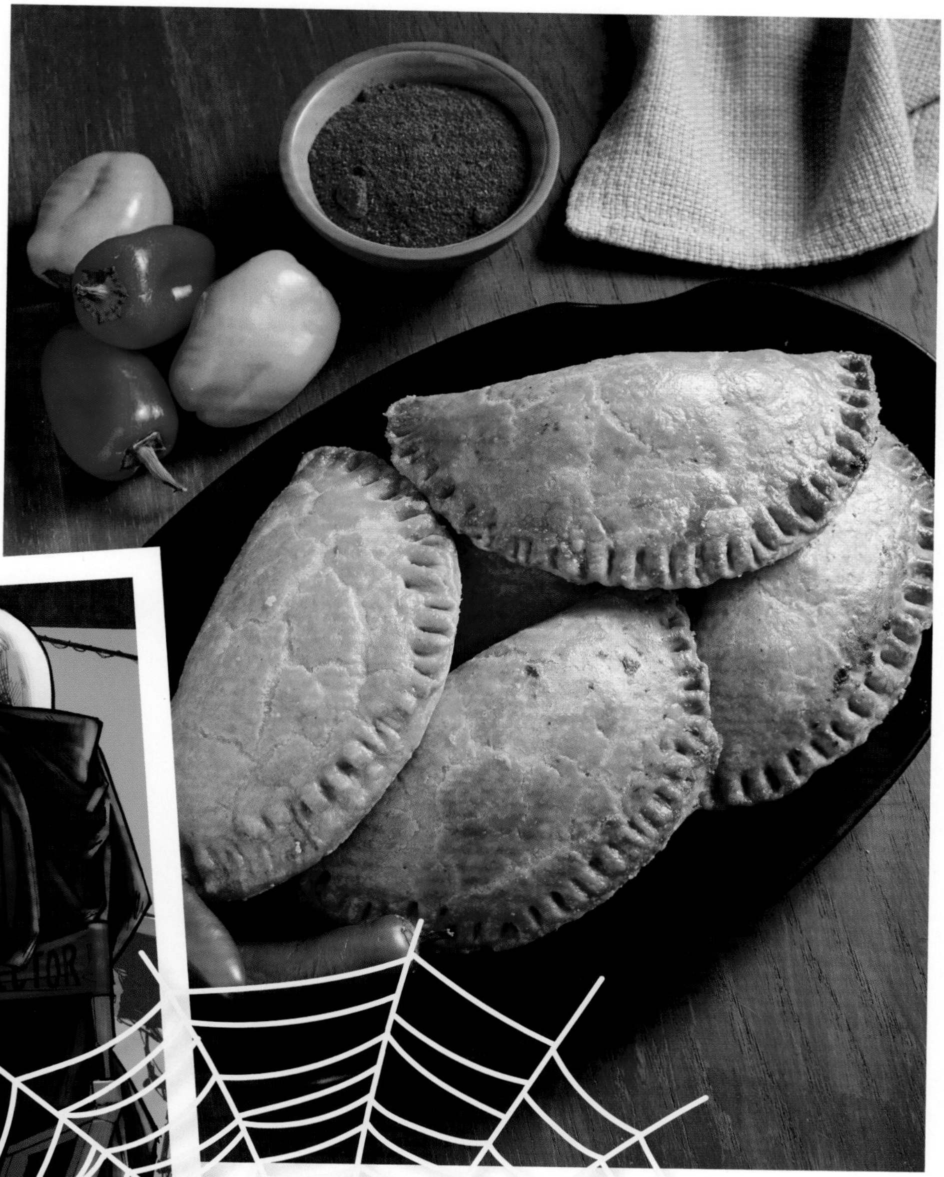

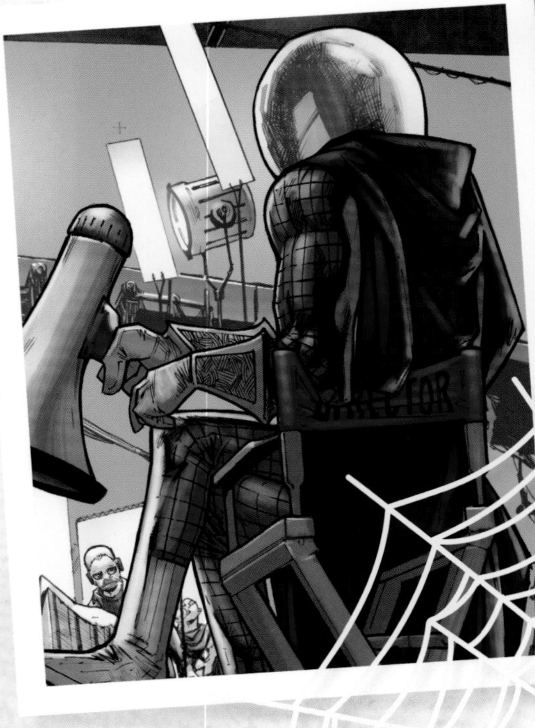

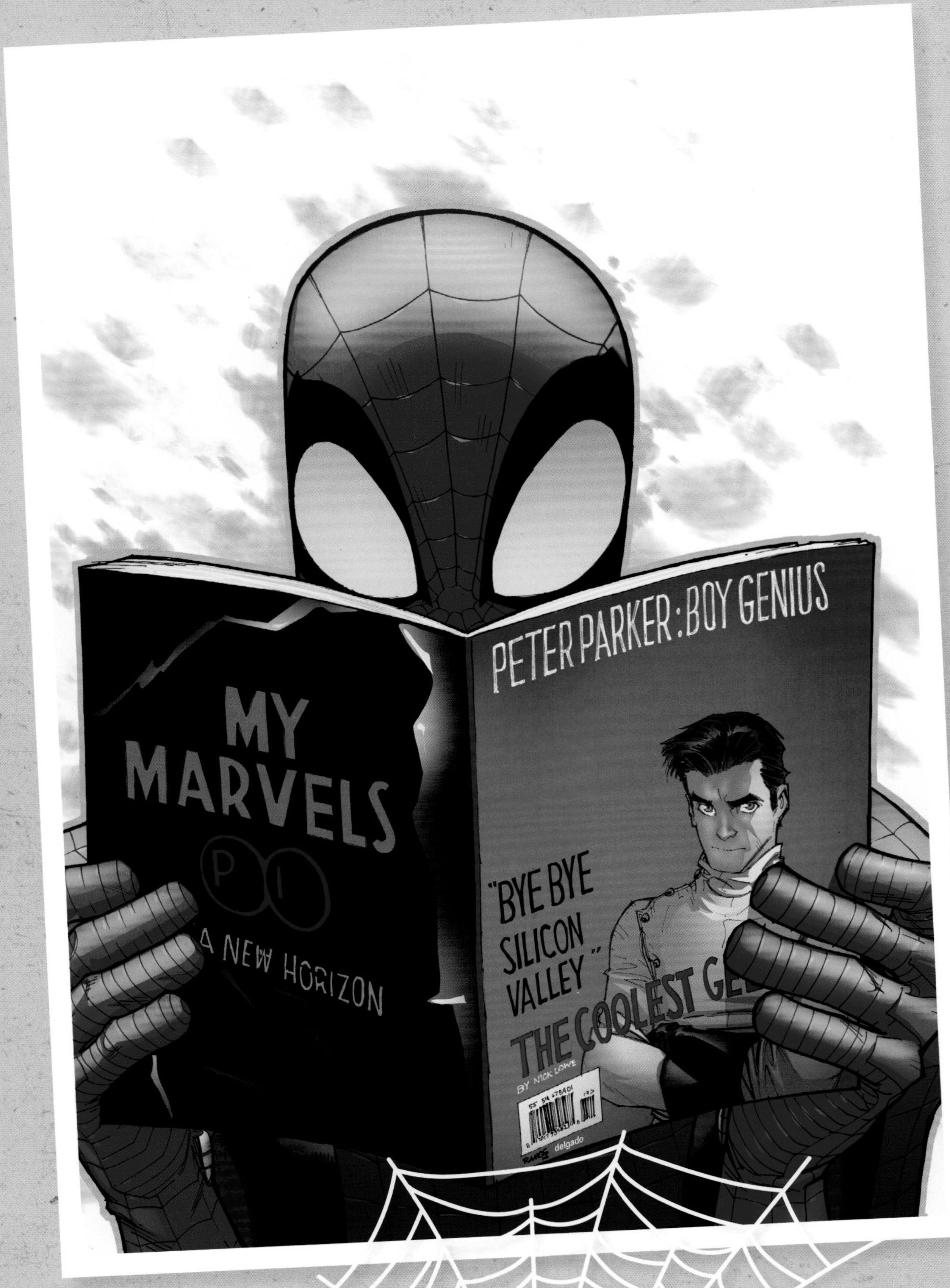
MY MARVELS
PI
A NEW HORIZON
PETER PARKER : BOY GENIUS
"BYE BYE SILICON VALLEY"
THE COOLEST
BY NICK LOWE
delgado

PETER PARKER'S FAVORITES

Well, he's not just a pretty face and provider of family breakfast secrets, not just a wizard at calculating focal length and aperture speed. Queens's own Peter Parker also wants to contribute a recipe or two to this shindig. Figures I'd throw the guy a bone, since he was kind enough to put me on payroll at Parker Industries. I'm turning this section over to Parker for the next two recipes, as I feel he knows this part of town almost as well as I do.

When I heard that Spidey was putting this book together, I figured: I've been along for the ride with the wall-crawler till this point, why stop now? I mean, I was just a promising science student at Midtown High, but thanks to Spidey, I was able to pursue my true passion, freelance photography! It's not like a stuffy lab can ever measure up to the fun of chasing after him and his super villains all over the tri-state area. Even though I love stuffy labs. And beakers. And groundbreaking innovative scientific discoveries . . . Yeah, I owe that wall-crawler a lot. (Why are we friends again?)

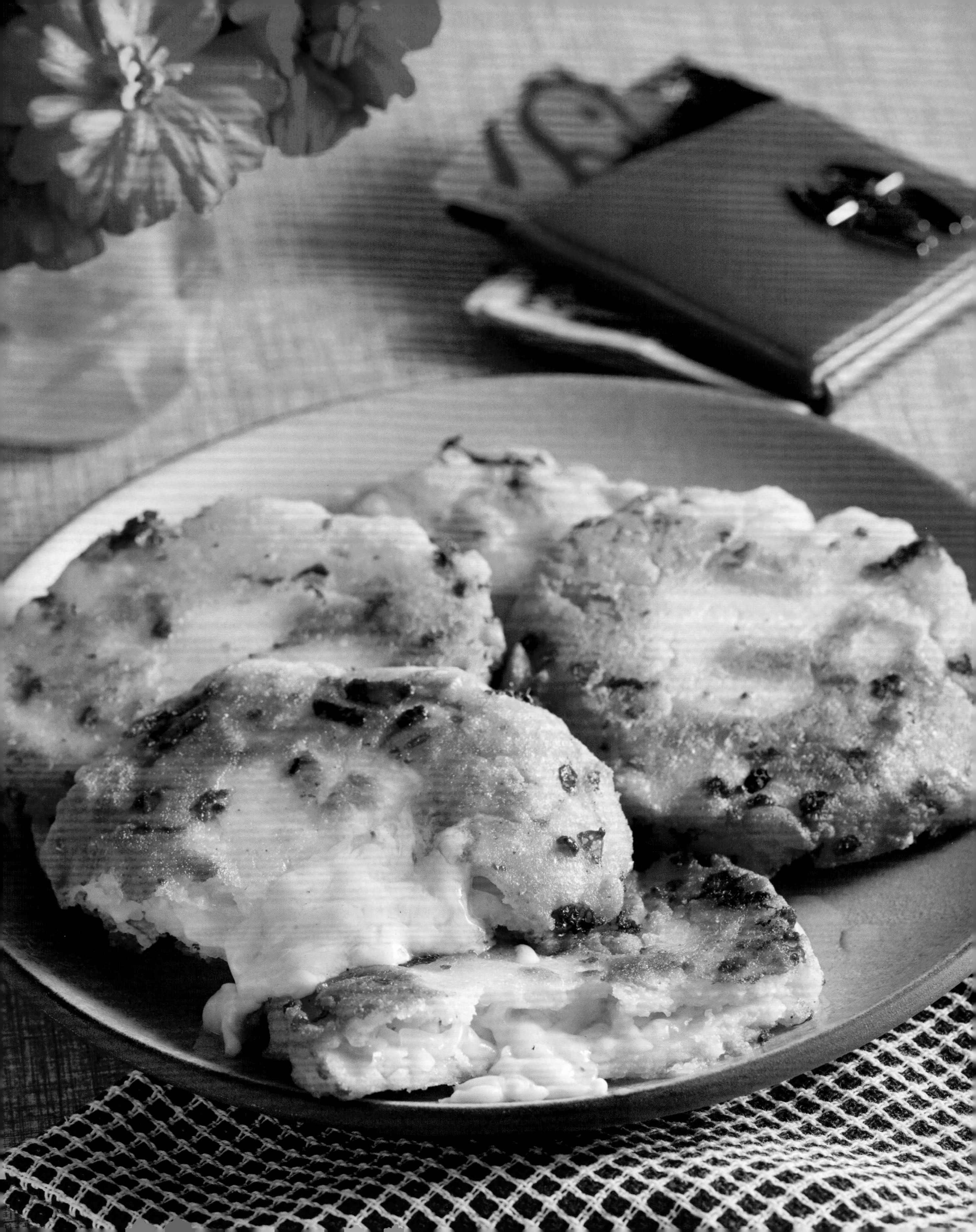

CHEESE AREPAS

GF | V
YIELD:
6 TO 8 AREPAS
PREP TIME:
20 MINUTES

Thinking back to our roots together, my first recipe ties back to when I had just sold my first set of Spidey pics to J. Jonah Jameson. My first job, my first paying gig. I was thrilled, and rich (I thought). I was so ecstatic that I got off at the wrong train stop on my way home and ended up in East Elmhurst. Right in front of a Colombian restaurant that seemed to be calling to me. I answered the call and ordered this cheese dish on a lark. Good choice, Parker—it served as the capper to an amazing day. It became a bit of a tradition to stop by there during high school, either to celebrate selling more photos or to drown my sorrows when I didn't make the sale. Cheese Arepas, my inner artist's comfort food and some of Queens's Finest.

2 cups milk or water

2 cups masarepa

1 teaspoon salt

¾ pound shredded mozzarella

2 tablespoons butter

2 tablespoon canola oil

1. Combine milk, masarepa, and salt in a bowl and mix well. Then stir in a quarter of the shredded mozzarella.

2. Portion your mix into sixteen golf-ball-size spheres.

3. Place one ball into a sandwich bag and press down, forming a flat disk. Set your disk aside and repeat, using the same sandwich bag, until you have sixteen disks.

4. Apply the remaining cheese evenly across the top of eight of your sixteen disks.

5. Cover each of your cheesy disks with one of the eight opposing halves. If needed, use more water to get them sticky enough to seal by gently pressing all the way around the edge of the circle. You should have 8 white burger-patty-looking pucks at the end.

6. Melt the butter with canola oil on a griddle or skillet, then reduce to medium low heat. Cook each arepa until golden on both sides, carefully turning until it's done. This should take about 3 to 4 minutes per side. To test if your arepas are fully cooked, tear one open slightly to confirm that the cheese is fully melted.

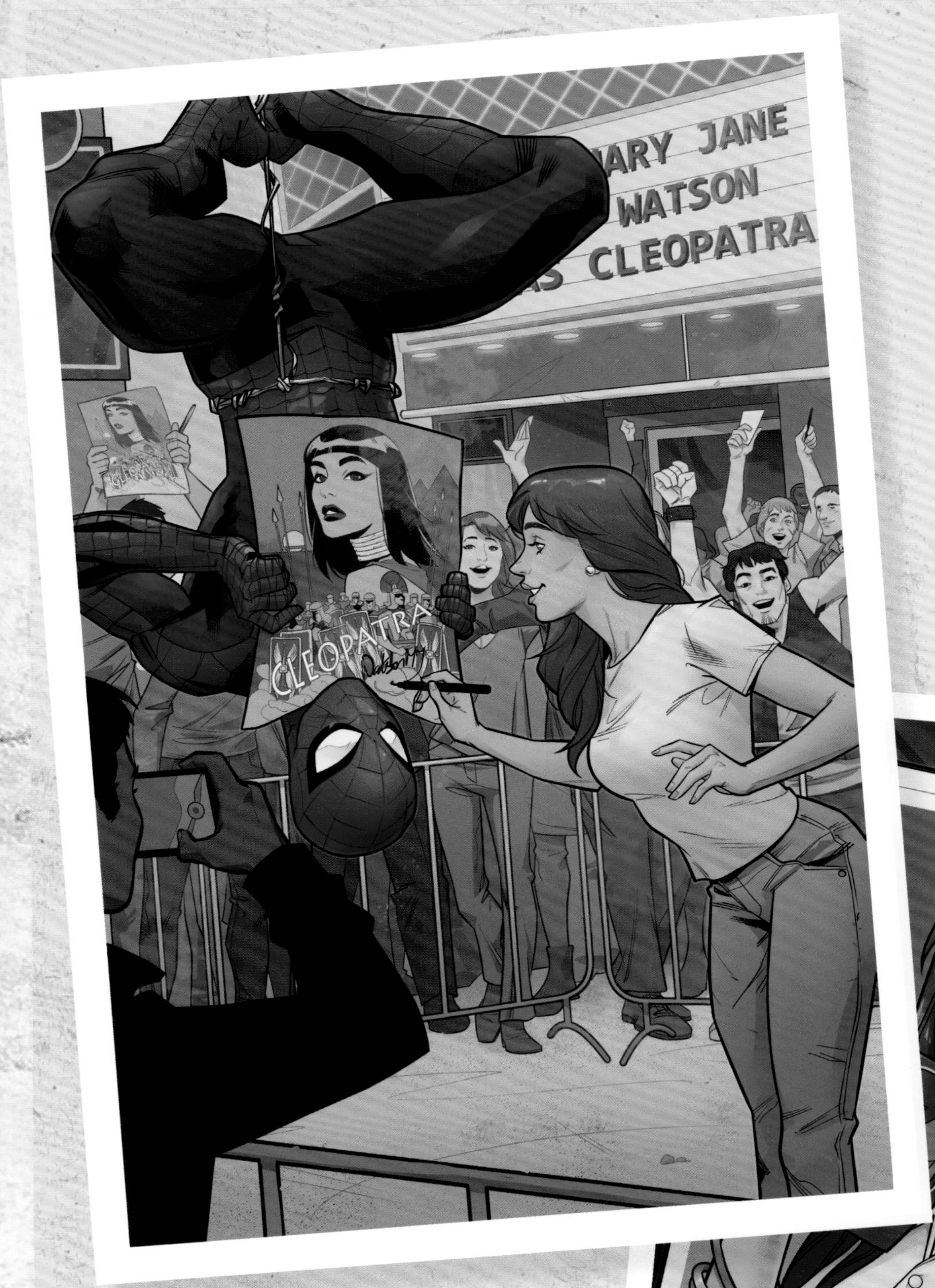
ARY JANE
WATSON
AS CLEOPATRA
CLEOPATRA

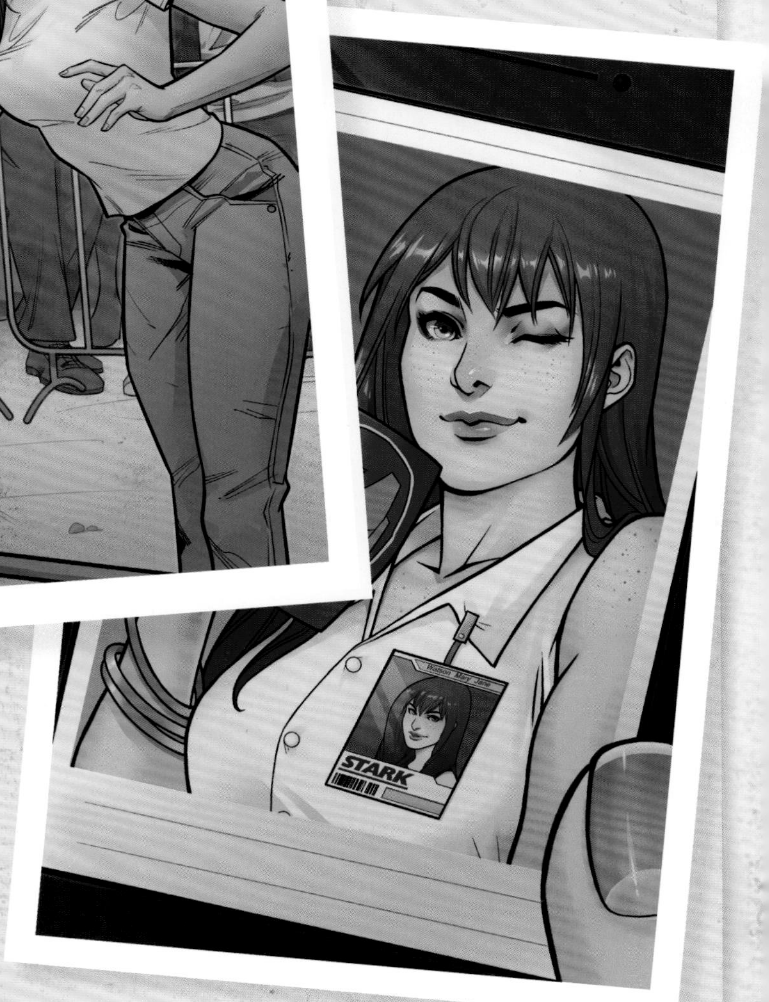
STARK

PASTRAMI SANDWICH

YIELD:
1 SANDWICH

PREP TIME:
15 MINUTES

The story behind this recipe revolves around one of Aunt May's favorite pastimes, telling her nephew "I told you so." Back when I was in school, she was on a mission to fix me up with the niece of Anna Watson, our next-door neighbor. May Parker is like a mother to me, so I naturally avoided this introduction at all costs. And then I actually met Mary Jane Watson. Well played, Aunt May, well played. Mary Jane's first words to me were "Face it, Tiger, you've hit the jackpot!" And man, was she spot-on with that one. As outgoing as I was reserved. We just clicked, you know? She was easily one of the most down-to-earth, funny, and giving people I've ever met. She did theater in high school, and, when we went to college, she was a psychology major. She made friends easily and could have gone anywhere in New York, any night of the week. She could have been taking in all that this town's nightlife had to offer, while I burned the midnight oil at the science lab at Empire State University. But she chose to hang with me for some reason. Afterward, we'd ride back into Forest Hills on my motorcycle. (Yes, I owned a motorcycle. Johnny Blaze I was not, but I had my moments.) And we'd tear into a pastrami sandwich at the only all-night deli still open in the neighborhood. We talked for hours. It's the best sandwich in the world, but I know I'm biased, and the company has a lot to do with it.

12 ounces pastrami, sliced ¼ to ⅛ inch thick

2 tablespoons deli mustard

2 slices rye bread

1 half-sour pickle

1. Gently spread and warm your pastrami in a toaster oven or pan with a touch of water so that it doesn't dry out.

2. Spread the mustard on two slices of rye bread.

3. Stack the pastrami up on one slice of the bread. It should look very generous. Top with the other slice and cut in half with a serrated knife.

4. Plate and serve with a pickle.

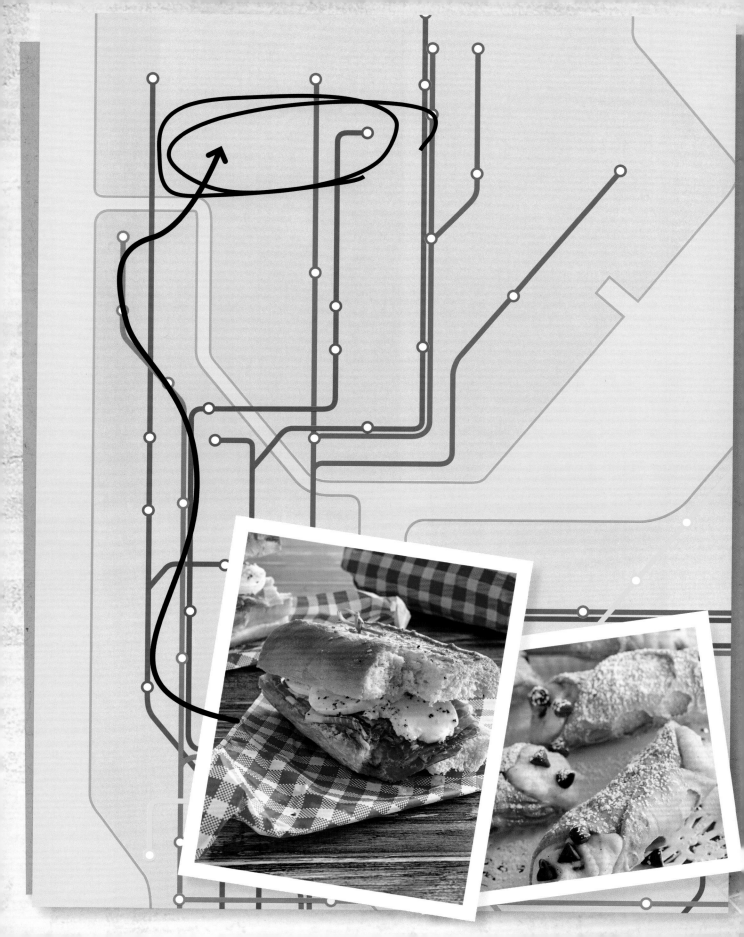

2 THE BRONX

Welcome to the Bronx, the borough so nice, it's the only one with a "the" in front of it. (Why is that?) Not my usual stomping ground, which has nothing to do with that *other* baseball team, or the fact that the whole place seems to be one perpetual slope—the things you notice as you're web-swinging uphill . . . But the people are great and so are the eats.

Maybe that's why super heroes tend to be frequent visitors, despite the long subway ride. I know the Hulk, back in his more monosyllabic days, loved busting up East Tremont for some strange reason. I mean, he'd just swing into town, cause a ruckus on the Grand Concourse, and leave. Of course, you could say the same for some tornados and most sports fans.

Which is not to say I'm trying to give vthe Bronx a bad name. Perish the thought. This book is about food, and it gets no better than the Bronx. Let's dive in with it.

CHOPPED CHEESE SANDWICH

YIELD:
1 SANDWICH

PREP TIME:
30 MINUTES

Now, you can find this rather inventive cheese dish at any bodega worth its salt. I, however, have found out the hard way, from foe-turned-friend the Prowler (hi, buddy!), that the home of *the* chopped cheese is indeed, the Bronx. He turned me on to this dish after a team-up to take down Jack O'Lantern. (Hey, I don't tease you about your villains, and you agree to do likewise.) The team-up happened in Midtown, on Spring Street, in Manhattan, but the Prowler insisted on taking me to the Bronx to prove his point. At midnight, I might add. I said it could wait until morning. Prowler emphatically begged to differ. So there we both were, atop the 4 train, going local like we were questing for a grail or something. Pronounced travel time aside, it was worth the trip.

2 tablespoons butter

½ cup diced sweet onion

8 ounces ground beef patty

1½ teaspoons salt

1½ teaspoons pepper

3 slices American cheese

One 6-to-8-inch seeded roll

2 tablespoons mayonnaise

3 slices beefsteak tomato

½ cup shredded iceberg lettuce

Ketchup

1. In a medium skillet on medium-high heat, melt butter and start cooking onions until fragrant, about 3 minutes.

2. Make space on your pan to add your burger patty, keeping onions cooking as well. Season the patty with salt and pepper.

3. Once charred on one side, about 3 minutes, flip and start charring on the other side.

4. You'll know your patty is cooked through by breaking it up a bit to confirm there is no pink or redness left. When it reaches that point, and the onions are a great golden color, add the three slices of American cheese to the top of the beef.

5. Give it a few seconds for the cheese to soften, and then, with a spatula, chop the meat, onions, and cheese a few times until you make a gooey, beefy mess. Taste and add more salt and pepper if needed.

6. Slice your roll in half lengthwise and spread mayo on each side. Using a spatula, lay the beefy mess on the bottom side.

7. Top with sliced tomato, shredded lettuce, and ketchup if you'd like. Cover tightly with the top of the roll. Cut in half horizontally and enjoy!

SMOKED SALMON BAGEL SANDO

YIELD:
1 SANDWICH

PREP TIME:
10 MINUTES

It's a little out of the way, but this tiny deli in Norwood makes the best Smoked Salmon Bagel Sando. I found it while chasing a villain by the name of Slyde. His suit is coated with a frictionless chemical that allows him to move as if the laws of physics don't apply. He's near impossible to catch, and I had been meaning to break out a special web formula I'd invented for just that purpose. However, it was this sandwich that won the day. Slyde had me exhausted and figured he could stop by said deli to pick up his usual before resuming his crime wave. The pit stop gave me enough time to string him up, the web formula really stuck the landing, and the discovery of this bagel dish was a welcome bonus.

1 everything bagel, made day-of, if possible

½ cup whipped cream cheese

½ pound smoked salmon or lox

2 to 3 thin slices ripe tomato

1. Carefully slice the bagel in half lengthwise and spread each side with 2 ounces of whipped cream cheese.

2. Layer the salmon on one side, being sure it's evenly arranged, folding when possible to create more volume. Your salmon slices should equal the thickness of one bagel half.

3. Top the salmon with enough thinly sliced tomato to cover the fish.

4. Top with the remaining bagel half and slice down the middle.

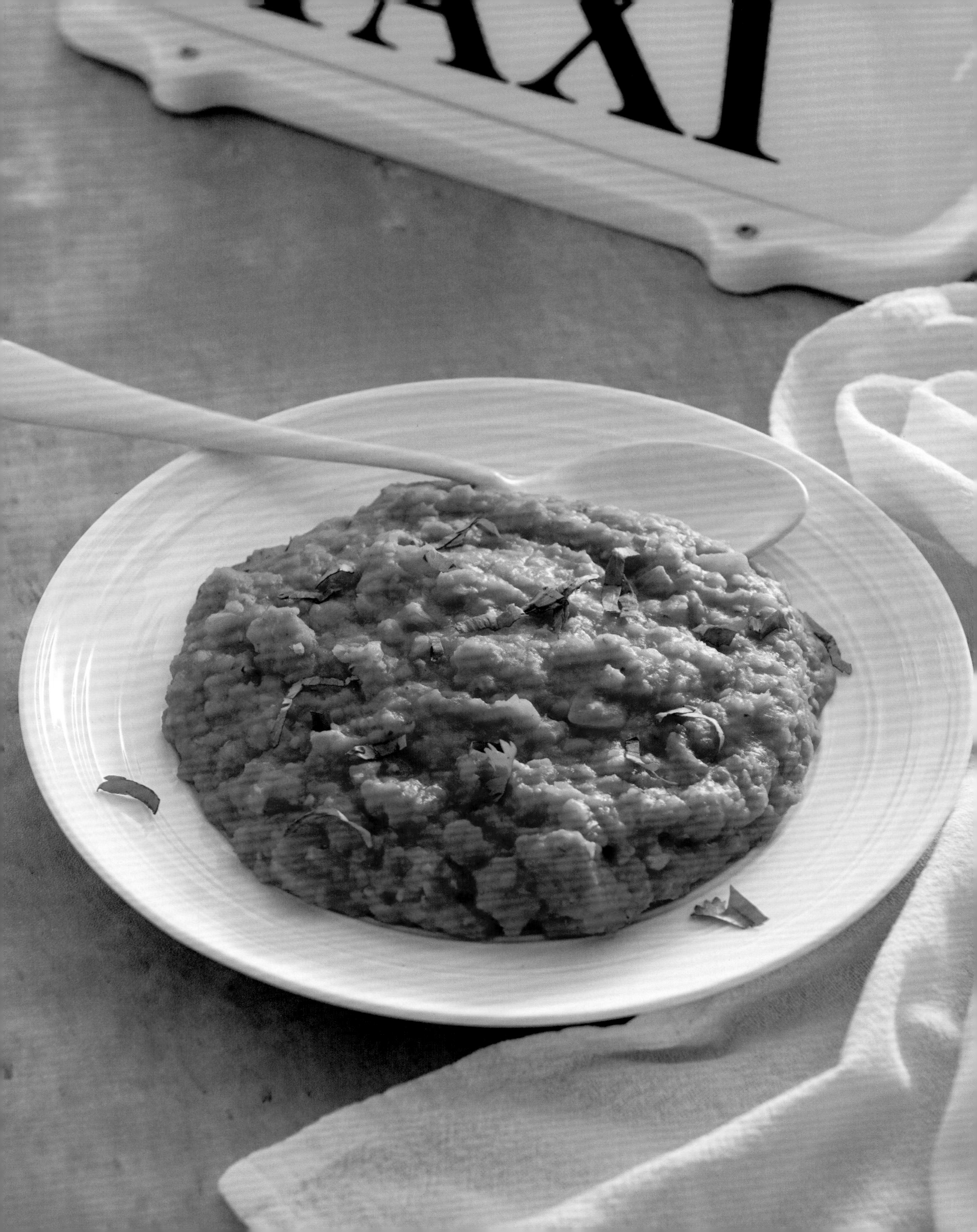

SAVORY RED LENTILS

GF | V
YIELD:
6 SERVINGS
PREP TIME:
1 HOUR

This recipe comes by way of Moon Knight, of all people. We ended up working a case together near Gun Hill Road. It's funny. At the time, he mentioned offhand that he didn't get up to the Bronx that much. Soon as the crime had successfully been fought, it was like a switch flipped and suddenly he knew the entire borough like the back of his hand. I'm talking deep, intimate knowledge. Like how New York cab drivers know every side street and the *exact* time of day to take each one—sort of like that. He took me to a deli where everyone seemed to know him, and the owner was kind enough to whip up this dish for us. He even said he'd be happy to part with the recipe, to be shared among friends. That Moon Knight, he's got layers to him, that's for sure.

4 tablespoons extra virgin olive oil

1 cup diced sweet onion

2 cloves garlic, minced

1 tablespoon minced ginger

2 tablespoons tomato paste

2 teaspoons ground cumin

1 teaspoon ground turmeric

1 teaspoon ground ginger

1 teaspoon ground coriander

1½ cups red lentils

4 cups vegetable stock

Salt and pepper

½ bunch cilantro, stemmed

1. In a 2-quart pot, sweat the onion, garlic, and minced ginger in the extra virgin olive oil for approximately 3 to 5 minutes.

2. When fully tender and aromatic, turn the heat to low. Add tomato paste, cumin, turmeric, ground ginger, and coriander. Cook for 5 minutes.

3. Add the lentils and vegetable stock. Simmer until lentils are fully tender, around 30 to 40 minutes. Season with salt and pepper to taste. Serve and add the cilantro for garnish.

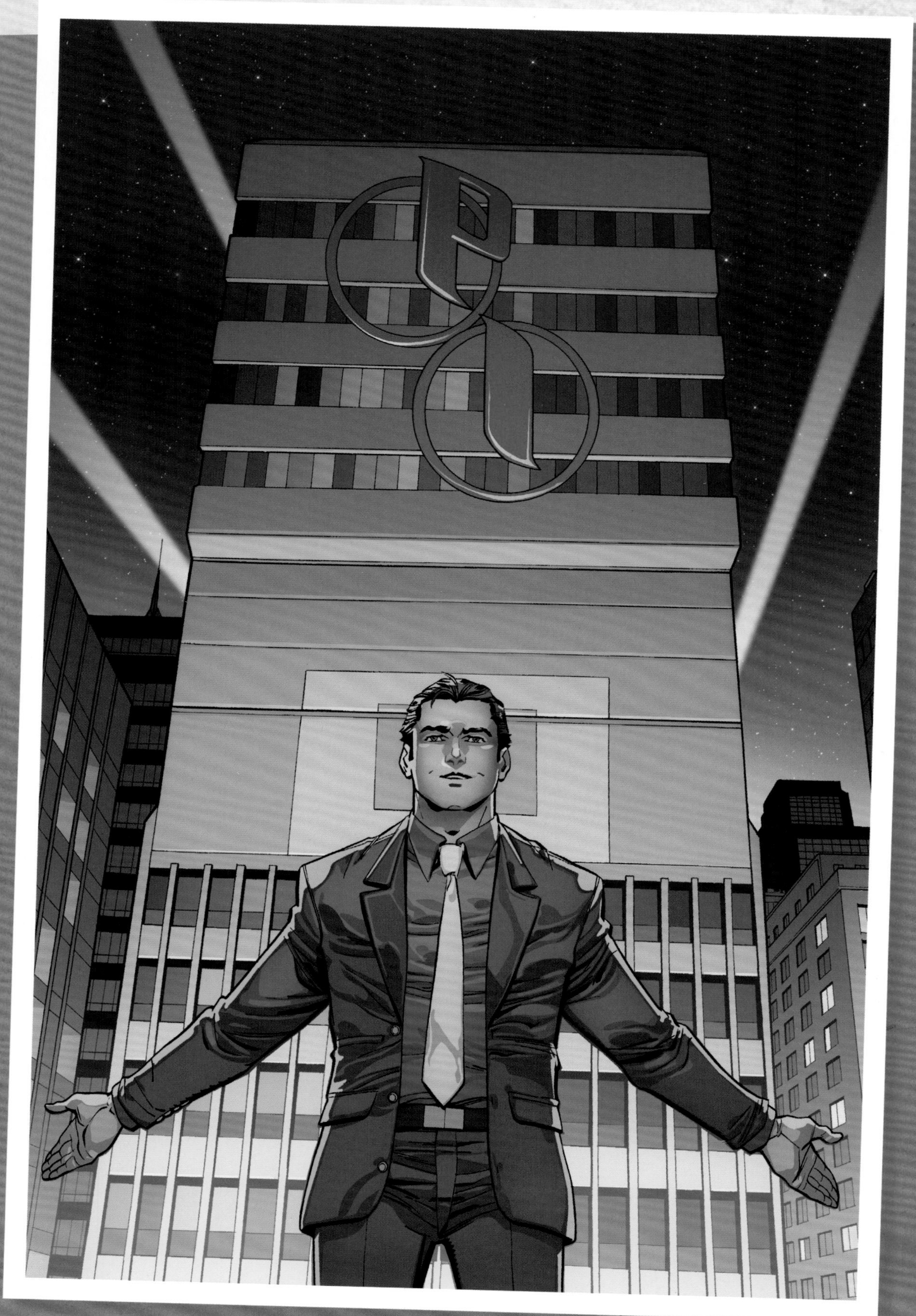

PERNIL ASADO

GF

YIELD:
6 TO 8 SERVINGS

PREP TIME:
8 HOURS TO MARINATE, PLUS 4 TO 6 HOURS TO COOK

I briefly mentioned that Peter Parker isn't just famous for taking my pictures. Well, he was also a titan of industry not too long ago. And on top of that, he had me on payroll as a bodyguard/corporate symbol of his company, Parker Industries. Hey, it worked for Stark Enterprises, and I'm much more handsome than Iron Man. Those were good times, while they lasted. Love that guy, but Peter's bad "Parker luck" is legendary. Anyway, we would make runs up to a Parker Industries' R&D lab up in the Bronx and were *enchanted* by the aroma of this Cuban dish. We didn't even know it existed until we happened upon this neighborhood restaurant not more than a stone's throw from the Parkchester lab. After that, we always found another "work" reason to head up to the Bronx for Pernil Asado. That Parker—a heck of a boss, that guy. When picking up lunch he told me it was a nice change of pace from the hustle of running a multimillion-dollar tech firm. Have I mentioned I miss that job? No? I *so* miss that job.

FOR THE MARINADE:

3 tablespoons salt

5 tablespoons minced garlic

½ cup chopped cilantro

2 tablespoons chopped oregano

1 tablespoon cracked black pepper

1 cup lime juice

1 cup orange juice

Zest of 2 oranges

Zest of 4 limes

½ cup olive oil

For the pork:

6 to 8 pounds bone-in pork shoulder

½ bunch cilantro, stemmed

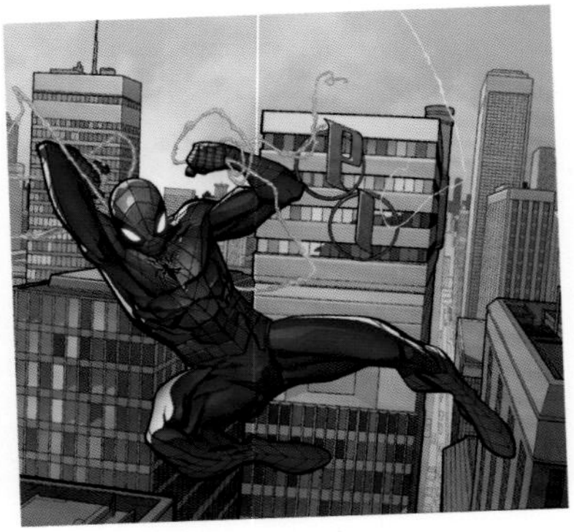

1. Combine all the ingredients for the marinade in a large bowl and mix well.
2. Place the pork in a deep roasting pan. Using a paring knife, cut one-inch-deep incisions all over the pork shoulder. Pour the marinade over the meat and jam as much marinade and herbs into the incisions as you can. Cover tightly with plastic wrap or a lid, refrigerate, and let marinate for at least 8 hours.
3. Remove the pork shoulder from the fridge and let it sit on the counter up to one hour to take the chill off. When you're ready, preheat your oven to 350°F.
4. Re-cover pork tightly with two layers of plastic wrap and then two layers of aluminum foil. When the oven is hot, place the pork in and roast for 4 to 5 hours.
5. After 4 to 5 hours, check your pork carefully. When you peel back the foil and plastic, tons of steam will rush out and can burn you. The pork should be jiggly and super moist. Take a spoon and check the resistance of the meat. The spoon should easily slide all the way in until it reaches the bone. If not, wrap the meat tightly again and keep cooking.
6. When the meat is fully tender, remove foil and plastic and place back in the oven and roast until its beautifully caramelized. You'll know that's happened when you can really smell it!
7. Remove the meat and let rest. Carefully place on a serving platter and garnish with lots of cilantro.

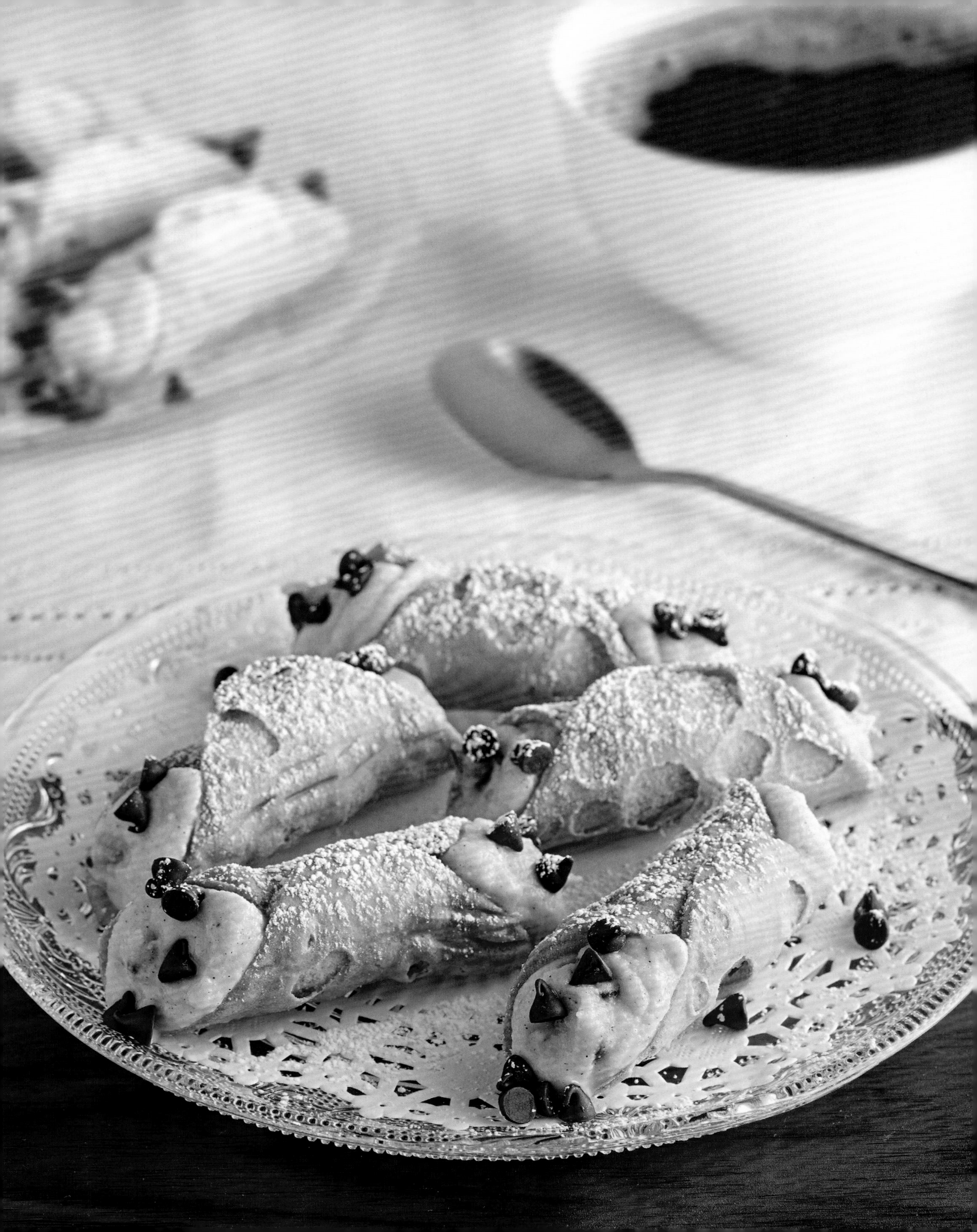

CANNOLI

YIELD:
12 TO 16 MINI CANNOLI

PREP TIME:
30 MINUTES

You have Caesar Cicero to thank for this recipe. Yes, that guy. Yes, the Maggia underboss, YES HIM!! Well, not him exactly, it's not like he baked these things for his hench goons while extorting, strong-arming, and intimidating his enemies (allegedly). But this was a closely guarded recipe of his personal chef, who I ran into when I raided his Bronx mansion trying to rescue a friend of mine. I was content to exit stage left, but my friend picked up on Cicero being as protective of this recipe as he was about the less-than-legal deal he was brokering. Let's just say I can multitask when motivated. I made a point of finding the recipe in a box in the chef's kitchen before we left.

EQUIPMENT:

1 piping bag

16 ounces ricotta

½ cup powdered sugar, plus 1 tablespoon for dusting

1 orange, zested

1 teaspoon vanilla paste

½ teaspoon cinnamon powder

½ cups mini milk chocolate chips (plus 4 tablespoons for garnish)

16 mini cannoli shells

1. Start with your filling, combining ricotta, ½ cup powdered sugar, orange zest, vanilla paste, and cinnamon powder in a mixer and whip until smooth and airy, like a super light frosting.

2. Remove the whisk and, using a spatula, fold in chocolate chips, gently spooning the filling over on itself until mixed.

3. Scoop as much filling as manageable into a piping bag and cut a hole around ¾ of an inch wide in the bottom.

4. Insert the piping bag halfway into the first cannoli shell, from the left side. Once you've packed half the shell with filling, repeat on the right side. Do the same for the rest of the cannoli.

5. To serve, put a couple dabs of filling on the plate to keep the shells from rolling. Place the cannoli on top of the dabs and arrange to your liking. Use the 4 additional tablespoons of chips to garnish each open end of your cannoli. Finally, dust with 1 tablespoon of powdered sugar.

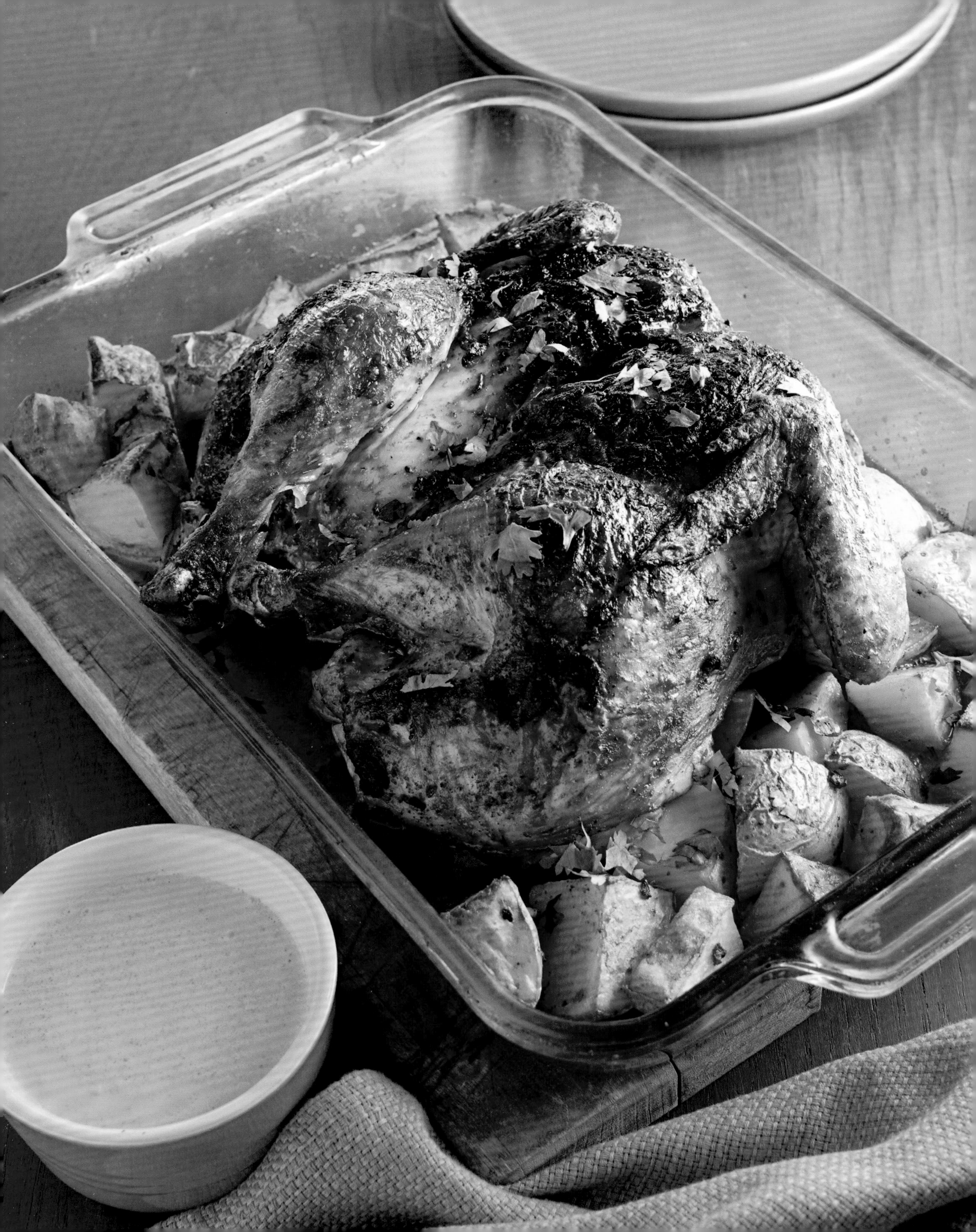

PERUVIAN ROAST CHICKEN

GF

YIELD:
2 TO 4 PORTIONS

PREP TIME:
OVERNIGHT MARINADE,
PLUS 2 TO 3 HOURS

The Beetle is one of my oldest foes, and yet every time I tangle with him, I'm struck by the fact that his early costume had a weakness that I didn't notice immediately. See, this one time on Morris Avenue, a battle took us straight through the front of a Peruvian restaurant. The chef, Ricardo, was one tough cookie. Rather than run, he dumped a scalding hot pot of soup on the Beetle. The guy inside the power suit, insulated. The servos in his power suit, not as much. Shorted his costume out and saved the day. I got this roast chicken recipe from Ricardo as thanks for sticking around to help him clean up afterward.

FOR THE MARINADE:

1 whole chicken, approximately 3 pounds

2 teaspoon ground cumin

¼ cup aji panca

¼ cup aji amarillo

½ cup canola oil

4 tablespoons soy sauce (gluten-free versions available, if preferred)

7 tablespoons water

2 teaspoons salt

1 teaspoon black pepper

1 teaspoon oregano

4 tablespoons white vinegar

1½ tablespoons grated garlic

FOR THE POTATOES:

4 Yukon Gold potatoes cut in 2-inch pieces

2 teaspoons kosher salt

1 teaspoon cracked black pepper

4 tablespoons olive oil

FOR THE CILANTRO SAUCE:

½ cup sour cream

½ cup mayonnaise

1 cup packed cilantro leaves

1½ ounces lime juice

1 small clove garlic, grated

2 tablespoonse aji amarillo

1 teaspoon salt

1. To spatchcock your chicken, remove the backbone with a knife or kitchen shears. Start at the top, where the neck is, and cut down along the joints on either side until you get to the tail. Once this bone is removed, press down on either side of the breast and fully open up the chicken. You can remove the center bone, or keel bone, with your fingers.

2. In a mixing bowl, whisk the cumin, aji panca, aji amarillo, canola oil, soy sauce, water, salt, black pepper, oregano, white vinegar, and garlic to create your marinade.

3. In a pan or deep bowl, lay the chicken in the bottom and cover liberally with the marinade. Cover in the fridge and let sit overnight, or for at least 6 hours.

4. When you're ready to cook, preheat your oven to 350°F and turn on its interior fan.

5. In a roasting pan, mix the potatoes with 2 teaspoons of salt, 1 teaspoon of pepper, and 4 tablespoons of olive oil. Top this with your chicken, flesh side down. Don't worry if the marinade is dripping all over the potatoes.

6. Roast the chicken in the oven until the thickest parts measure 155° to 160°F, about 50 to 70 minutes. If the poultry starts to brown too fast, you can always cover it with foil. When the chicken is done, remove it from the oven, set aside, and let it rest.

7. To make the cilantro sauce, combine sour cream, mayonnaise, cilantro leaves, lime juice, garlic, aji amarillo, and salt in a blender and puree until smooth. Place in the refrigerator and chill until it's time to serve.

8. To serve, cover a platter with the roasted potatoes and place your roasted chicken on top. Spoon the pan drippings over the chicken and potatoes. Serve with the cilantro sauce on the side.

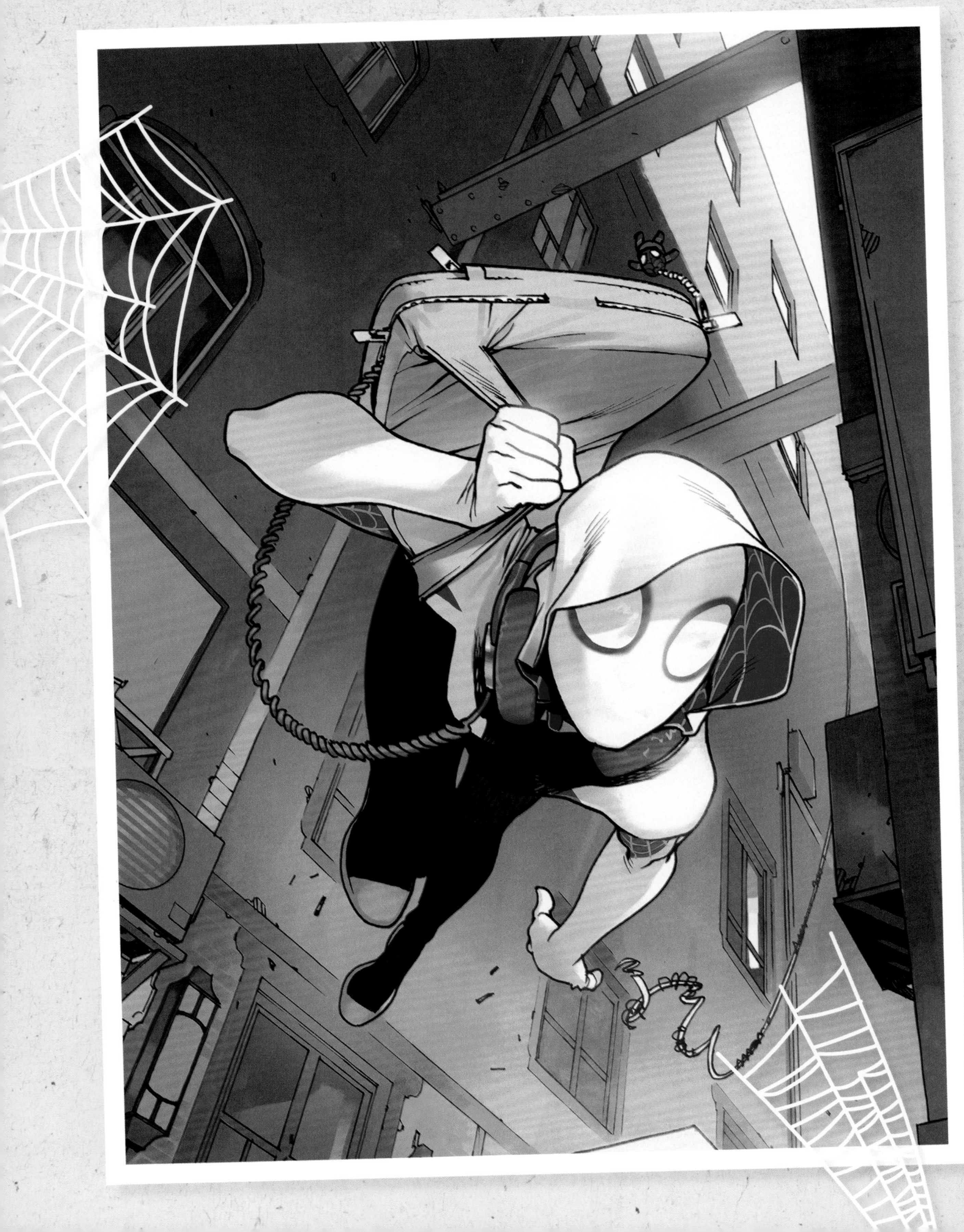

GHOST-SPIDER'S SELECTIONS

I'm going to turn these last two recipes over to a guest in our universe, an amazing Spider-Woman in her own right, and a crime fighter who can pull off a white suit with more swag than Moon Knight ever could. Heroes and heroines, I give you Ghost-Spider.

Hi folks. I'm sending these recipes via my friend, Spidey, and he's promised he'll take care with my identity. I hear it doesn't go so well for super heroes in this universe when they're discovered. Anyway, I think it's safe to share that I'm a university exchange student from a neighboring universe. At night, I usually fight crime back in my own dimension, where everyone knows my name. Like that show you guys have here. Note to Spidey: When you see this, can you remind me of the name of that show? Anyway, my symbiote costume and I love it in your universe. Especially the food. My powers come from this living, breathing colony of spiders. And they need to eat. Just not brains or whatever that Venom guy feeds his suit, ugh. So, while my symbiote chows down on kale chips (my suit loves a high-cellulose diet), I like to explore the Bronx of your universe and feed the girl behind the Ghost-Spider.

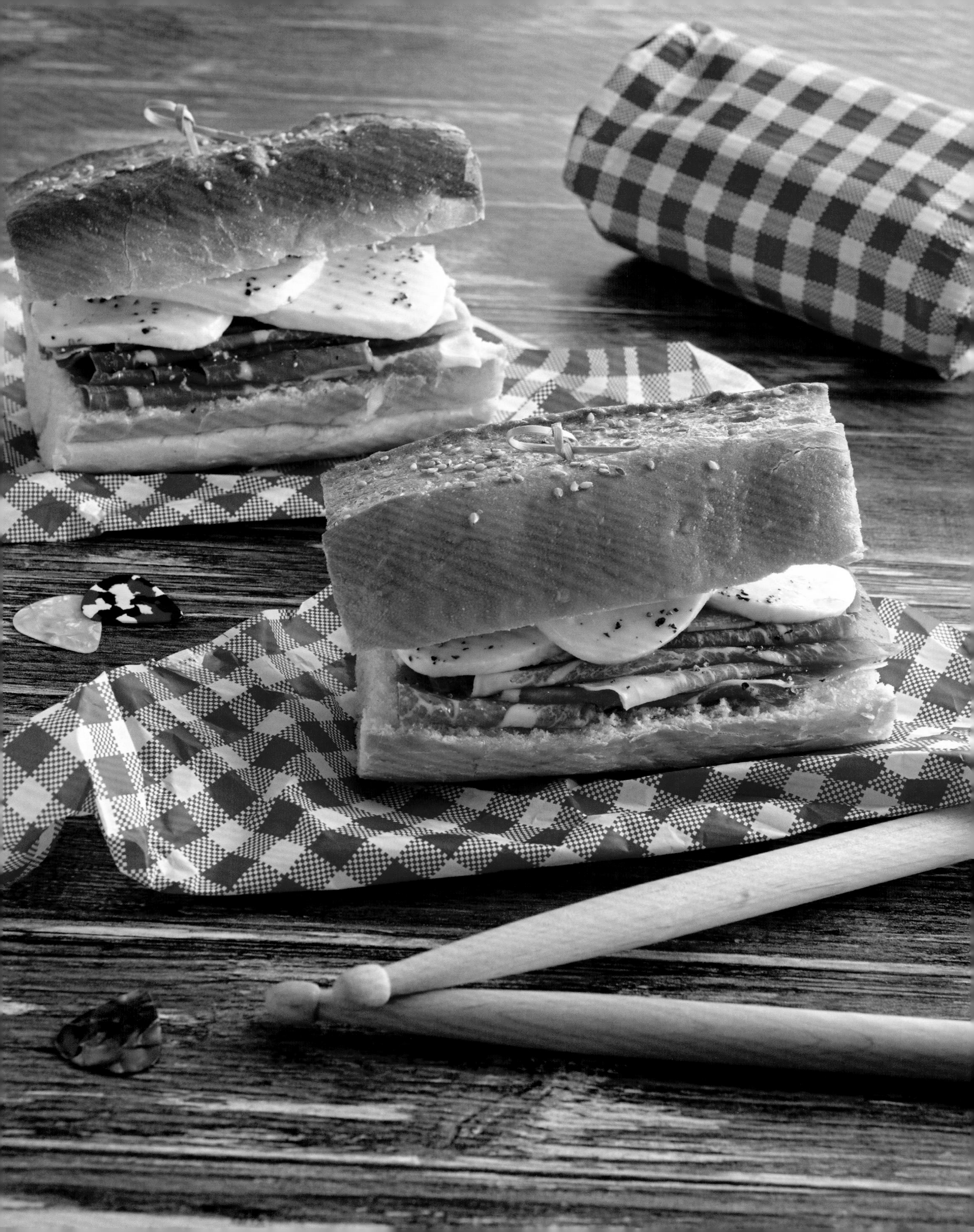

PROSCIUTTO MOZZARELLA SANDWICH

YIELD:
1 LARGE SANDWICH

PREP TIME:
15 MINUTES

I'm in a band back home, and a fight with your dimension's Scorpion recently made me late for band practice. Again. *But it's not my fault.* Interdimensional commutes are the worst. So as a peace offering, this time I stopped by a deli on Fordham Road before jumping back to my dimension. If this prosciutto sandwich can soothe the savage glare I get regularly from our band leader, then it's not just food, it's manna from heaven.

One 8-inch sesame seed roll, about 4 inches wide

16 slices prosciutto, sliced thin from your deli

8 ounces freshest mozzarella possible, or mozzarella packaged in water, cut ½-inch thick

2 tablespoons extra virgin olive oil

1 teaspoon flaky sea salt

1 teaspoon cracked black pepper

1. Slice the bread lengthwise. On the bottom half, gently layer the prosciutto, folded on itself to create height evenly across the sandwich.

2. Place the mozzarella over the prosciutto all the way across the sandwich, creating a slight overlap between each piece of cheese to look like shingles on a rooftop.

3. Liberally dress the mozzarella and prosciutto with the extra virgin olive oil and season with sea salt and fresh cracked pepper.

4. Place the other half of the bread on top, gently cut in desired portions with a serrated knife, and serve.

MULTIDIMENSIONAL EGGPLANT PARMESAN

YIELD:
2 SERVINGS
PREP TIME:
2 HOURS

Remember when I mentioned that everyone knew who I was back home? Well, that includes my dad, who is a cop. In fact, he's *the* cop. A police captain in my version of New York. Kind of a problem considering I was wanted for a murder I didn't commit. But I know you've all been there. Dinner was awkward around my house before he found out who I was. Now we're mending fences. Slowly. So on those nights when I'm not at band practice, but somehow still running late to get home (it really is the interdimensional commute, I swear), I stop by this pizzeria on Belmont Avenue and pick up this eggplant Parmesan for me and my dad. He lived off this dish when he was a beat cop. Best eggplant Parm in two dimensions. And he would know, so you can't go wrong with this recipe.

FOR THE EGGPLANT:

1 medium eggplant, cut into 6 slices, each ⅓ inch thick

3 tablespoons kosher salt

32 ounces of your favorite tomato sauce

1 ½ cup shredded mozzarella

6 leaves fresh basil

2 tablespoons extra virgin olive oil

FOR THE BREADING:

2 cups panko

1 teaspoon black pepper, ground

1 tablespoon salt

1 tablespoon oregano

¼ cup grated Parmesan

4 eggs

4 tablespoons water

2 cups flour

TO FRY:

1 ¼ cup canola oil

¾ cup extra virgin olive oil

1. Slice the eggplant into ⅓-inch slices and season liberally with the salt. Layer them on paper towels on a tray or plate for at least one hour before you want to bread them. This will pull some of the bitterness and moisture from them.

2. Take 1 cup of panko and pulse it in a food processor. This finer grind will help coat the eggplant. Keep the remaining cup as is to add another texture.

3. Combine the two sets of panko, black pepper, salt, oregano, and Parmesan in a mixing bowl.

4. Crack the eggs into a separate bowl, beat well, and add water.

5. Pour the flour into a third bowl and line it up next to the other two as your breading station.

6. Coat each slice of eggplant well, starting with the flour, then the egg mix, and ending with the breading mix. Set eggplant aside on a rack.

7. Combine canola oil and olive oil and heat in a large frying pan or pot with enough wall height to prevent splashing or overflow. Preheat your oven to 375°F and turn on the fan.

8. Test your oil by dropping a bit of egg mix or breading into it. The mix should fry up immediately. When ready, gently lay a slice or two of eggplant into the oil at a time, depending on pan size. Always lay the slice away from you, so that if the oil splashes, it doesn't reach your hands. Carefully fry on both sides until golden. Reserve back on your baking rack. Repeat with all slices.

9. Once you're done frying, spoon your favorite tomato sauce onto each slice of eggplant and cover with shredded mozzarella. Each slice takes about ½ cup of sauce and ¼ cup of cheese.

10. Set the smothered slices on a sheet tray and place on a rack in the oven. Bake until the cheese is fully melted.

11. Spoon a bit of warmed tomato sauce onto the center of a plate and place a slice of eggplant on top. From there, stack as many layers of eggplant on top as you wish to serve. Garnish with basil and 2 tablespoons of extra virgin olive oil.

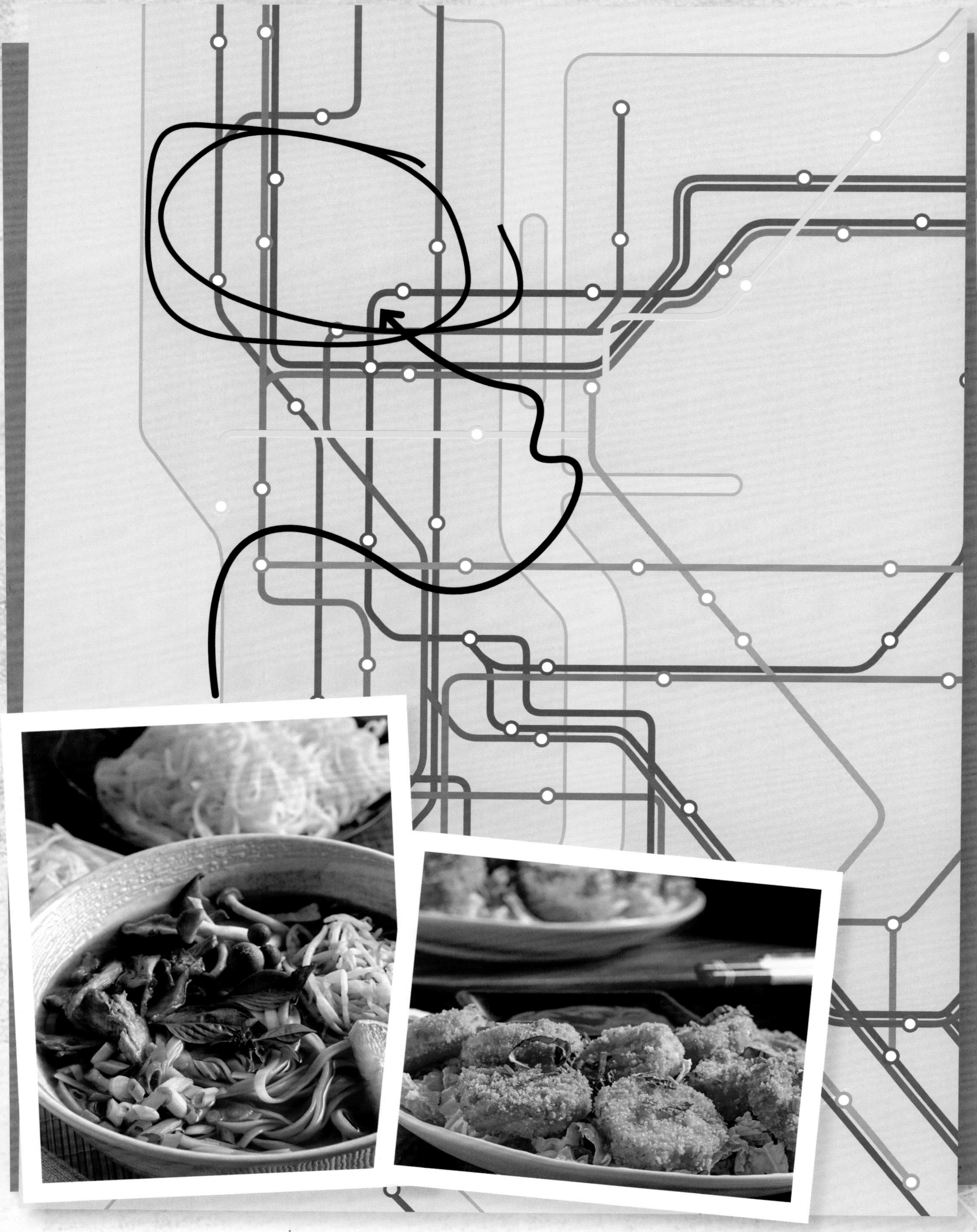

3 MANHATTAN

There's nowhere else in the world
like the Island of Manhattan. Which
is why so many of us super heroes
choose to call this place home. I mean,
seriously, I'm surprised the skies
over Midtown don't come with their own
traffic lights for all of us, swinging,
flying, gliding, jumping, and otherwise
clogging the flight pattern. There's
an energy to this town. It's the city
that never sleeps—that goes for the
crime around here as well as the food.
I don't watch over this borough alone,
and there's no way I was going to
tackle this part of the book by myself
either. We'll have contributions from
more of my Spider crew, and a slew of
other notable names and faces, enough
to cover dishes from the Bowery to the
Heights, Harlem to the Met Cloisters,
and all points in between.

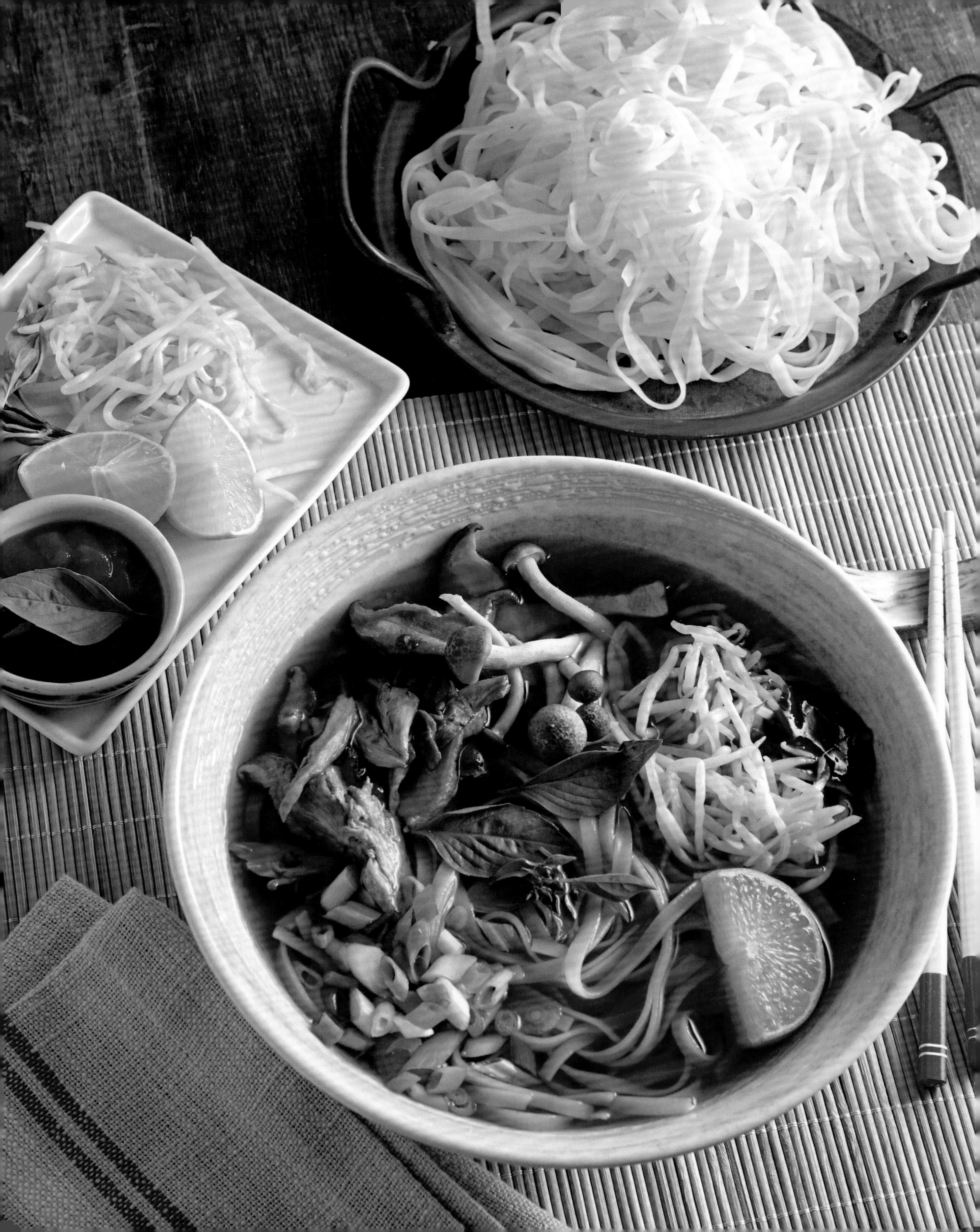

VEGAN PHO

V+

YIELD: 2 BOWLS

PREP TIME: 45 MINUTES

Juggernaut, a man who needs no introduction. Because he'll just barge right in and introduce himself. Here's how he introduced me to pho. Everyone's least favorite human wrecking ball was on a rampage, and only one man could stop him. Thor. Thor was that one man, but of course he wasn't available, so the responsibility fell to me. I buried Juggernaut in about forty feet of quick-drying cement. Brilliant, right? Wish I did that before he spent about three hours pounding me into one big five-foot-eleven spider bruise (my everything hurts to this day just thinking it). Anyway, flash forward a few years and the Juggernaut has mellowed a tad. He finds me, tells me he wants to make up for the hurting he put on me all those years earlier. Turns out he's learned that breaking bread versus heads heals many wounds. A lesson he picked up from his stepbrother Charles Xavier (yeah, I know, families are complicated). Early on in this mea culpa tour, Juggy developed a love for pho, and to this day uses it as a peace offering. He found a great spot on Delancey for us to bury the hatchet. It's some great pho, which I didn't know I loved until now, and the vegan option tickled my taste buds in a way I didn't expect. I forgave Juggy for our tussle. And pho this good almost makes me forget the pain he put me through. Almost.

- 8 cups vegetable stock
- 1/4 cup dried shiitake mushrooms
- 1/4 cup thinly sliced ginger
- 1 cinnamon stick
- 2 pieces star anise
- 1 bunch scallions, sliced thin
- 1/2 bunch Thai basil, stemmed (with stems set aside & saved)
- 3 tablespoons soy sauce
- Kosher salt
- 1 cup bean sprouts, washed and stemmed
- 1 cup 1/4-inch-sliced fresh shiitake mushrooms
- 1 cup 1/2-inch-sliced fresh oyster mushrooms
- 1 package beech mushrooms, trimmed
- 1 teaspoon ground black pepper
- 8 cups water
- One 16-ounce package bánh pho
- 2 tablespoons hoisin
- 2 tablespoons sriracha
- 1 lime, cut in wedges

1. Preheat oven to 450°F.
2. In a large pot, combine vegetable stock with dried shiitake, ginger, cinnamon, star anise, and half of the sliced scallions. Bring to a simmer on the stove and then turn off heat immediately.
3. Add 6 Thai basil stems and let steep for 10 minutes. Strain into a separate bowl to preserve the broth, pressing all the stock from the shiitakes and scallions. Keep the broth warm and season it with 2 tablespoons of soy sauce and salt to taste.
4. Combine all the fresh mushrooms in a mixing bowl and season with 1 teaspoon of salt, the remaining tablespoon of soy sauce, and 1 teaspoon black pepper. Spread on a nonstick baking tray and roast in the oven until cooked, about 10 minutes. Reserve warm.

CONTINUED ON PAGE 58

CONTINUED FROM PAGE 57

5. In a separate pot, bring 8 cups of water to a full boil and turn off heat. Add the pho noodles to the water and fully submerge. Let sit until *just* soft, about 4 minutes. Strain from hot water and portion out the desired amount of noodles into two deep soup bowls. Rinse remaining noodles in cold water and store in an air-tight container for another day.
6. Bring your broth back up to a simmer.
7. In each of the two soup bowls now filled with noodles, top one quadrant with roasted mushroom mix and another with bean sprouts. In the remaining half of the bowl, add scallions and a few leaves of Thai basil. Pour 3 cups of broth over the noodles and serve with a side of hoisin, sriracha, cut limes, and more of the Thai basil.

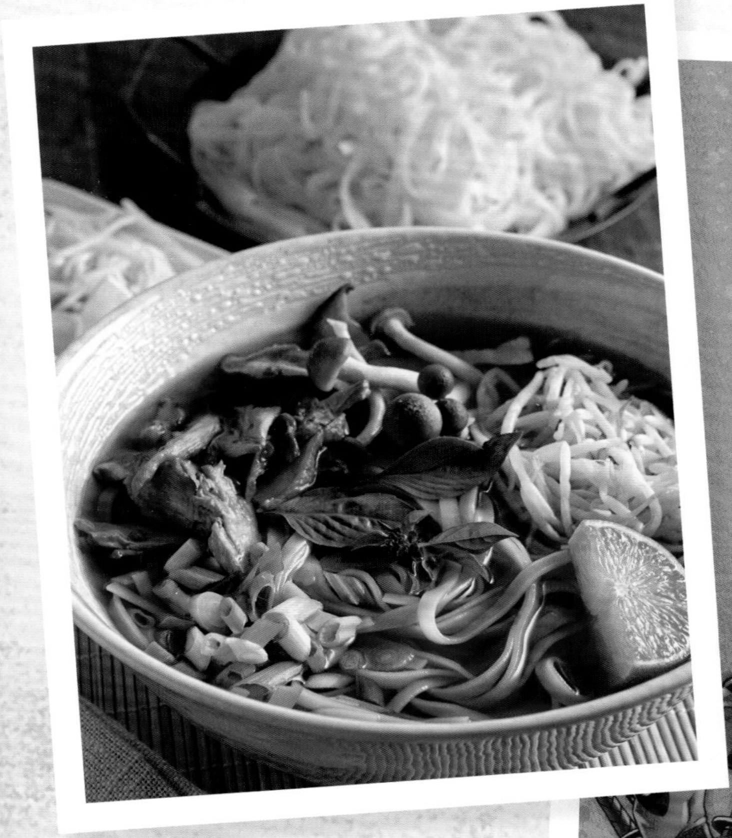

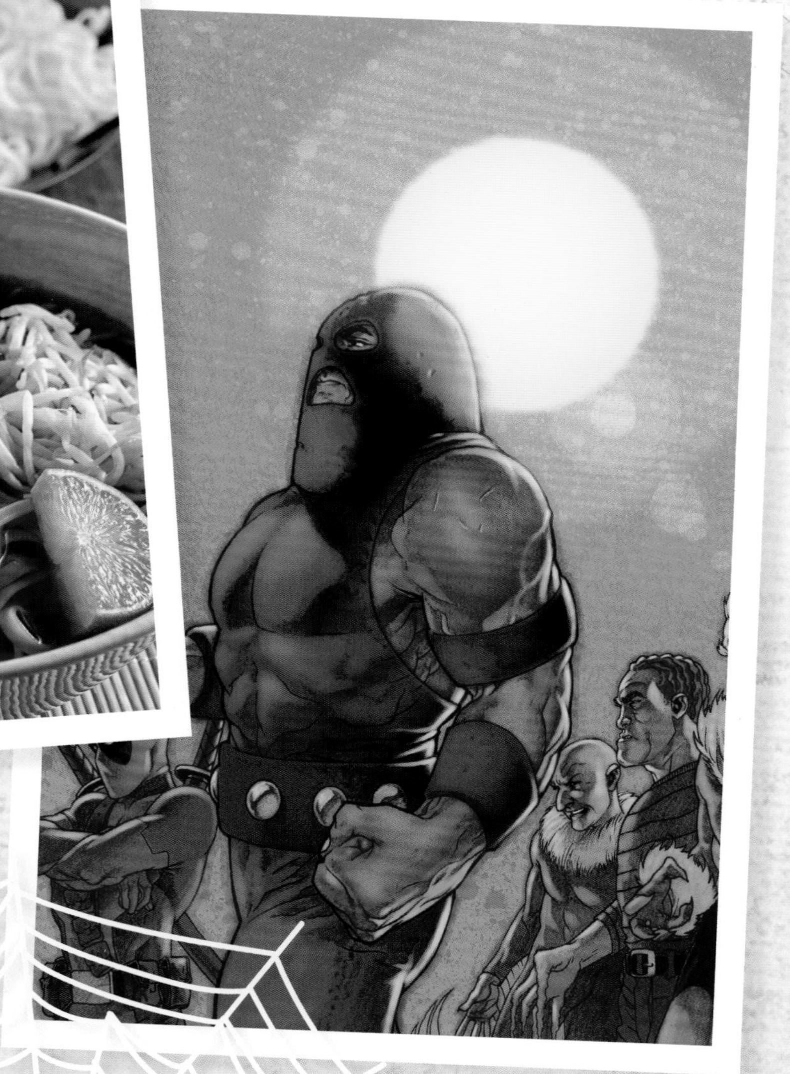

MANHATTAN CLAM CHOWDER

GF

YIELD:
6 SERVINGS

PREP TIME:
90 MINUTES

Any sports fan worth their salt knows that Boston and New York hold the sort of feelings for each other usually reserved for the Richardses and the Von Dooms. Well, it's not just sports. Ask Captain Marvel. What? We hang out! Anyway, when we do, we tend to argue about everything. Massachusetts vs. New York: There's nothing "further, higher, faster" than that rivalry. But I *think* I convinced her of the merits of authentic *Manhattan* Clam Chowder.

Okay, I didn't get an admission from her exactly, but she did ask for seconds of this recipe.

Nice try, Spidey.

4 tablespoons extra virgin olive oil

6-8 slices bacon, cut into ½-inch pieces

3 cloves garlic, sliced thin

1¼ cup small-diced carrots

¾ cup small-diced celery

¾ cup small-diced fennel

1½ cup small-diced onion

1½ pounds Yukon potatoes, diced small

32 ounces clam stock

One 28-ounce can San Marzano chopped tomatoes, including the juice

2 sprigs thyme

1 bay leaf

1 teaspoon ground black pepper

10 ounces clam meat, fresh shucked or frozen

1 tablespoon Old Bay seasoning

Kosher salt

4 tablespoons flat-leaf parsley, cut into fine chiffonade

1. In a 16-quart braiser or stockpot, add olive oil and render bacon till crispy, about 3 to 5 minutes. Remove the bacon and blot on paper towel.

2. Add garlic to the pot and quickly sauté on medium-high heat for 1 to 2 minutes.

3. Then add carrots, celery, fennel, and onion, sweating till tender, about 6 to 8 minutes.

4. Add the potatoes and then the clam stock, tomatoes, thyme, bay leaf, and black pepper.

5. Simmer until all the vegetables are just tender, about 20 minutes, on medium-low heat. Remove the thyme and bay leaf.

6. Add the clams and bring back to a simmer for 3 to 5 minutes. Season with Old Bay and salt to taste.

7. Ladle soup into bowls and garnish with bacon and parsley.

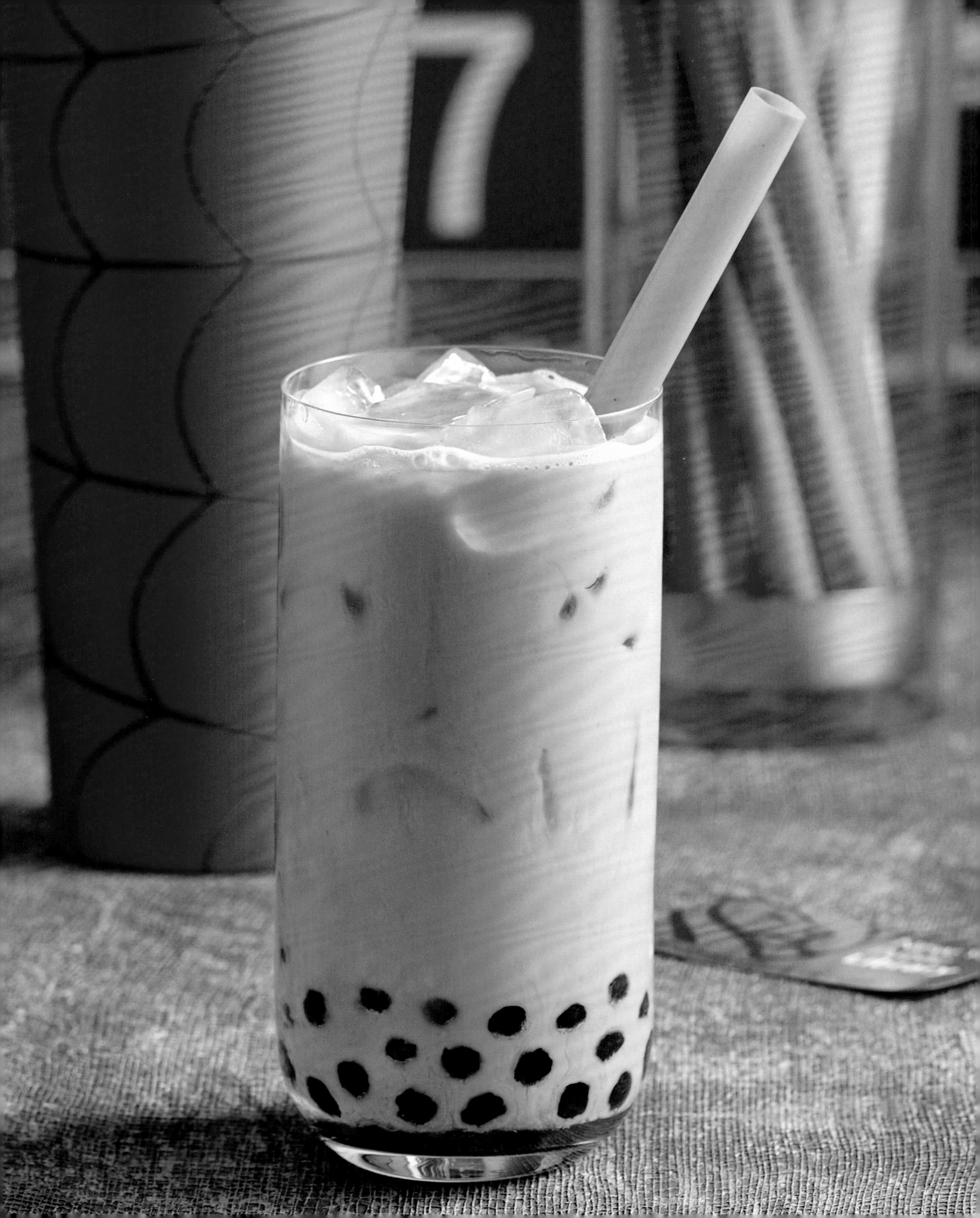

BUBBLE TEA

GF | V

YIELD:
2 SERVINGS

PREP TIME
45 MINUTES

We've reached Midtown. And this recipe has been a lifesaver for me as, for those of you who have not noticed, this red and blue unitard does *not* have a short-sleeved option. Summers can be toasty here in New York, and in Midtown especially, when the asphalt seems to radiate a heat I can feel even as I swing above Seventh Avenue. That's when a cold cup of Bubble Tea is the move to make. It's sweet, but not too sweet, and portable. The perfect grab-and-go drink as I swing through Koreatown.

½ cup honey

8½ cups water

½ cup tapioca pearls

2 tablespoons matcha powder

3 cups unsweetened almond milk

OPTIONAL:

Wide, tapioca-size straw

1. Combine the honey and ½ cup water in a pot and bring to a simmer until homogenized. Reserve and chill.

2. Bring the remaining 8 cups of water to a boil and add the tapioca. Simmer until the tapioca is done to your liking and strain. It should be easily chewy. Rinse the pearls well in cold water. Cover them in the honey syrup and chill.

3. With a hand blender or regular blender, combine matcha and almond milk and blend until completely emulsified.

4. In large glass, spoon ⅓ cup of tapioca into the bottom, add ice, then pour in matcha milk. Adjust to the sweetness of your liking by adding more of the honey syrup if needed. Drink with a tapioca-size straw, if possible. Save the rest of your tapioca for later!

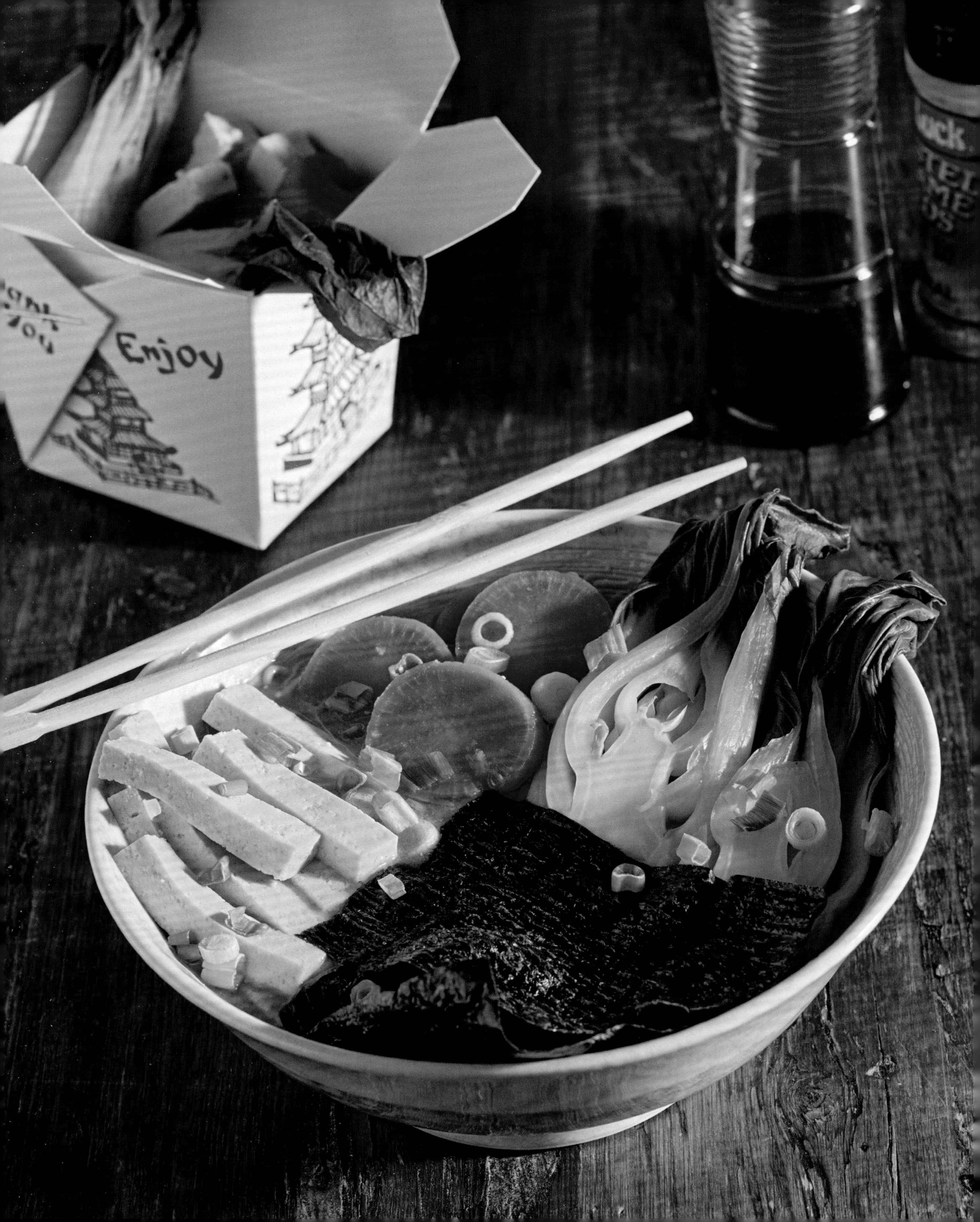
Enjoy

V

YIELD: 2 BOWLS

PREP TIME: 40 MINUTES

MISO RAMEN

If Bubble Tea is my on-the-go treat, this miso dish is my "pick up a bowl, find a perch along the side of the Empire State Building, and call it a day" recipe. I was turned on to Miso Ramen by a delivery driver named Kenji. Right place wrong time for Kenji. His scooter, my fight with Klaw, the master of sound. I was impressed. Kenji got knocked off his ride and yet he didn't spill a single order. At least not on the ground. It all got me pretty good as I caught him. Not my most graceful moment, but the smell of that heavenly miso broth stayed with me. I mean, it really stayed with me—I was picking ramen out of my web shooters for days. Later, I circled back around to see how he was doing. He was so grateful he promised me ramen on the house and even shared this recipe.

4 heads baby bok choy, cut in half and blanched tender

10 cups vegetable stock

¼ cup thinly sliced ginger

¼ cup shiitake mushroom stems

1 cup sliced shiitake mushrooms

10 tablespoons red miso paste

2 tablespoons soy sauce

Salt and pepper

4 ounces firm tofu, cut into 2-inch-long batons, each ½-inch thick

Two 3½-ounce packs ramen noodles, highest quality available

6 slices pickled daikon

8 sheets toasted, salted nori

2 tablespoons sliced scallions

1. Bring a medium pot to a boil with 4 cups of water on high heat. Drop the bok choy in and cook for 3 minutes, until a knife can easily pass through its base. Remove and dunk the bok choy in ice water until cold. Reserve.
2. In a large pot, bring vegetable stock to a simmer with the ginger and shiitake stems. Let steep for 10 minutes. Then strain into a separate pot, pushing out all the juice.
3. Bring the steeped vegetable stock to a boil again, adding shiitake slices and the red miso paste. Then add the soy sauce to taste, as well as salt and pepper if needed.
4. Remove a cup of broth and put it in a small sauté pan on medium-high heat. Add the blanched bok choy and the tofu to heat them up.
5. Add two packs of ramen noodles to the miso soup base and cook until al dente.
6. Using chopsticks or tongs, divide the noodles between two large bowls and ladle in broth and shiitakes to cover. Tuck bok choy into one side of each bowl. Then do the same with the tofu batons.
7. Next to the tofu, place the slices of pickled daikon. In the remaining empty space, lean your toasted nori on the side. Garnish with sliced scallions.

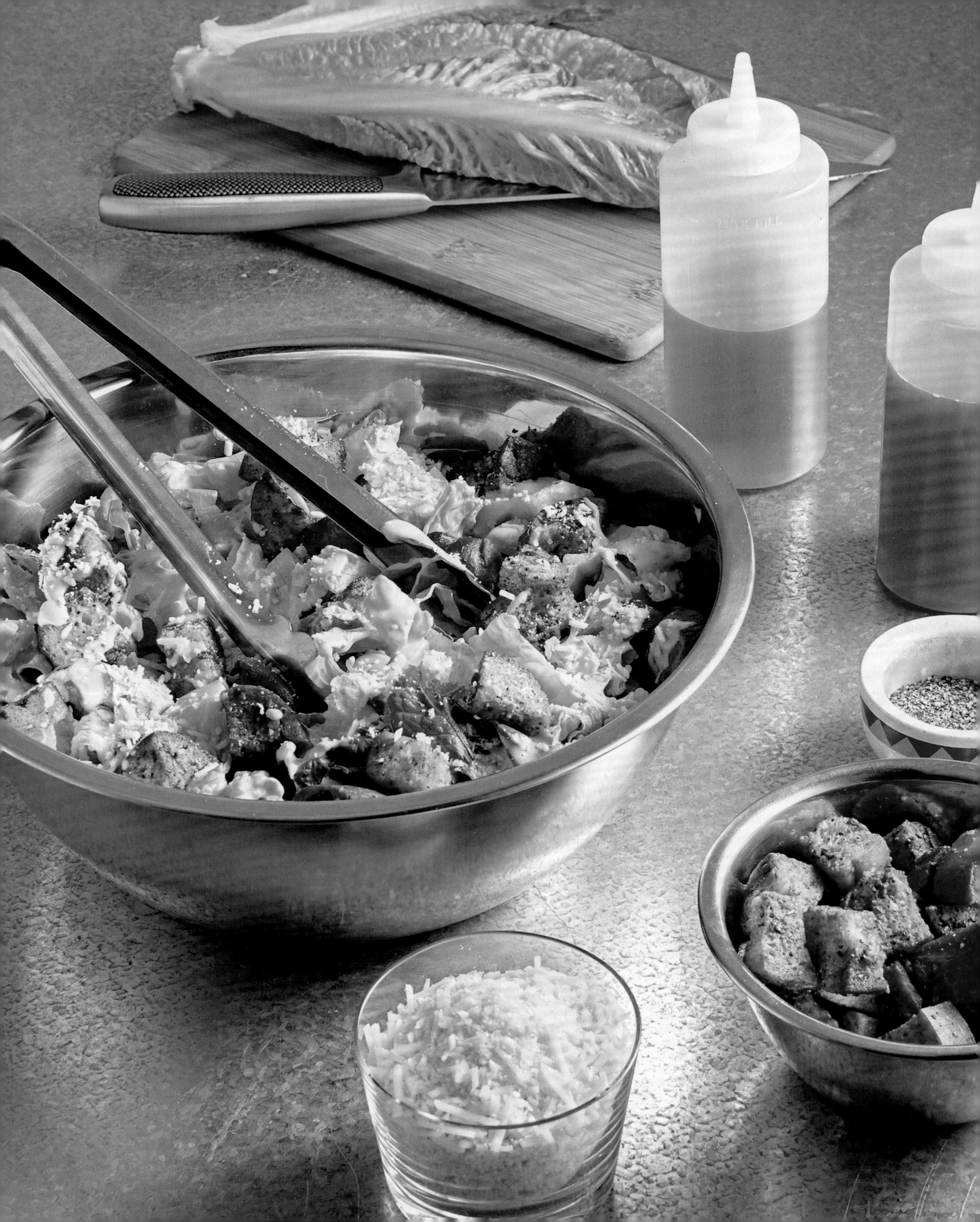

CAESAR SALAD

YIELD:
2 TO 4
PORTIONS

PREP TIME:
40 MINUTES

I try to take every villain I face off against seriously. I really do. I swear. But when a guy like Plantman decides to wage war on a regional salad chain, well, let's just say I'm glad this mask hides the expression on my face. Long story short, and an industrial-strength dose of herbicide later, Plantman's down for the count and I'm getting a salad named after me on the menu. I told them my name is Caesar. All things considered, that's a win in my book.

FOR THE CROUTONS:

4 tablespoons butter

2 ounces olive oil

1 ounce grated Parmesan

2 teaspoons oregano

1 teaspoon chile flakes

1 tablespoon garlic, minced or grated

2 teaspoon salt

1½ teaspoon cracked black pepper

2 cups cubed Italian bread

For the dressing:

2 egg yolks

½ ounce lemon juice

2 teaspoon Dijon mustard

1 tablespoon anchovies

1 small clove

2 tablespoons grated Parmesan

1 teaspoon salt

6 tablespoons olive oil

FOR THE SALAD:

1½ cups romaine hearts, cut diagonally in 2-inch chunks.

2 tablespoons grated Parmesan

2 tablespoons Parmesan shards

Cracked black pepper

1. Preheat oven to 350°F.

2. To create your crouton seasoning, melt butter together with the olive oil in a small pan on medium heat. When fully melted, add Parmesan, oregano, chile flakes, garlic, salt, and pepper. Stir and mix well.

1. Cut you bread into 1-inch cubes. Once you have enough for 2 cups, add this to a large bowl and pour your seasoning over the bread until cubes are evenly covered.

2. Spread the seasoned bread on a baking sheet lined with foil or parchment paper and bake approximately 20 minutes, or until croutons are golden and toasted, pausing to stir halfway through.

3. Make your dressing by combining egg yolks, lemon juice, Dijon mustard, anchovy, clove, grated Parmesan, and salt in a food processor. Once smooth, stream in the olive oil until emulsified

4. On a large platter or in a bowl, combine romaine hearts and 2 tablespoons grated Parmesan with the croutons and dressing. Top with the shards of Parmesan and add cracked black pepper to taste if desired.

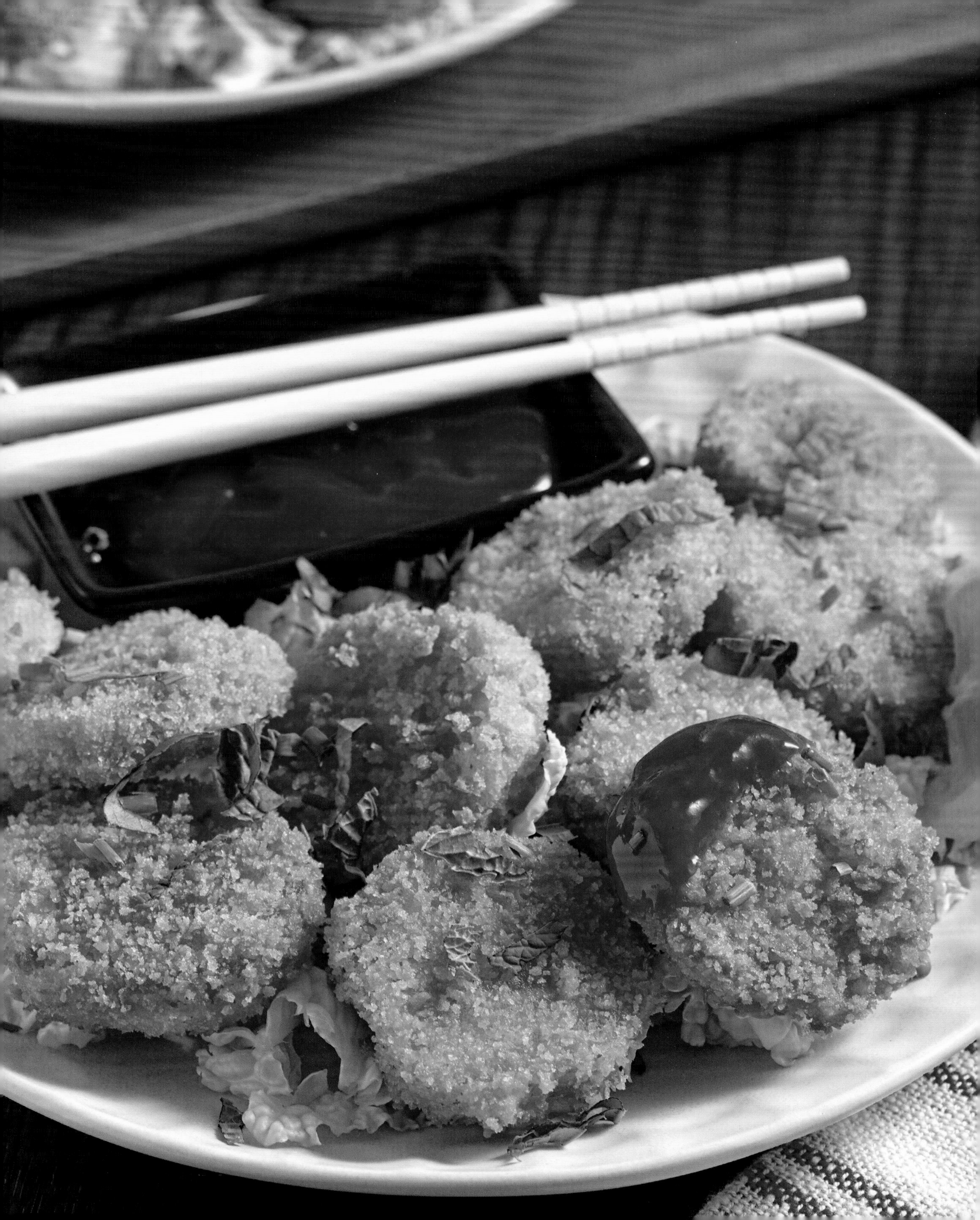

SWEET POTATO KATSU

V

YIELD: 4 PORTIONS

PREP TIME: 1½ HOURS

Hi, I'm Peni. And this recipe comes from me and Spider. We're psychically bonded and we pilot SP//dr, our giant mech suit. I used to think it would just be me and Spider forever, fighting crime together on our world. Then I met your Spider-Man and the rest of the Spider-Verse. I wasn't sure I could trust all these new people at first, but Spider had a good feeling about them. I'm glad he did. Now I pop into this universe from time to time to visit with Ghost-Spider and Araña. They take me all over town for the best vegan meals. This recipe comes from one of my favorite places! The owner of the restaurant even lets me park SP//dr out front. Which is super nice since this suit is nearly nine feet tall. But Ghost-Spider and Araña let me know that New Yorkers get kind of weird about parking. So now I just pick up this katsu to go, or make it at home. Thanks for reading this, and I hope you enjoy the recipe, friends!

2 large sweet potatoes
2 teaspoons kosher salt
1 teaspoon cracked black pepper
2 tablespoons extra virgin olive oil

FOR THE SAUCE:

¼ cup ketchup
¼ cup Worcestershire sauce
2 tablespoons light brown sugar
1 tablespoon soy sauce

FOR BREADING:

2 cups all-purpose (AP) flour
1 cup aquafaba (water from chickpea cans)
1 ½ cups panko

FOR FRYING:

6 cups canola or preferred frying oil

FOR PLATING:

½ head cabbage, freshly shredded
4 lemon wedges
8 leaves basil, cut into chiffonade
4 tablespoons minced chives
12 leaves mint, cut into chiffonade

1. Preheat your oven to 300°F.
2. Wash the sweet potatoes well and peel them. Cut widthwise into ¾-inch-thick slices. Season potatoes with salt, pepper, and olive oil. Then lay them on a rack.
3. Bake for about 15 minutes, until a fork just pierces easily. They should be slightly undercooked. Let cool to room temperature.
4. In a small bowl, make your tonkatsu sauce by combining the ketchup, Worcestershire sauce, brown sugar, and soy sauce.
5. Set up your breading station with three containers: one with flour, one with aquafaba, and one with panko.
6. Starting with the flour, coat the sweet potato slices. Then dip them in the aquafaba. Dunk into the panko bowl last, pressing firmly so the crumbs stick to the potatoes. Set them aside on a tray.
7. Heat the oil in a large frying pan or pot with enough wall height so that the oil won't splash out or overflow.
8. Test the oil by dropping a bit of the breading in. It should fry up immediately. If ready, gently lay a slice of breaded sweet potato in the oil. Always lay the slice away from you, so any splashing oil doesn't reach your hands. Carefully fry potatoes on both sides, flipping with a spatula, until lightly golden. It should be about 2 minutes per side. Reserve on a paper towel.
9. Fill a side dish with tonkatsu sauce and arrange a bed of shredded cabbage for the sweet potato to nestle against. Add a lemon wedge to squeeze later. Top your sweet potato katsu with the chiffonade of basil, chives, and mint.

KEBABS

SPIDEY: And now, for an ever so brief contribution from everyone's favorite former media magnet . . . I'm not printing this . . . I'm not printing this? Why did I even mention I was doing this book to you? You get one, J.J., you get one of these and that's it. Folks, here's J. Jonah Jameson with a few words:

JJJ: Thank you, Spider-Man, for this opportunity to address the costumed menaces of this city directly *JONAH!!*

JJJ: Now, back in my day, we didn't have fancy ray beams and lightning coming out of every place. We just had a pen, our wits, and a drive to get to the truth. It's what made me such a determined *AND MODEST* journalist, a shrewd and nurturing publisher, and now the head of an ever-expanding podcasting empire. We're all heroes in our own unique ways. *SURE WE ARE*

JJJ: This cookbook's attempt to bring some unity to the community reminds me of the times when my team would have to pull together to put a late-breaking story to bed. I'd make a point to go and get food for all the reporters . . . so they'd stop complaining and focus on their work. There was a restaurant just across the way from the *Daily Bugle* that would keep their kitchen open for us at my request. Served the best kebabs in town. Those moments made me proud to be a newshound. And I'd like to share this particular recipe with you good folks. Consider it a peace offering, if nothing else. I know I've made your lives difficult in the past, and if the wall-crawler and I can bury the hatchet after all these years, then anything's possible.

SPIDEY: I'm shocked, and stunned, and speechless. That actually ended up being . . . nice? That's the word I'm looking for, right? Nice? Thank you, JJJ. You stuck the landing on that one.

GF

YIELD:
4 PORTIONS

PREP TIME:
1 HOUR AND 10 MINUTES

- Wooden skewers (or metal as an alternative)
- 2 pounds beef tenderloin
- 1 sweet onion
- 2 cloves garlic
- 2 teaspoons chopped fresh thyme
- 2 teaspoons dried oregano
- 1 cup extra virgin olive oil
- 1 teaspoon smoked hot paprika
- 2 ounces lemon juice
- 1 teaspoon ground coriander
- 2 tablespoons kosher salt
- 1 teaspoon ground black pepper
- 8 ounces tzatziki

1. If using wooden kebab skewers, soak them in water for at least 30 minutes. If using metal skewers, skip to step 2.
2. Trim the fat from the beef tenderloin and cut into 1-inch cubes. Slice the sweet onion into 1-inch pieces. Grate the garlic and chop the thyme.
3. Combine beef, garlic, thyme, oregano, olive oil, paprika, lemon juice, coriander, salt, and pepper in a bowl. Let sit for at least an hour to marinate.
4. Assemble skewers, alternating meat and onion until all sticks are equally apportioned.
5. Grill on medium-high heat, turning frequently, for about 10 minutes.
6. Serve with tzatziki.

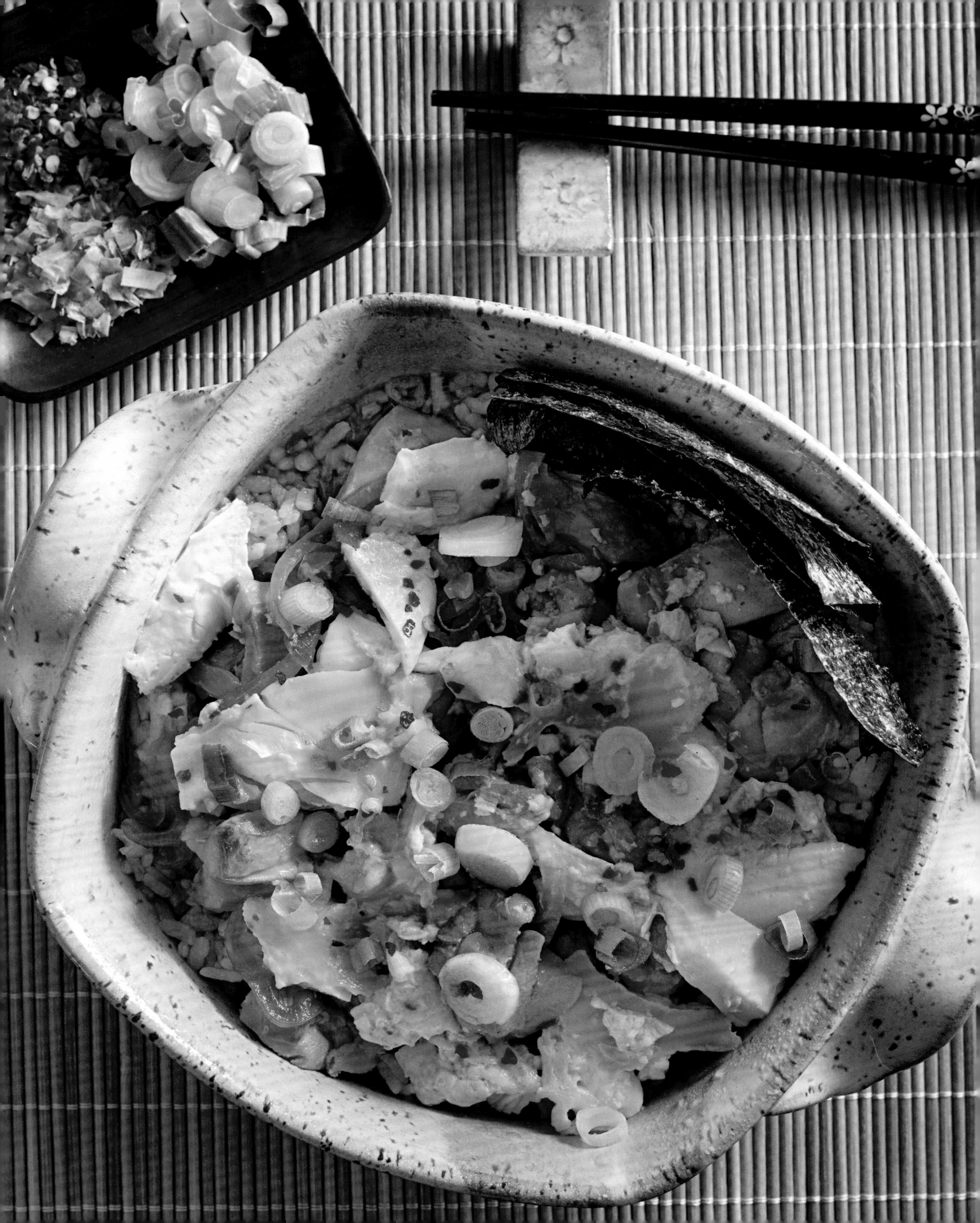

YIELD:
4 PORTIONS
PREP TIME:
1 HOUR

OYAKODON

Despite having the greatest kung fu teachers (I'm getting to this story later, I swear), I don't often get the chance to punch "outnumbered-by-ninjas" off my Baddie Bingo card. Well, lucky (?) for Ambassador Kenzo Uchiyama, I was the only thing standing between him and the uber-deadly clan of assassins known as the Hand. And lucky for me, it all happened right in front of the United Nations, so I've got some witnesses. You know who has been through one of those us-versus-like-thirty-shuriken-and-katana-wielding-crew situations? Wolverine, Daredevil, Black Widow. And now me.

So, guys, when do we all meet and compare notes? At the next potluck maybe? Anyway, the ambassador insisted I dine with him after saving his life. Yes, I was underdressed for a formal government function. But I stayed and learned about this incredible dish from his chef.

- 4-by-4-inch sheet of kombu
- 3 cups water
- 2 tablespoons bonito flakes
- 2 cups white sushi rice, uncooked
- 1 1/4 pound boneless, skinless chicken thighs
- 3 tablespoons sugar
- 5 tablespoons low-sodium soy sauce
- 2 cups dashi
- 4 tablespoons water
- 1 cup thinly sliced onion
- 4 eggs
- 6 tablespoons sliced scallions
- Chile flakes
- 1 pack seasoned nori

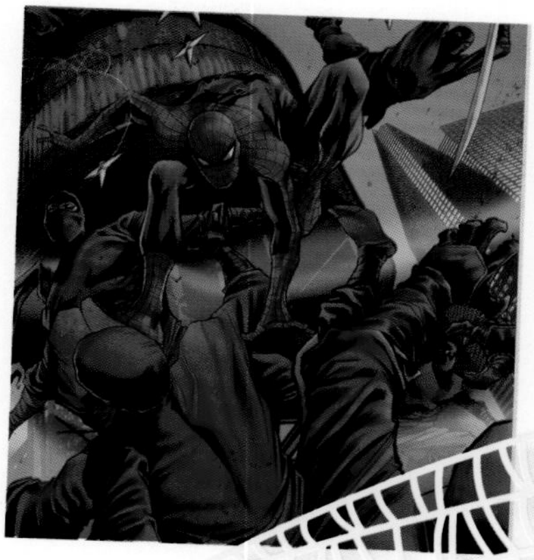

1. Rinse kombu with cold water, place in a pot, and fill with three cups of water.
2. Bring to a simmer, remove from the heat, and add the bonito flakes. Cover and let steep for 20 minutes. Strain and reserve the liquid, tossing the kombu and bonito.
3. Cook the sushi rice in either a rice cooker or in a pot and keep it warm.
4. Cut chicken into 1-inch cubes.
5. In a large pot, combine the chicken, water, sugar, soy sauce, and dashi. Cover with a lid and let simmer until sauce begins to thicken, about 5 minutes.
6. Add the onions and stir well, continuing to cook until the sauce is tight and begins to cling to your spoon and the onions are super tender. Taste and adjust the seasoning if needed.
7. Crack in 4 eggs and gently give them a stir, breaking up the yolks. Cover with a lid and cook for about 2 to 3 minutes to achieve an over-easy quality to your egg. Keep covered longer if you like.
8. Spoon the rice into a bowl and top with the oyakodon. Season with scallion, chile flakes, and seasoned nori.

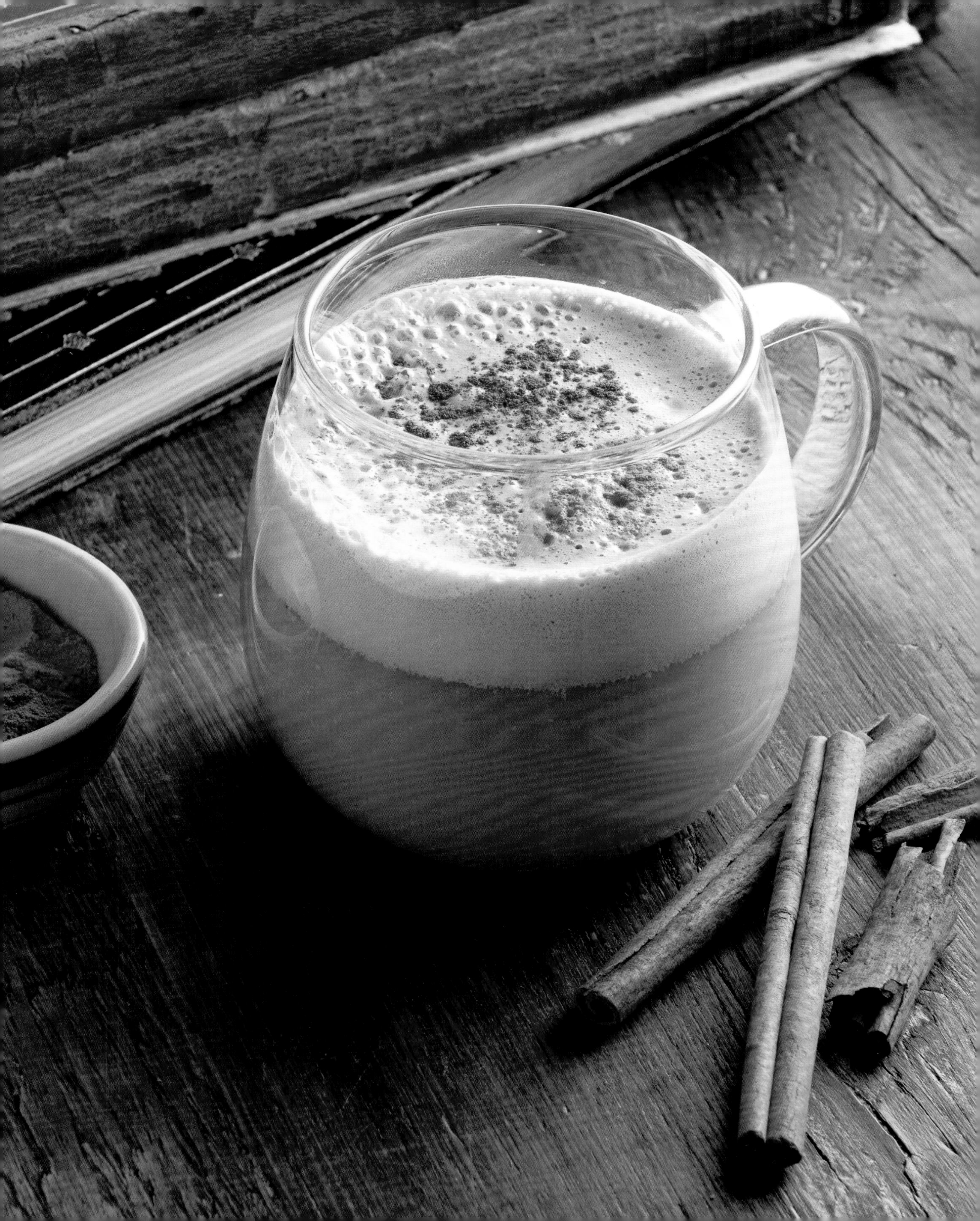

CHAI LATTE

GF | V+

YIELD:
2 SERVINGS

PREP TIME:
20 MINUTES

Remember the time when I was an outlaw? No, not that time. Not that one either. I know the one you're thinking about and it's not that either. You know what, it doesn't matter. The point is, I think it's safe to share that I was hiding out with some of the Avengers at the home of Doctor Strange. Me, Luke Cage, Wolverine, Bucky dressed as Captain America. We had some fun. And Wong, Doctor Strange's right hand, had to put up with all of us. The man's patience knows no bounds. Anyway, Wong had this great Chai Latte recipe he picked up traveling around India on his way back to Nepal one time. So, whenever we needed a jolt to keep our spirits up but our jitters down, he had this at the ready. Perfect for any fugitive from the law. Now, I'm not saying that will ever happen to *you*, but here's the recipe just in case.

20 ounces unsweetened oat milk or other nondairy milk (a gluten-free version if preferred)

2 teabags of your favorite black tea

1 cinnamon stick

2 star anise pieces

1 tablespoon fresh ginger, smashed

1 teaspoon vanilla extract

2 tablespoons agave syrup

1 pinch cinnamon powder

1 pinch turmeric powder

1. In a small pot, combine everything except the cinnamon and turmeric powders. Heat until hot and steamy. Let steep until you like the strength of the tea.

2. Strain everything into another pot, whisking or using an immersion blender to aerate and create a foam.

3. Pour into two coffee cups and be sure to spoon in some of the foam.

4. Dust with cinnamon and turmeric powder and enjoy!

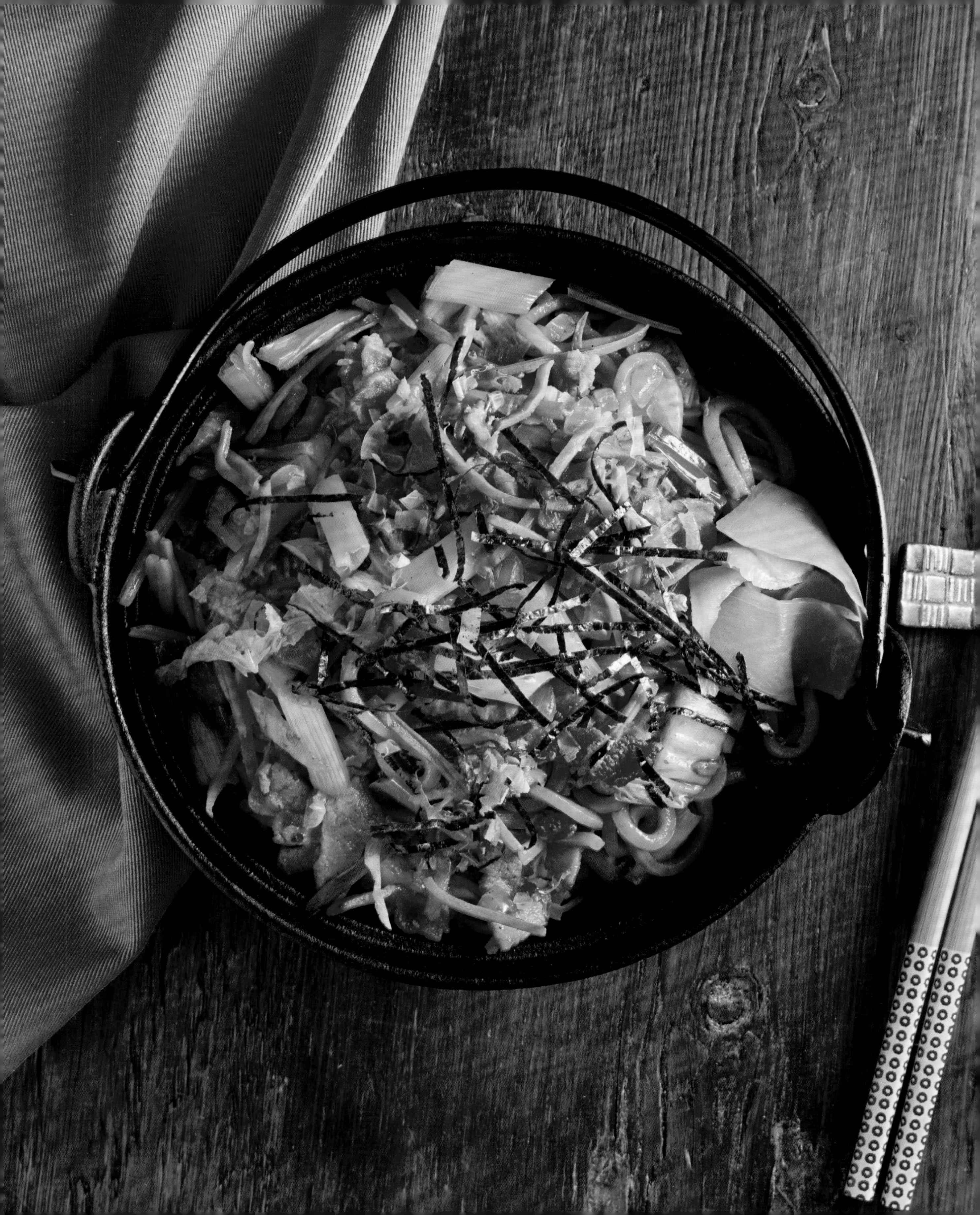

YAKISOBA

YIELD:
1 TO 2 PORTIONS

PREP TIME:
30 MINUTES

Just so I can get this on the record, not every member of our esteemed NYPD is out to "GET SPIDER-MAN!" In fact, Captain Yuri Watanabe went to bat for me on more than one occasion. Yuri was tough as nails, and we made one heck of a team for a time. I called us "Quippy and Lacey" . . . strangely, she wasn't a fan. During a stakeout, she once took out this delicious-smelling dinner she'd brought from home. And she offered some to me. Eventually. I think the growling stomach, the sad Spidey eyes, and the winning sense of humor won her over. I haven't seen her in a while, but I fondly remember this stir-fry dish, made with love—or at least tacit like—by Yuri.

FOR THE SAUCE:

1 tablespoon oyster sauce
1 tablespoon ketchup
1 tablespoon brown sugar
1 tablespoon soy sauce
1 tablespoon Worcestershire sauce

FOR THE NOODLES:

6-8 strips of bacon
1/3 cup sliced sweet white onion
1/2 cup julienned carrots
1/2 cup wide-julienned green cabbage
1 bunch scallions, cut into 1-inch pieces
1 teaspoon ground black pepper
8 ounces yakisoba noodles or other stir-frying noodles
1 tablespoon bonito flakes
1 tablespoon finely cut dried seaweed
1 tablespoon red pickled ginger

1. Put a pot of water on to boil.

2. In a small bowl, mix the oyster sauce, ketchup, brown sugar, soy sauce, and Worcestershire sauce to make your yakisoba sauce. Alternatively, if you can find prepared yakisoba sauce, please use it!

3. In a large nonstick pan, render the bacon until halfway crisp, using medium heat for approximately 12 minutes.

4. Add onions and carrots to your pan of bacon. Sauté until they are almost tender, about 4 minutes.

5. Add the cabbage, scallions, and black pepper to your pan, continuing to sauté. Don't be afraid to get a bit of char on your cabbage. The ideal texture is a bit crunchy.

6. Drop the noodles into the pot of boiling water and cook until just tender, about 2 minutes.

7. Drain the noodles into a colander and shake out most of the water. Add them to your stir-fry, tossing and mixing well.

8. Add the sauce, mixing one last time. Turn off heat and plate your dish.

9. Garnish your plate of noodles with bonito flakes, seaweed, and red pickled ginger.

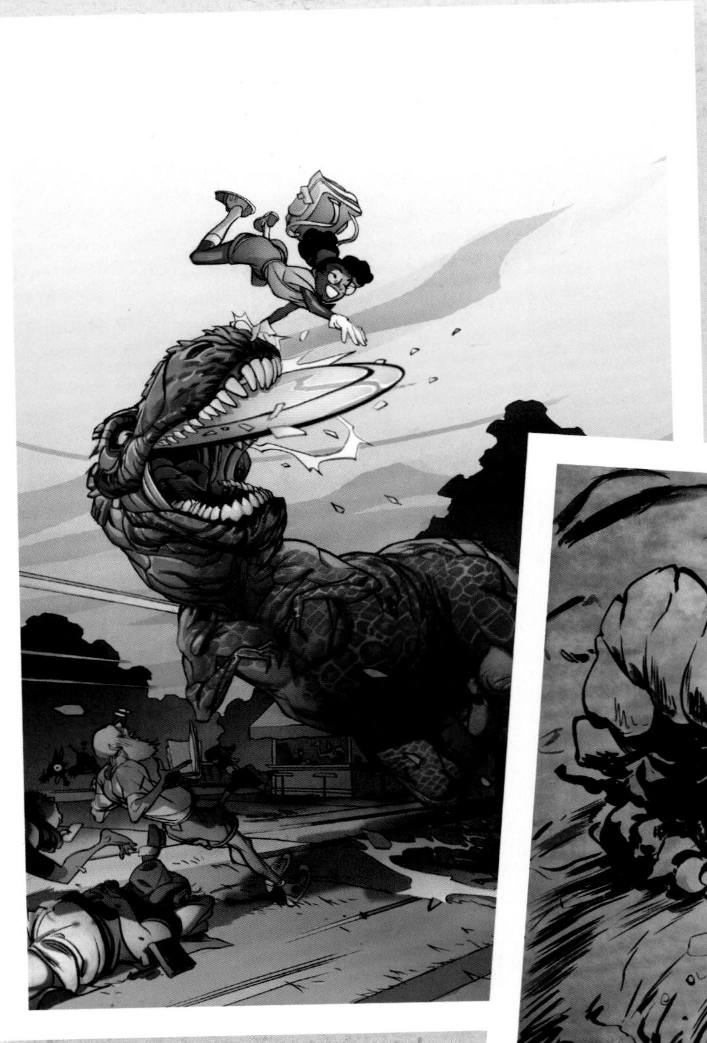

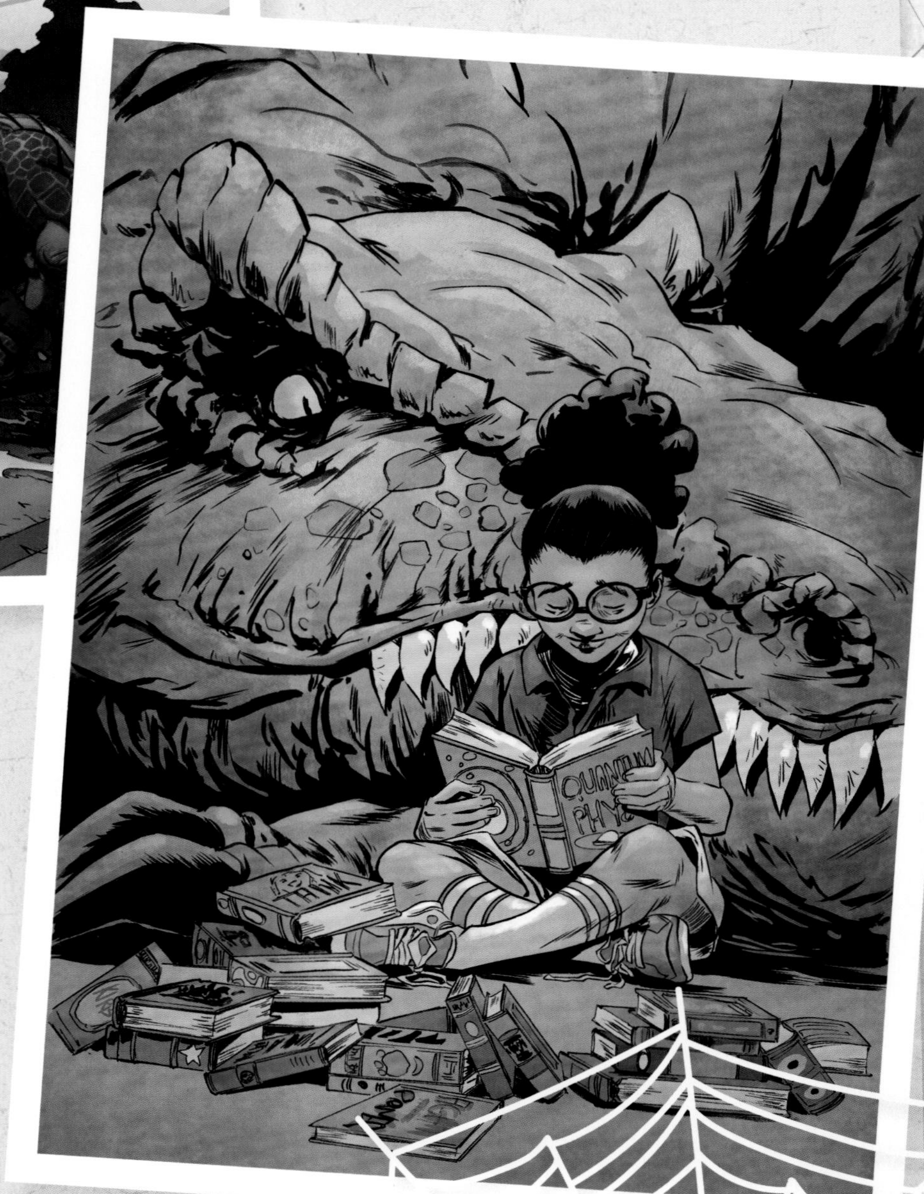

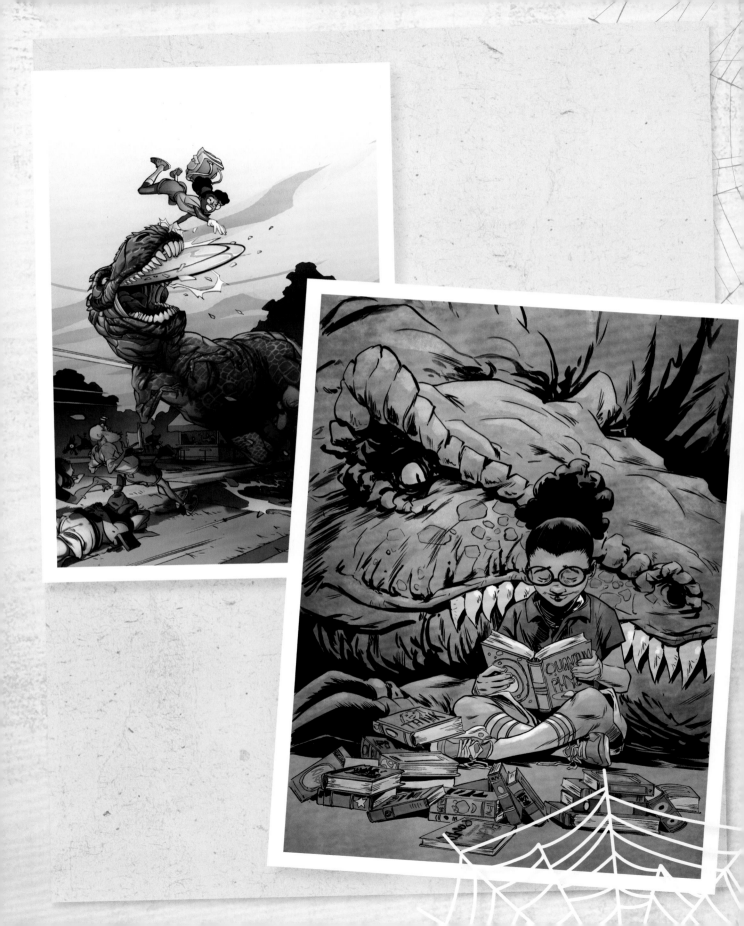

DIRTY WATER DOGS

YIELD:
4 HOT DOGS

PREP TIME:
45 MINUTES

Where do a two-ton cherry red dinosaur and his preteen prodigy best friend grab a bite to eat? Anywhere they want to. Now, I've seen some classic duos since getting into the crime-fighting biz. Power Man and Iron Fist, Captain America and the Falcon, to name a few. Moon Girl and Devil Dinosaur are a unique pairing in a category all their own. She's a Reed Richards –level super genius and he's a time-misplaced dinosaur. They make an impressive team. And I'm not just saying that because the big guy is really intimidating. (Those museum fossils undersell the teeth on those things. So. Many. *Teeth*.) I had been itching to ask Moon Girl since they first burst on the scene: How do you keep DD fed? Turns out, Moon Girl's not just *science* smart. Apparently, Big Red's been a sucker for dirty water hot dogs since he and Moon Girl first teamed up. She approached a local wiener franchise with locations all over the city, who agreed to make Devil Dinosaur their official mascot. All she asked for in return was all the dogs DD could eat. They of course had no idea what they signed up for. But at least DD is happy. For all our sakes.

2 tablespoons canola oil

3 cloves garlic, sliced thin

2 sweet onions, diced small

½ cup water

½ cup ketchup

2 teaspoons hot sauce

¼ teaspoon cinnamon

Kosher salt

1 quart beef stock

1 teaspoon smoked paprika

4 hot dogs, skinless all beef

4 hot dog potato rolls, warmed

Mustard

1. Heat the canola oil in a sauté pan on medium heat and add ⅔ of the garlic. Sweat until almost golden, about 2 minutes.

2. Add the onions and sauté until they're soft and translucent, using medium-high heat for about 4 minutes.

3. Deglaze the onions by adding ½ cup of water. Then stir in the ketchup, hot sauce, and cinnamon. Keep on medium heat for 15 to 20 minutes. Sauce should become thick at this point. Season with salt to taste.

4. In a separate pot, bring the beef stock to a simmer with the remaining third of the garlic, as well as the smoked paprika.

5. Turn the heat on your pot to low and add the hot dogs to the beef stock. Let simmer until they are super plump, approximately 10 minutes.

6. Add a hot dog to a bun and top with onion sauce, as well as mustard if desired.

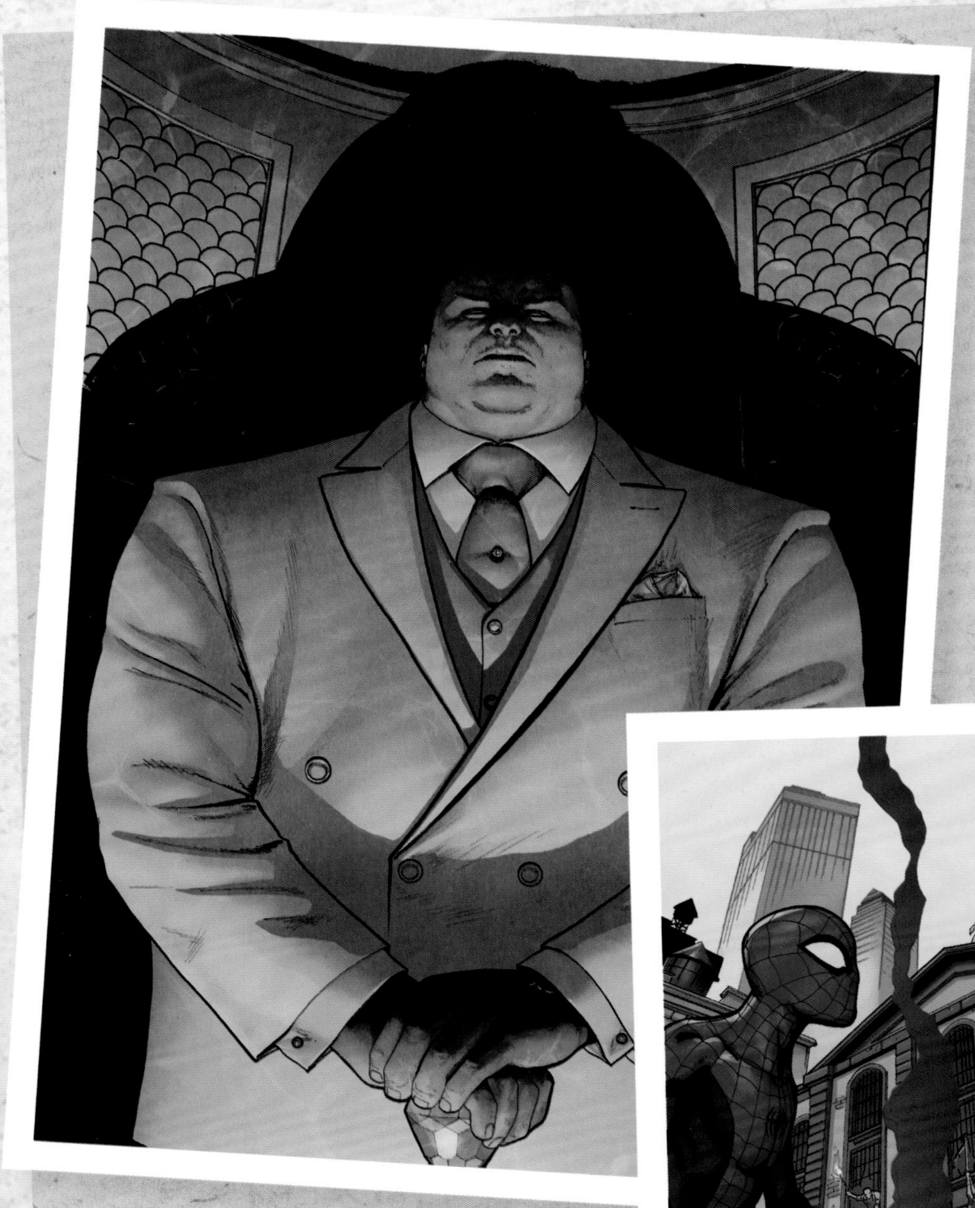
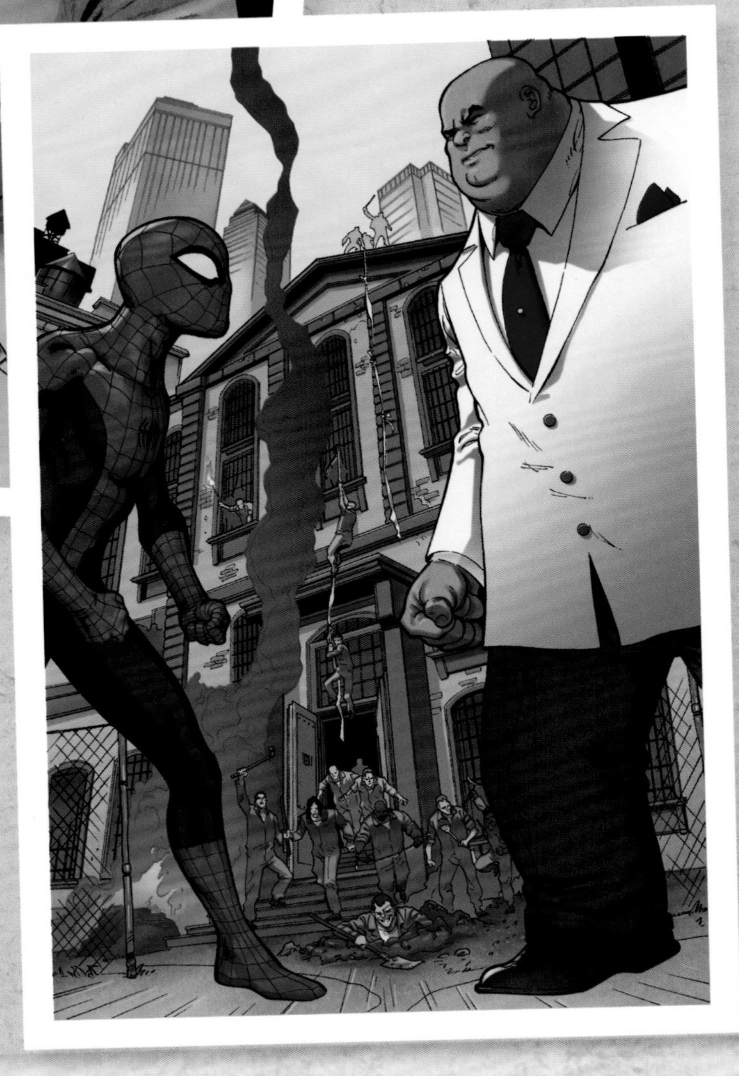

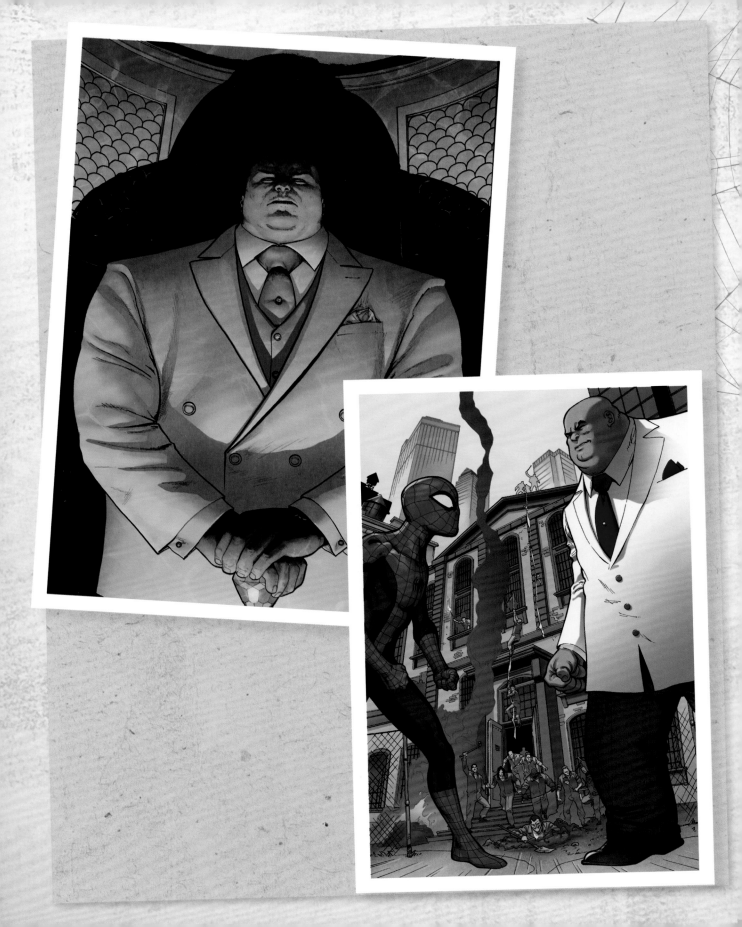

EGGS BENEDICT

GF | V

YIELD:
1 SERVING

PREP TIME:
30 MINUTES

Before Wilson Fisk became a seemingly permanent dance partner for my good friend Daredevil, the Kingpin and I used to tango on the regular. Not going to say I miss him; he hits like a truck that has little baby trucks for fists. This recipe comes from a confrontation I had with him as he was eating breakfast on his veranda. I was stern, I was determined to confront Wilson, call him out for his crimes. That was kind of hard to do while the Eggs Benedict on his plate was just sitting there looking awfully tempting. It smelled so good, I might have gotten a bit distracted. I did a half-hearted tough-guy speech. Pretended to leave, swung around to the kitchen to plead with his personal chef for the recipe. I have no shame. Enjoy.

FOR THE HOLLANDAISE:

2 egg yolks or ¼ cup of
  pasteurized egg yolk
1 tablespoon water
Salt
1 cup melted butter
1 tablespoon lemon juice
1 pinch cayenne pepper

FOR THE BENEDICT:

2 tablespoons olive oil
1 pound triple-washed
  spinach
Salt
1 quart water
1 tablespoon white vinegar
2 eggs
1 English muffin (gluten-
  free versions available,
  if preferred)
Pepper
1 tablespoon minced chives

OPTIONAL:

4 ounces salad mix
1 tablespoon of your
  favorite dressing

1. Fill a medium pot with two inches of water and set it to simmer on the stove. Lower the heat until just a bit of steam is coming off it.

2. Crack two eggs, keeping only the yolk. Alternatively, use ¼ cup of pasteurized egg yolk. In a bowl wide enough to sit on top of your pot, add egg yolks, 1 tablespoon of water, and a pinch of salt. Mix well.

3. Place yolk-filled bowl on top of your pot and whisk vigorously—not letting the egg cook by removing the bowl when it gets too hot. Slowly drizzle in the melted butter, whisking as you do. Continue until the butter is fully incorporated and the hollandaise is thick and airy. Add the lemon, more salt, and cayenne. Keep warm.

4. In a sauté pan, add olive oil, spinach, and salt to taste. Sauté until spinach is *just* wilted. Remove from pan and keep warm.

5. In a medium pot, add your remaining quart of water and your white vinegar. Bring to *just* before a simmer about 180°F. Gently crack two eggs into a cup and then pour them into the pot, one at a time, stirring the water as you do. Keep the eggs moving in a circle until the whites begin to set. It should take approximately 3 to 4 minutes to poach.

6. While the eggs are poaching, split the muffin and toast.

7. When the egg whites have fully formed and are no longer translucent and the yolk is set in, remove the eggs with a slotted spoon and blot on a paper towel. Season with salt and pepper.

8. On a plate, build your Benedict. On each half of your muffin lay down spinach and then an egg. Spoon hollandaise over everything and top with chives.

9. Serve with a side salad dressed with your favorite dressing if you like.

CHICKEN OVER RICE

Daredevil here. As a born-and-raised resident of Hell's Kitchen, I promised I'd send in something that captures what this neighborhood means to me. As you know, I keep my ears to the ground around here, but I can't be everywhere, listening in on everything. Fortunately, my favorite food truck chef, Aariz, is plugged into the community. I appreciate his skills as an informant, but his skills as a cook are unparalleled. His recipe for Chicken Over Rice is truly special, but it's a well-guarded family secret. He's provided a version he's comfortable sharing. As for the original recipe, I like his chances of keeping that secret. He's got his own Guardian Devil watching over him, after all.

FOR THE CHICKEN MARINADE:

- 2 tablespoons ground cumin
- 1 tablespoon hot smoked paprika
- 2 teaspoons ground turmeric
- 1 teaspoon ground coriander
- ½ teaspoon ground ginger
- ¼ teaspoon ground clove
- ½ teaspoon ground cinnamon
- 1 teaspoon ground black pepper
- 12 ounces boneless, skinless chicken thighs
- ½ cup extra virgin olive oil
- 2 lemons, juiced
- 1 tablespoon kosher salt

FOR THE RICE:

- 2 tablespoons butter
- ½ teaspoon turmeric
- ½ teaspoon cumin
- ½ teaspoon oregano
- 1 cup basmati rice, rinsed well
- 2 cups chicken stock
- 1 teaspoon kosher salt

1. Combine all eight marinade spices in a bowl and mix well. Reserve half for another time.

2. In a 1-gallon ziplock bag or reusable container, combine 2 tablespoons of your spice mix with the chicken thighs, olive oil, lemon juice, and salt. Mix well and refrigerate for an hour.

3. Preheat your oven to 375°F and turn on interior fan.

4. In a small pot or rice cooker, melt two tablespoons of butter and toast the turmeric, cumin, and oregano. When fragrant, add the rice and toast for a minute.

5. Pour in the chicken stock, cover, and cook rice on medium-low heat for about 25 minutes. Season with salt to taste.

6. In a small mixing bowl, combine the mayonnaise, Greek yogurt, lemon juice, parsley, and sugar. Add salt and pepper to taste and adjust the consistency with water if needed. It should be a bit runny.

7. Take the chicken out of the fridge and set on a nonstick tray or broiling rack. Set in your oven and roast the chicken until cooked, about 25 minutes, basting with the marinade and juices if you have the time.

GF

YIELD:
2 SERVINGS

PREP TIME:
90 MINUTES

FOR THE WHITE SAUCE:

1 cup mayonnaise

½ cup Greek yogurt

1 tablespoon lemon juice

½ teaspoon chopped fresh parsley

1 teaspoon sugar

Kosher salt

1 teaspoon ground black pepper

2 tablespoons water

FOR PLATING:

Two 5- to 6-inch pitas, oiled and gently toasted (option to omit for gluten free dish)

6 ounces romaine lettuce hearts, cut in ½-inch strips

1 cup large-diced tomato

OPTIONAL:

1 high-quality egg

8. When the chicken is cooked, let it rest for 5 to 10 minutes and then cut it into ½-inch strips.

9. Rub a touch of olive oil on the pitas and warm them in the oven for 4 minutes.

10. To plate, spoon a bed of rice down first, then place half of the cut chicken on top. Let some of the juice from the pan drip on top. Behind the rice and chicken, tuck a bed of romaine lettuce. Top with tomatoes and a couple of wedges of pita. Dress the chicken rice generously with white sauce and hot sauce to your liking.

SPIDEY'S TASTY TSUKUNE

If life gives you lemons, you make lemonade. If life puts you in the path of a rampaging Molten Man, you make tsukune. As a motto, it needs work. Opening this up to my all my fellow super heroes: Bring your suggestions to the next potluck. The point is that, in *our* line of work, in *this* city, you've got to be able to roll with the punches. Which is what I was doing when tall, gold, and fiery tried to punch me during a tussle on the Upper West Side. Unfortunately, when I rolled out of the way, his fist kind of went through the walls, ceiling, and floor of the popular Japanese restaurant behind me. The couple who owned it were so good-natured about the whole thing. They said their super villain insurance would cover the repairs and that they could probably get a little publicity out of it. All they asked of me was if I'd lend my name to these spicy meatballs to help generate buzz. See, rolling with the punches. Or maybe the moral of the story is always get super villain insurance?

EQUIPMENT:

Eight 8-inch wooden skewers
Latex gloves (or nitrile for those with latex allergies)

FOR THE MEATBALLS:

4 tablespoons finely minced onion
$\frac{1}{2}$ pound ground chicken thigh
$\frac{1}{2}$ pound ground chicken breast
2 tablespoons panko bread crumb
1 teaspoon cracked black pepper
1 teaspoon kosher salt
2 tablespoons sliced scallions, for garnish

FOR THE TARE:

1 cup soy sauce
$\frac{3}{4}$ cup water
6 tablespoons sugar
2 tablespoons peeled and thin-sliced ginger
2 tablespoons scallion greens
2 tablespoons dry shiitake or any available mushroom scraps
1 lemon wedge

OPTIONAL:

1 high-quality egg

1. If possible, soak the wooden skewers in water the night before.

2. Mince the onion finely and rinse thoroughly. Then drain and squeeze off excess water.

3. Combine all the meatball ingredients and mix thoroughly. Keep mixing until it is bouncing and almost tacky. Set aside until you're ready to form the skewers.

4. Combine the soy sauce, water, sugar, peeled ginger, scallion greens, and dry shiitake and heat on medium until sugar is melted and liquid comes to a simmer to make your tare (glaze and dipping sauce).

5. Let cool to room temperature and strain. Separate half for basting and half for dipping later.

6. This next step is very "hands-on," so wear gloves if possible. Using an amount you feel comfortable with, form an oblong meatball on the pointed side of a skewer. Six tablespoons per skewer is a good amount. If the meatball was mixed well enough, it should stick to the skewer with no issue.

7. Heat the oven to around 375°F and turn on its fan. Lay the skewers on a foil-covered pan that has been lightly greased and cover the exposed skewers with foil to keep them from burning.

8. Begin cooking your skewers, turning them little by little. After a few turns, start to apply sauce to baste them. Continue to alternate between turning, basting, and heating for about 5 to 10 minutes. The more love and attention you give them, the better they will come out.

9. Cook them until they are firm with a bit of bounce. If the edges of your meatballs start to shrivel, it's a sign they are overcooking. There's not a lot of fat in these, so overcooking will dry them out.

10. To plate, pour the tare you set aside for dipping into a side dish. If you're feeling adventurous, add an organic egg yolk to the center. You can also cut the tare with water to adjust the salt. Brush the skewers once more with the basting tare and garnish with sliced scallions and a wedge of lemon.

YIELD:
8 SKEWERS

PREP TIME:
OVERNIGHT, PLUS 40 MINUTES

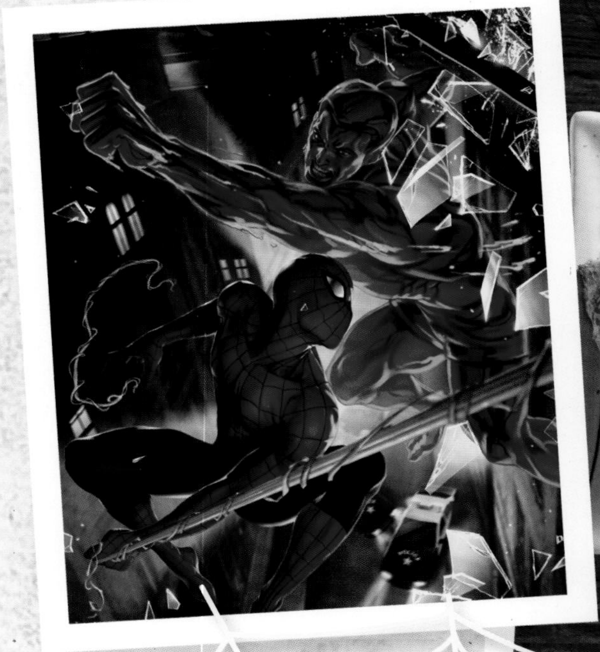

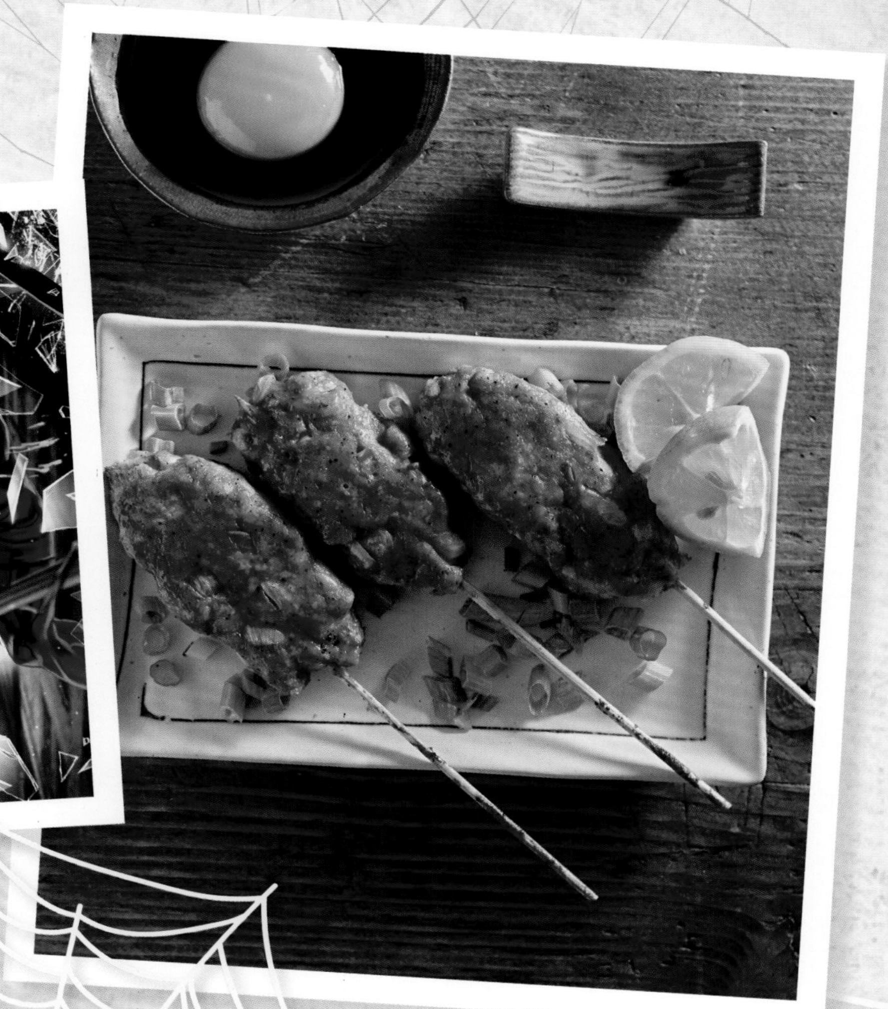

FRIED CHICKEN AND WAFFLES

We're making our way uptown for this next one. And while I'm a fan of chicken, and I'm a fan of waffles, I had no idea chicken *and* waffles could be such an amazing fusion until I trailed Tombstone to his favorite soul food restaurant on Malcolm X Boulevard. One of the more surreal nights in my decorated crime-fighting career. I was spoiling to mix it up with Tombstone. Never wanted to get into a fight more than I did that night. I burst through the window prepared to throw down, and it's a packed house. Everyone stops. Looks at me. And keeps eating. I make a beeline for Tombstone, who just puts his hands up and offers me a plate. I'm seething, but then I notice that everyone, and I do mean everyone, is looking at me. Tombstone explained what he knew everyone in there was thinking: "You have two options: Sit and eat. Or leave. But you're not making it out of here if you start a super fight while I'm enjoying this food." Fair point. So I sat. And I ate. The meal was on him and, despite myself, it was a delightful one. I got up to leave and the owner gave me two other options: Help clean up the glass and board up the window I busted. Or prepare to start doing dishes to clear my debt. Yes, folks, uptown is unique.

FOR THE CHICKEN:

6 cups all-purpose (AP) flour
6 tablespoons onion powder
6 tablespoons garlic powder
1 tablespoon chipotle powder
1 tablespoon dried thyme
2 tablespoons ground black pepper
2 tablespoons kosher salt
1 quart buttermilk
One 3½-pound chicken, cut into 8 parts: legs, thighs, breasts, and wings

FOR FRYING:

2 quarts canola oil

1. Combine the flour with the onion powder, garlic powder, chipotle, and thyme, as well as 1 tablespoon each of pepper and salt. Divide this mix into two containers.

2. Set up a breading station consisting of three bowls: flour mix, buttermilk, and flour mix again.

3. Season the chicken with 1 tablespoon each of salt and pepper, drop it into your first bowl of flour mix, then wet thoroughly in the buttermilk, and dredge in the last bowl of flour mix, getting the chicken super shaggy.

4. Preheat your oven on to 375°F and make sure your waffle iron is on.

YIELD:
4 PORTIONS

PREP TIME:
2 HOURS

FOR THE WAFFLES:

4 cups flour
½ cup sugar
3 tablespoons baking powder
1½ teaspoons kosher salt
8 egg yolks
8 egg whites
3 cups milk
12 tablespoons melted butter

TO PLATE:

8 ounces maple syrup
12 ounces hot sauce

5. Set up a high-wall crock for frying and add 6 cups of oil to it. Set up a frying thermometer so you can see the oil's temperature.
6. When the oil is at around 320°F, start frying the chicken. Begin with the thighs and legs, frying each piece until it's beautifully golden all over and cooked. This should take about 6 to 8 minutes. Remove from the oil and rest on a rack.
7. Get the oil up to 350°F and fry the breast and wings until they are golden, too, which should take another 6 to 8 minutes. Reserve on the rack.
8. Start on your waffles. Take out a separate bowl and combine 4 cups of flour with the sugar, baking powder, and 1½ teaspoons of salt.
9. Crack eight eggs, separating the yolks and whites into different bowls. Combine the egg yolks with milk and stir into the flour mix to create your batter. Then stir in the melted butter.
10. In the other bowl, whip the egg whites until they are stiff. Then gently fold them into the batter.
11. Spray your waffle iron with baking spray, load with batter, and go. Most waffle makers will tell you when they are done, but it should take about 4 minutes.
12. While the waffles are cooking, transfer the fried chicken to a tray in the oven to heat and crisp up, at 375°F for about 5 minutes.
13. To plate, serve with a waffle on the bottom and a piece or two of chicken on top. Be sure to include maple syrup and hot sauce on the side.

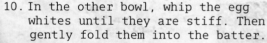

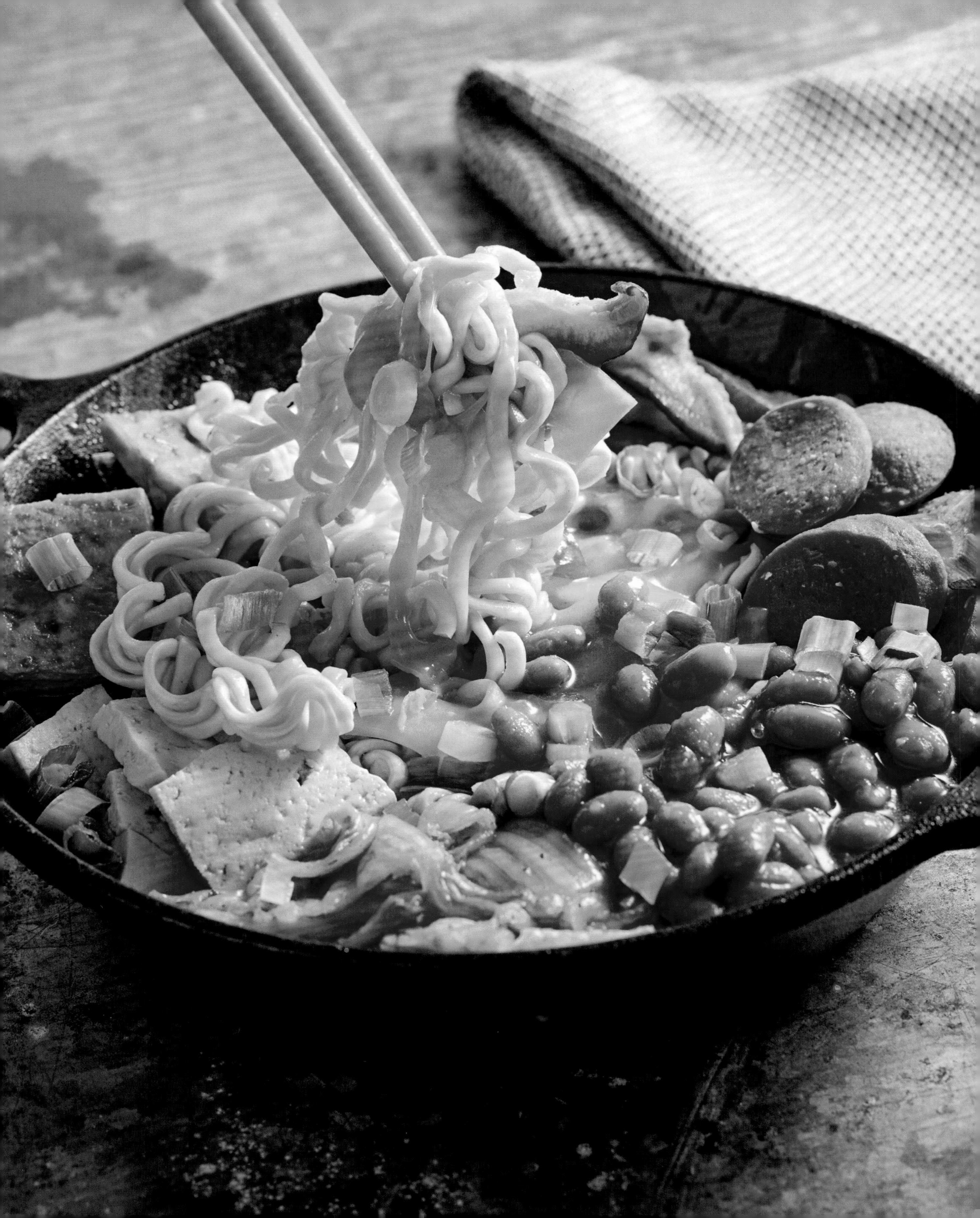

ARMY STEW

YIELD:
4 PORTIONS

PREP TIME:
30 MINUTES

When I need to think—you know, get away from it all, while still being in the middle of it all—I hit the Empire State Building. I swing on up to the observation deck after hours and take in the sights of the city. Up there, the sounds of traffic on Thirty-Third Street seem far away. I have the run of the place thanks to a deal I made with Freddy, who works the late shift on the deck three nights a week. He's pretty much stuck on duty until he goes out for lunch at about midnight. Meanwhile, the only Korean restaurant in the area that makes his favorite Army Stew closes at 11 p.m. He offered to buy me a bowl if I made the two-block, 110-story run for him. As deals go, this was a win-win. He got lunch, and I got an introduction to this cornucopia of spicy meats. We've kept it up ever since.

1 can processed pork, halved, then sliced into ⅓-inch pieces

4 hot dogs, sliced on a ⅓-inch bias.

12 ounces tofu, halved, then sliced into ⅓-inch pieces

1 cup shiitake mushrooms, sliced thin

1 cup kimchi, sliced in 1-inch squares

8 cups stock of your choosing, or water

1½ teaspoons Korean chile flakes

2 tablespoons gochujang

2 teaspoons fish sauce

1 tablespoon soy sauce

1 pack spicy Korean ramen

8 ounces baked beans

2 slices American or cheddar cheese

4 scallions, sliced thin

OPTIONAL:

Steamed rice

1. In a 12- to-16-quart pot, form a ring around the bottom with your cut processed pork, hot dogs, tofu, shiitakes, and kimchi in groups. Leave the center clear.

2. Gently pour about 7 cups of stock or water in the center and turn the pot on to simmer with a lid.

3. In a separate bowl, add the remaining cup of stock. Whisk in the chile flakes, gochujang, fish sauce, and soy sauce. Keep whisking until the gochujang is dissolved.

4. Once your covered pot comes to a simmer, add the ramen noodles to the middle. Then pour in the bowl of seasonings. Finally, spoon the baked beans into an empty spot in the pot. Re-cover and cook until the noodles are al dente.

5. Top the cooked pasta with two slices of cheese, scatter the scallions all over, and serve family style with a cup of steamed rice if desired.

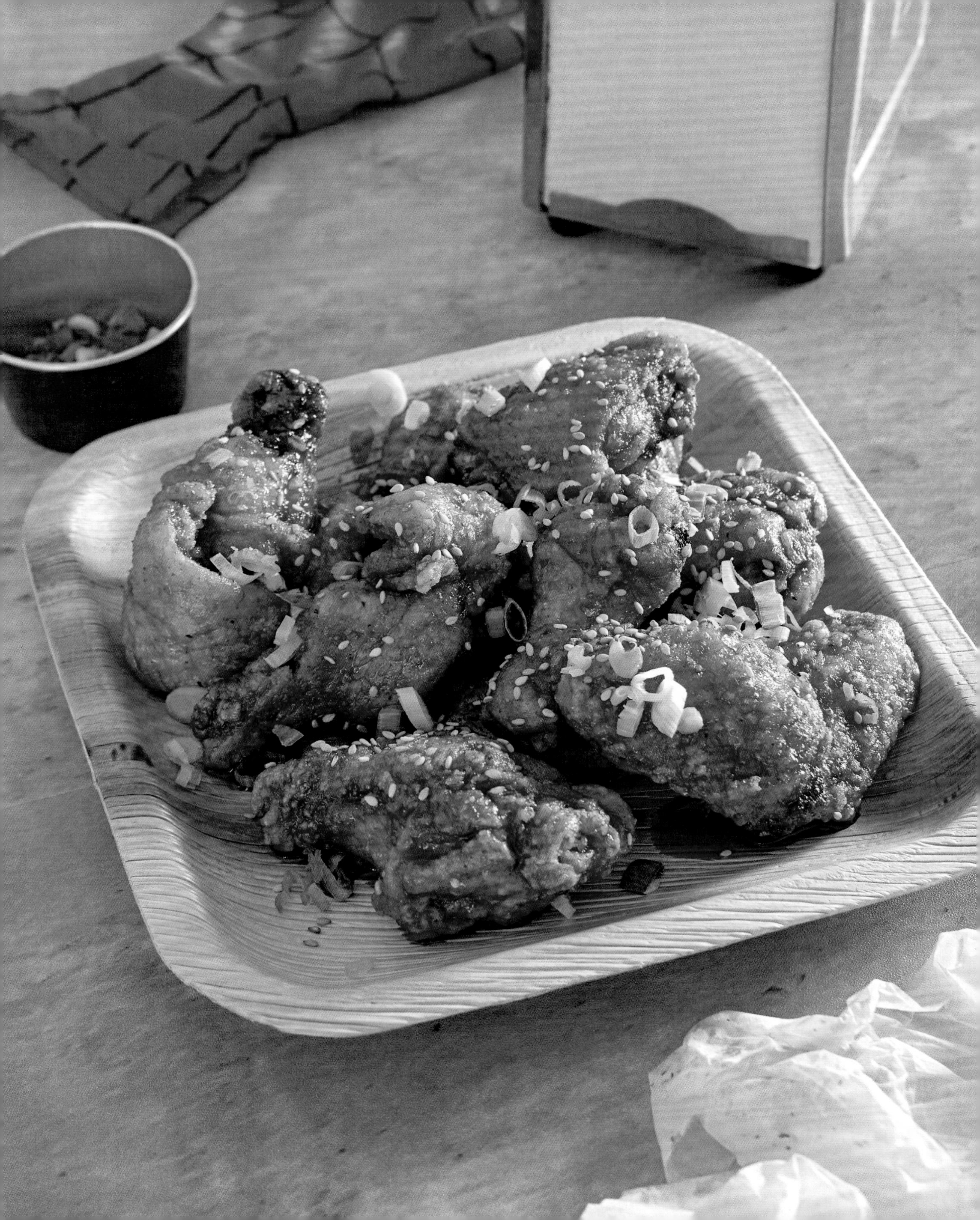

KOREAN FRIED CHICKEN

YIELD:
12 WINGS/
24 PIECES

PREP TIME:
45 MINUTES

You want to talk about a dish best made for guys who don't wear gloves? I give you this sticky, sweet finger food. It's a challenge for a grab-and-go guy like me, as this is an appetizer you cannot have just one of. Which leads to Spidey's number one conundrum when eating on the go: What do I do with the gloves? I'm among friends with this one, right? I feel like I can emote here. Where do you stash these things? Put them off to the side and I'm probably five blocks away before I realize I've left them on my last perch. Do I tuck them in my belt, do I tuck them under my mask? I know, I'm overthinking. But I love this dish, so if anyone figures out a workaround, just let me know. Thanks.

12 chicken wings, split, tips removed

6 cups canola oil

1 cup potato starch

2 teaspoons salt

1 teaspoon black pepper

1 teaspoon baking soda

½ cup gochujang

½ cup brown sugar

2 cloves garlic, grated

4 tablespoons grated ginger

2 tablespoons soy sauce

2 tablespoons honey

2 tablespoons rice vinegar

1 teaspoon toasted sesame seeds

2 tablespoons sliced scallion

1. If your wings aren't separated, simply cut them at all the joints and discard the wing tips.

2. Rinse the wings and pat dry.

3. In a large high-walled pot, put canola oil on to heat. Use a candy thermometer to monitor the temperature, aiming for 340°F. Meanwhile, preheat your oven to 375°F.

4. In a large bowl, mix the potato starch with salt, pepper, and baking soda. Then toss the wings in the mixture to coat. Lay wings on a rack until you're ready to fry.

5. Frying 5 or 6 at a time so your oil temperature doesn't drop too much, cook the wings until they are golden and cooked through, about 6 to 8 minutes per round. Set on paper towels to rest while you finish them.

6. In a large mixing bowl, blend together the gochujang, brown sugar, garlic, ginger, soy sauce, honey, and rice vinegar. If needed, add water to thin your glaze into a sauce-like consistency.

7. Place the wings in your glaze bowl and toss just enough to coat them.

8. Plate the chicken and sprinkle with toasted sesame and scallion.

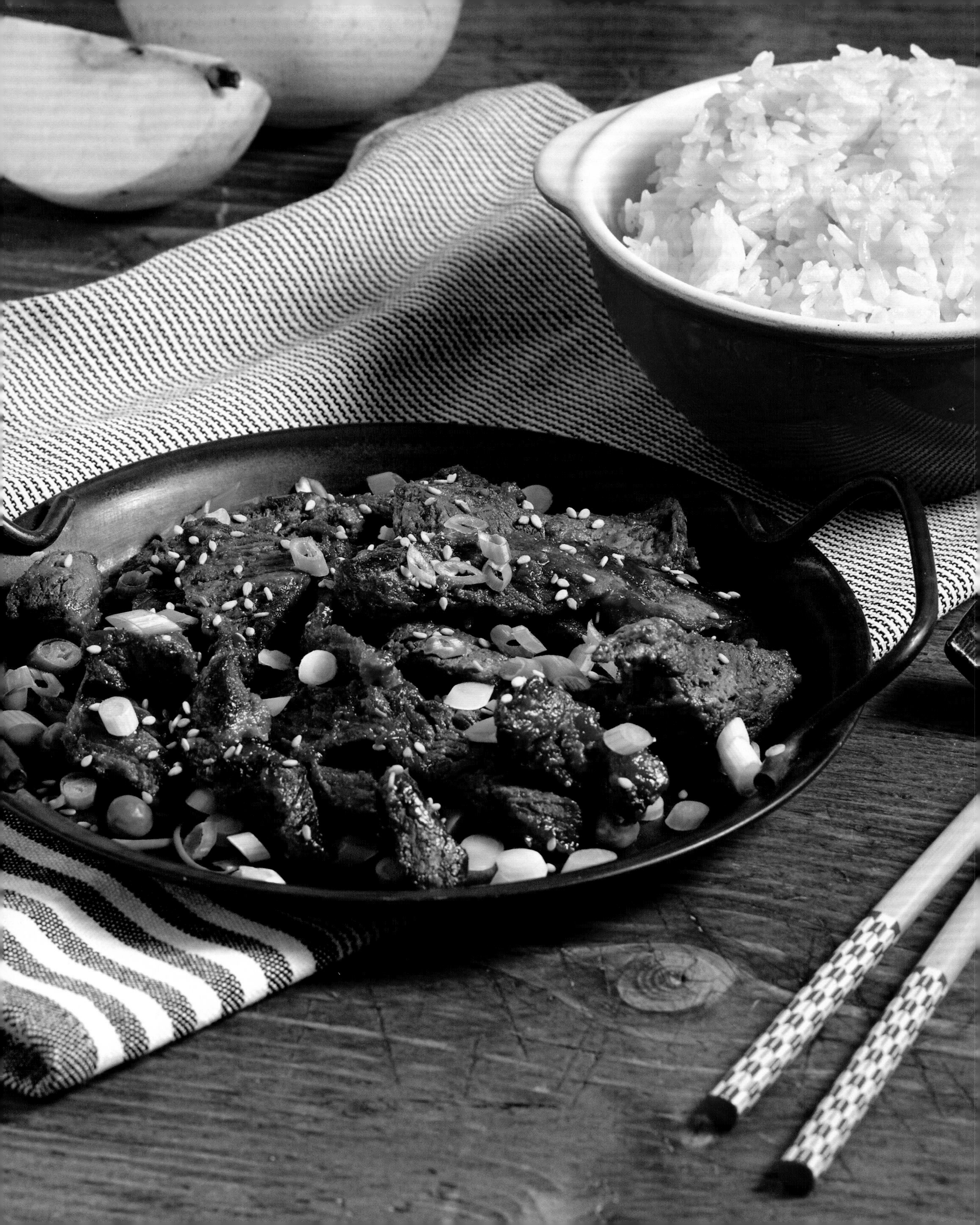

The incomparable Silk has written in with this next dish. She not only does whatever a Spider can, but, in many cases, does it better than I can. Which is awkward. But she's a heck of a hero and we need as many of those as we can get. So I let it slide.

YIELD: 4 PORTIONS
PREP TIME: 1½ HOURS

BULGOGI

Thanks for letting me participate, Spidey. This recipe is close to my heart. The one thing folks may need to know about me, for context on this one, is that I kind of had to hide out from a multiversal vampire named Morlun for a few years. Alone in, well, let's say an undisclosed location. I passed the time as best I could. But I desperately missed my family. And one thing you can't fake with supply rations is mom's home cooking. I did finally get to leave my hideaway bunker. And I wanted to share this recipe from my first night back home. This one comes straight from my mom, who still has the skills. Hope you enjoy it with good company!

2 cups short grain rice
½ large sweet onion
¼ cup peeled garlic
1 Asian pear, peeled and cored
¼ cup peeled ginger
1 cup + 3 tbsp soy sauce
2 tablespoons brown sugar
6 tablespoons sesame oil
1 tablespoon salt
1½ pounds beef tenderloin
1 bunch scallions, sliced thin
1 tablespoon toasted sesame seeds

OPTIONAL:
4 cups steamed white rice

1. Rinse 2 cups of short grain rice in a bowl. Place in a heavy-bottom pot and cover with 3 cups of water and lid. Turn on medium-high heat and bring to a simmer. Then turn down to low and continue to cook until the water has evaporated. Turn off the heat and let the rice sit, covered and warm, for at least 15 minutes.
2. Combine onion, garlic, pear, and ginger in a blender or food processor and puree until smooth.
3. Remove your mix from the food processor and whisk in soy sauce, brown sugar, sesame oil, and salt to complete your marinade.
4. Preheat your grill to medium-high heat or turn on the broiler.
5. Slice tenderloin into thin strips through the grain, cover in marinade, and let sit for at least 20 minutes.
6. Shake off excess marinade and grill tenderloin for about 4 to 5 minutes until well charred on all sides.
7. Arrange on a platter and garnish with scallions and sesame. Serve with a side of white rice.

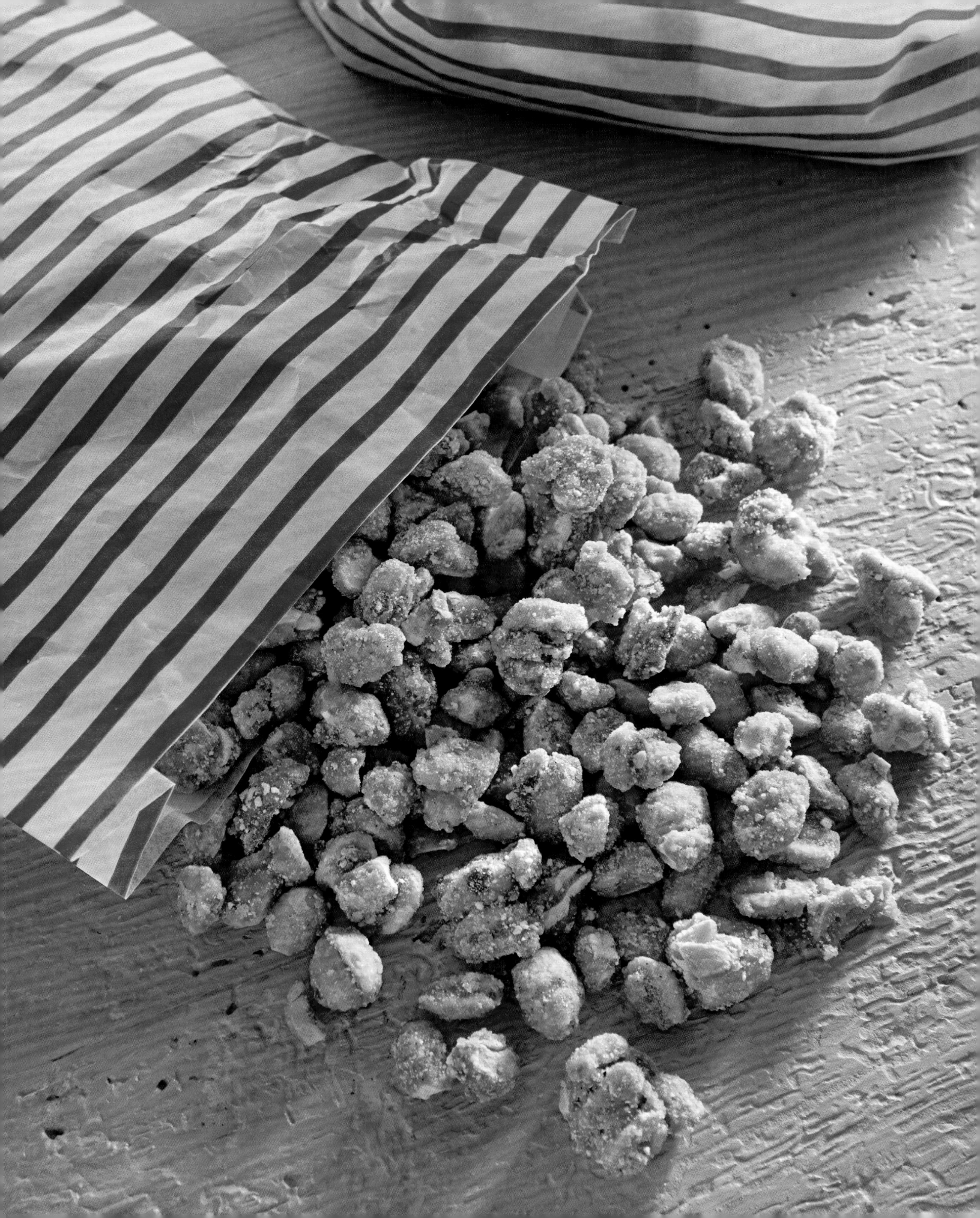

SWEET AND SALTY PEANUTS

GF | V+
YIELD:
2 SERVINGS
PREP TIME:
30 TO 45
MINUTES

Ah, the circus. Just the mention of it brings up memories from when I was a wee Spider-Lad seeing everything from the trapeze artists to the clowns for the very first time. I even got to feed the elephants. The smell of beer nuts takes me back to that. Though I try to block out a memory from a few years later, when I went back as an adult and had to tangle with the Circus of Crime for the first time. Let's just say they don't give me the same nostalgia feels. Though I will admit that fighting them center ring at Madison Square Garden did scratch my itch to ham it up in front of a capacity crowd. (I want to make a Spider-Ham joke so bad here, but he's a Multiversal treasure who deserves better than that. I really should be applauded for my restraint.) I suppose you can also chalk up some lapses in memory to the fact that their leader, the Ringmaster (so on the nose with that one), hypnotized me and sent me after Daredevil. Only some clever sleight of hand from old Horn Head and, oddly enough, the smell of beer nuts snapped me out of my stupor. I made sure to grab a bag, and the recipe, before I left MSG. Got to feed the elephants again, too.

½ cup water

1 ½ cups sugar

4 cups unsalted and unroasted peanuts

1 tablespoon kosher salt

4 tablespoons granulated honey (omit if vegan)

1 teaspoon vanilla paste

½ teaspoon cinnamon powder

1. In a large nonstick sauté pan, bring water and sugar to a simmer on medium-high heat.

2. Add peanuts and salt. With a wooden spoon, keep stirring and cooking continuously on medium heat.

3. After about 8 to 10 minutes, as sugar begins to crystallize, add honey, vanilla paste, and cinnamon powder. Remove from heat and pour onto greased parchment to cool a bit before serving.

4. Serve warm and enjoy.

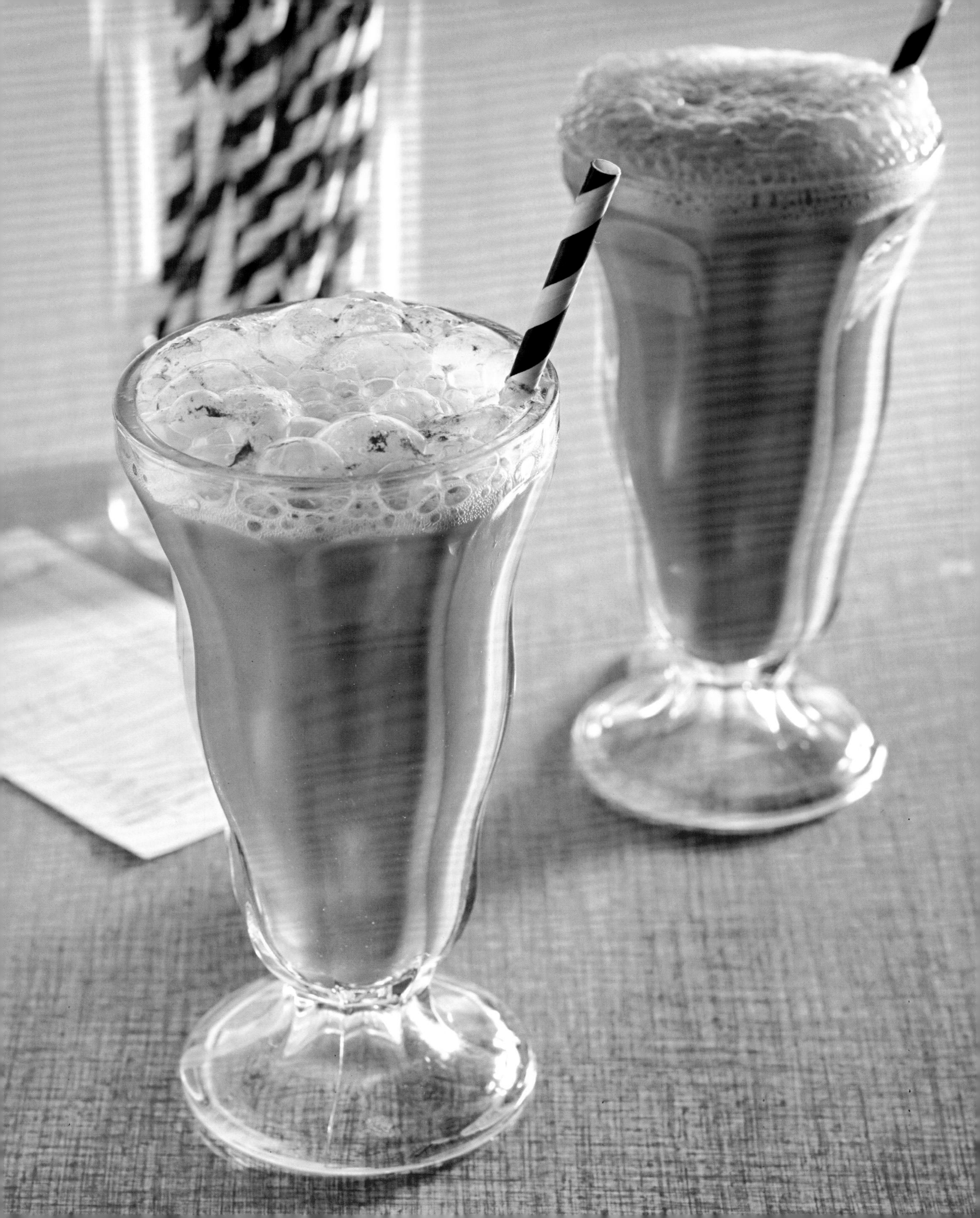

EGG CREAM

GF

YIELD:
1 GLASS

PREP TIME:
5 MINUTES

I'm over by the Roosevelt Island tram a lot. I mean, it's kind of odd how many of my, let's call them "tussles," have taken place on that thing. You'd think at least the occasional super villain might want to call it a day to relax and enjoy the spectacular view of the city. But what's a spider to do? I've learned to make the most of it. A guy gets familiar with the neighborhood when he's getting fired on, dropped from, and swung into its aerial tram. And that's how I found a spot a few blocks away that deals in nothing but the finest desserts. I tend to swing by anytime I'm roped into unplanned tramway acrobatics. The cakes and the cookies are to die for, but it's their signature egg cream that tends to hit the spot for me.

2 tablespoons chocolate syrup

¾ cup cold milk

¾ cup cold seltzer

1. In a pint glass, stir syrup and milk until fully mixed. While stirring, pour in seltzer using the back of the spoon to pour against.

2. You should have a nice foamy head. Serve immediately.

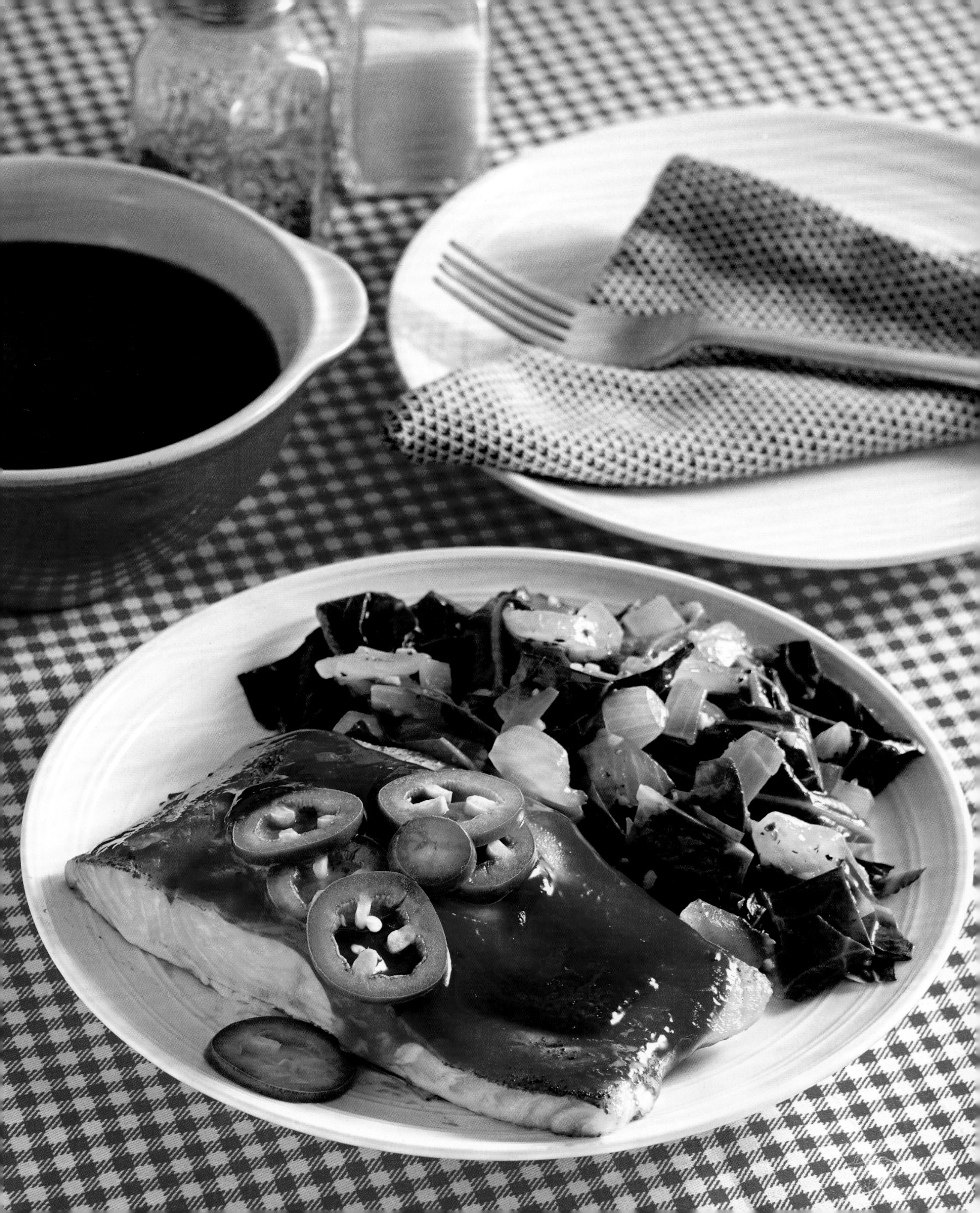

Here's one of Harlem's own. You've known him as the Falcon over the years, but he's currently literally flying the Stars and Stripes. Captain America has written in with a dish from the neighborhood we all hope you enjoy.

GF

YIELD:
2 SERVINGS OF SALMON,
4 TO 6 SERVINGS OF COLLARDS

PREP TIME:
1½ HOURS

BBQ SALMON AND COLLARDS

I started this off thinking: What better way to represent community than with one of my all-time favorite cookout dishes? After all, summer in Harlem is about being outside, experiencing everything along 125th from the street fairs to the music festivals to the block parties. But it's also about getting your eat on. This recipe takes me back to when my mother, sister, brother, and I would get together in front of my father's church and throw a potluck. You really get to know people over a good meal, and this recipe is inspired by my mom's traditional contribution. It slayed with everyone at these events, but I'm sharing an updated version of the recipe because she'd slay me if I let anyone have the original. On the plus side, mine's gluten-free.

FOR THE COLLARDS:

2 bunches collards, stemmed and cut in large strips

4 tablespoons olive oil

¾ cup chopped sweet onion

3 cloves garlic, smashed

2 cups vegetable stock

4 tablespoons champagne vinegar

2 teaspoons salt

1 teaspoon cracked black pepper

FOR THE SALMON:

1 jalapeño, sliced thin

6 tablespoons champagne vinegar

½ cup of your favorite BBQ sauce (gluten-free versions available, if preferred)

4 tablespoons Creole marinade or fish marinade (gluten-free versions available, if preferred)

Two 6-to-8-ounce fillets of salmon

6 to 8 cilantro leaves

1 lemon wedge

1. Turn on your grill to a high heat. Place the collards in a large bowl and rinse them with water, repeatedly, until the bottom of the bowl shows no sand or dirt.

2. In a large pot on the stove, sweat the onion and garlic in olive oil by heating on medium-high heat until aromatic and tender, about 3 to 5 minutes. Add the collards in parts, sweating and wilting them as you go until you can fit them all in the pot. Place a lid on top and sweat the greens until they're mostly wilted, approximately 6 to 8 more minutes.

3. Add the vegetable stock and simmer until just tender, about 20 to 30 minutes. Add the first 4 tablespoons of champagne vinegar, plus salt and pepper. Continue to cook until well balanced and tasty. Set aside and keep warm.

4. Cover the sliced jalapeños with the remaining 6 tablespoons of champagne vinegar and let sit in separate bowl to pickle for about 10 minutes.

5. Combine the BBQ sauce and marinade. Slather this all over the salmon and place the fish skin-side down on a well-oiled grill. Lower the lid and let cook for about 3 to 5 minutes, turning the fish occasionally until it easily releases from the grill.

6. Gently flip and baste the fish once more with additional sauce and cook for about 5 more minutes for a nice medium-done. Your salmon should be firm to the touch without breaking apart.

7. To plate, spoon out about a ½ cup of collards to each rimmed plate. Place the salmon on top, garnish with pickled jalapeños and cilantro, and add a lemon wedge.

YULE LOG

Next up, New York's favorite former hero for hire, and current favorite mayor, um, very much not-for-hire. Because that would be corruption. But first, let me set the scene with a little reenactment of how I convinced our man to write a recipe:

CAGE: You seriously got me for a Yule Log?

SPIDEY: Just go with it.

CAGE: A Yule Log?

SPIDEY: Luke? C'mon.

CAGE: Seriously, I'm the mayor of the largest municipality on the planet and you got me for a Yule Log?

SPIDEY: But . . . but . . . your catchphrase?

CAGE: (exasperated) Fine. But you owe me one.

And with that, here's his contribution to our fine cookbook:

POWER
STRENGTH
LUKE
CAGE

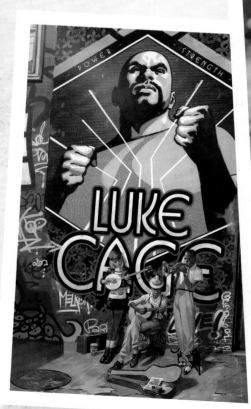

V

YIELD: 10 SLICES

PREP TIME: 3 HOURS

Hi, I'm Luke Cage, I've been known to say "Sweet Christmas" a whole lot. It used to help keep me from swearing. I am also a proud child of Harlem. And years ago, I did a meet-and-greet at a bakery in the neighborhood for an old friend of mine. We used this advertisement: "Free autograph with the purchase of this SWEET CHRISTMAS YULE LOG." I'm honored to serve the people of New York and can laugh about the early days of the campaign that got me here. But you can't, Spidey.

FOR THE CAKE:

- 2 tablespoons butter for greasing
- 6 large eggs
- ½ cup granulated sugar
- ¾ cup cake flour
- 1 teaspoon baking powder
- ½ teaspoon salt
- 6 tablespoons Dutch cocoa powder, plus 2 tablespoons for dusting
- ¼ cup canola oil
- ¼ cup milk
- 2 teaspoons vanilla extract

FOR THE GANACHE:

- 2 cups heavy cream
- 1 pound semisweet chocolate chips

FOR THE FROSTING:

- 1 cup softened cream cheese
- ½ cup mascarpone
- 2 teaspoons vanilla extract
- 1 pound powdered sugar, plus 2 tablespoons for dusting
- ½ cup Dutch cocoa powder

OPTIONAL:

- Decorations like meringue or chocolate-covered cookies in the shape of mushrooms

1. Preheat your oven to 350°F and prep a half sheet tray with parchment. Be sure to grease everything with butter.
2. In a mixer, using the whisk attachment, cream the eggs and ½ cup of sugar together until light and fluffy. This will take about 3 to 4 minutes, and it should be thick and airy.
3. In a separate bowl, sift together the cake flour, baking powder, salt, and cocoa powder.
4. Turn the mixer on slow and add in the bowl of flour mix by thirds, stopping to scrape the bowl and making sure the whisk doesn't knock any of the flour out of the bowl. Take care not to overmix at this stage or you'll risk forcing all the air out of the batter.
5. In another bowl, mix canola oil, milk, and 2 teaspoons of vanilla extract. Then stream this into the mixer until all ingredients combine to create a batter.
6. Pour the batter evenly on the prepped sheet tray and bake about 10 minutes, until spongey. To test, see if cake bounces back when pressed with a spoon.
7. Let the cake cool slightly while you lay out a lint-free kitchen towel and dust the top with cocoa powder. Then, while the cake is still warm, free it from the tray with a paring knife and flip it onto the towel.
8. Remove the parchment paper from the top of your cake and roll it up widthwise with the towel. Let it cool fully.
9. Prepare the ganache by heating a pot with the 2 cups of heavy cream to a simmer, then pouring it over a bowl containing the chocolate chips.
10. Let ganache sit for a few minutes, then gently stir until completely mixed. Be sure to scrape the bowl. Keep the ganache at room temperature.

CONTINUED ON PAGE 101

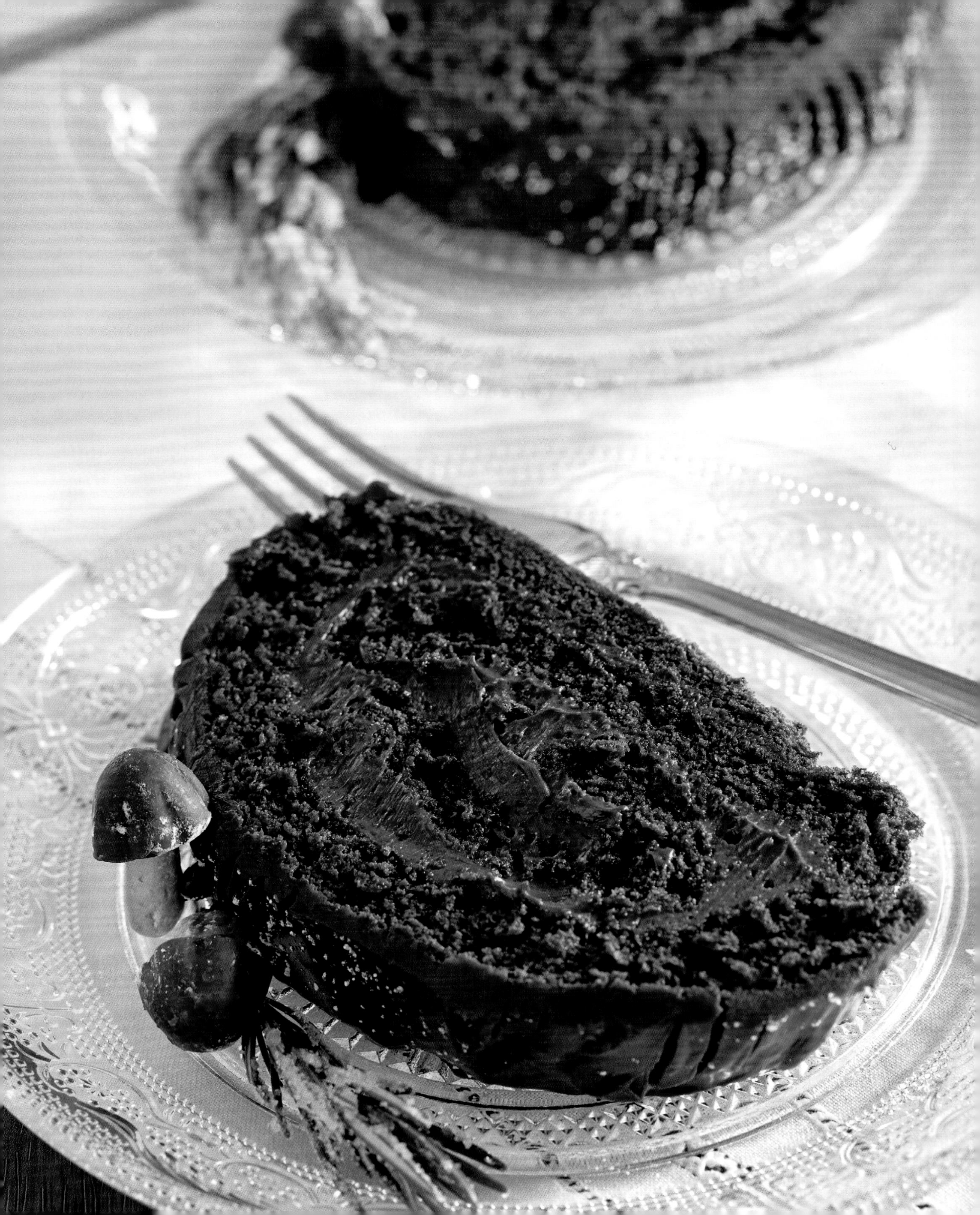

CONTINUED FROM PAGE 99

11. Make the chocolate frosting next. In a mixer, combine the cream cheese and mascarpone with 2 teaspoons of vanilla extract. Slowly add the pound of powdered sugar and the ½ cup of cocoa powder. Stop to scrape the bowl as needed until ingredients are fully mixed.

12. Once the cake is cool, unroll it and lay it flat, removing the towel. Spread the chocolate frosting evenly over the top of the cake.

13. Roll the cake again, without the towel this time, and rest it seam-side down on a platter. This will be easier since you've already trained the cake once with the towel.

14. Cut a section of your cake at an angle and reattach it to the main trunk like a branch. Let the whole thing set in the fridge for 30 minutes.

15. Take your refrigerated cake and spread the ganache evenly over the top of both branches of the log, moving in one direction. Then, trace groove marks into it with a knife or fork to look like tree bark. Dust with the remaining 2 tablespoons of powdered sugar.

16. Optional: Decorate with any premade decorations like meringue mushrooms and edible pine needles around the outside of the trunk.

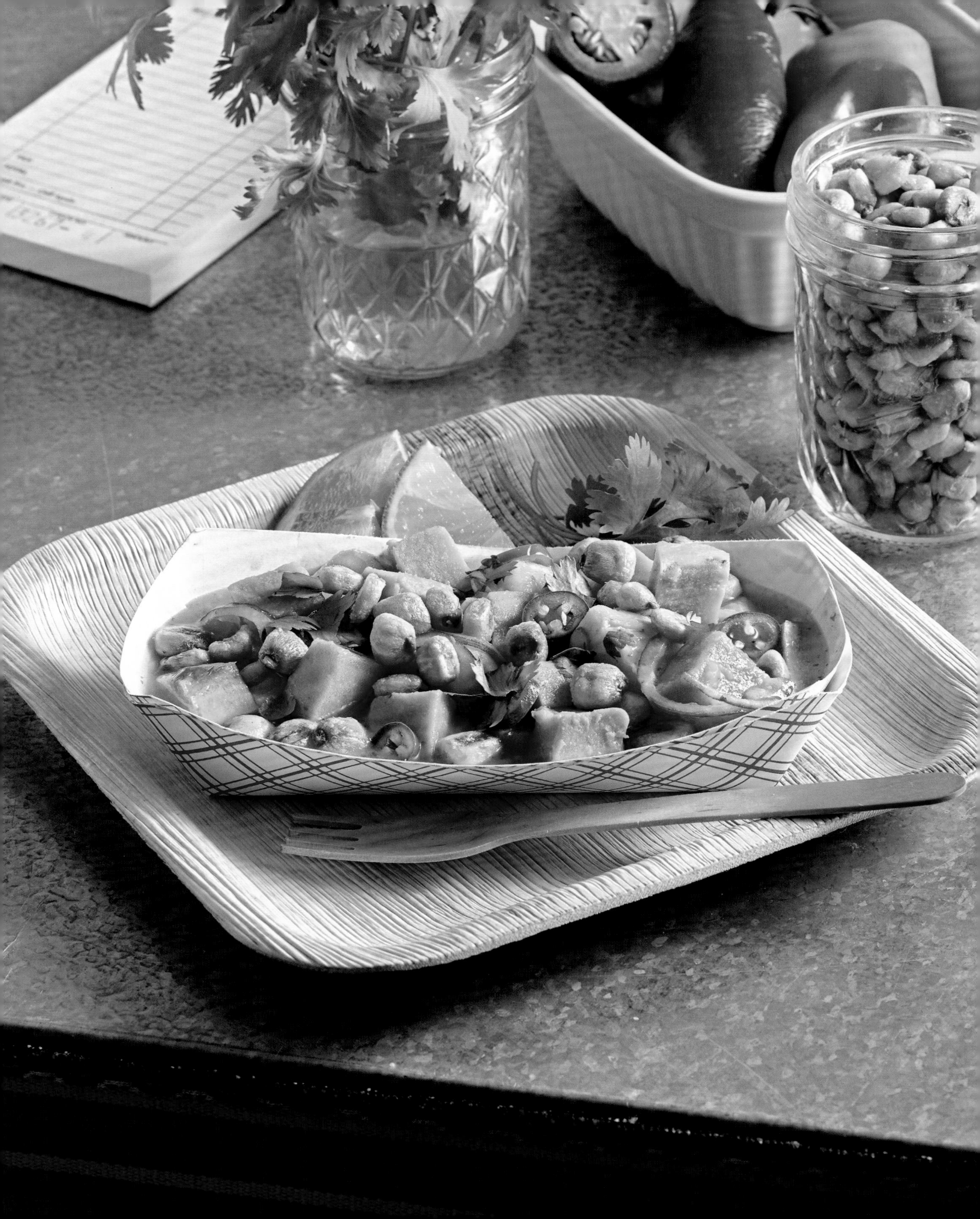

CEVICHE TIGERS MILK

GF
YIELD: 4 PORTIONS
PREP TIME:
OVERNIGHT, PLUS 2 HOURS

You all might have heard that I've tangled with the Lizard dozens of times. It's possible I've vented to some of you on occasion, or generally complained about it at one point or another. So it's been established that I know him well enough to say he's a good guy underneath all those scales. It just takes getting him out from under that hard green exterior. This involves a lot of empathy, an open heart, and a formula I've developed to turn him back to his human form. But getting him to take it often poses a challenge. I got inventive one time and grabbed this ceviche dish from a Peruvian food cart owner. The Lizard might hate my antidote, but he *loved* the ceviche. And I quickly became a fan as well.

FOR THE MARINADE:

1 cup fresh lime juice

½ cup fish stock, cold (gluten-free versions available, if preferred)

1 garlic clove

1 tablespoon cilantro stems (save leaves for garnish)

1 teaspoon kosher salt

2 tablespoons fresh chopped ginger

4 tablespoons aji amarillo paste

FOR THE CEVICHE:

1 large sweet potato, steamed, peeled, and small-diced (optional)

1 pound fluke or other firm sashimi-grade white fish, cut into ⅓-inch-thick slices

¼ cup of paper-thin, sliced red onion

2 serrano chiles, sliced thin

4 teaspoons extra virgin olive oil

½ cup corn nuts

½ bunch cilantro, stemmed

1 tablespoon flaky sea salt

4 lime wedges

1. Wrap a sweet potato in foil tightly and bake in a 350°F oven for 30 minutes. A fork should sink in easily, but the potato should not be shriveled or mushy. Cool, unwrapped, in the fridge overnight.

2. To make your marinade, blend lime juice, fish stock, garlic, cilantro stems, kosher salt, ginger, and aji amarillo paste together. Chill for an hour. Then strain through a fine sieve and set aside.

3. In a medium mixing bowl on ice, add the sliced fish and onion. Cover with the fish stock marinade for at least 20 minutes before serving.

4. Spoon the ceviche into four small bowls, being sure to divide the fish, onion, and marinade equally between them.

5. Peel and dice your sweet potato. Then garnish with equal amounts of sweet potato, chiles, and olive oil.

6. Finish each bowl of the ceviche with corn nuts, cilantro leaf, a touch of sea salt, and a lime wedge.

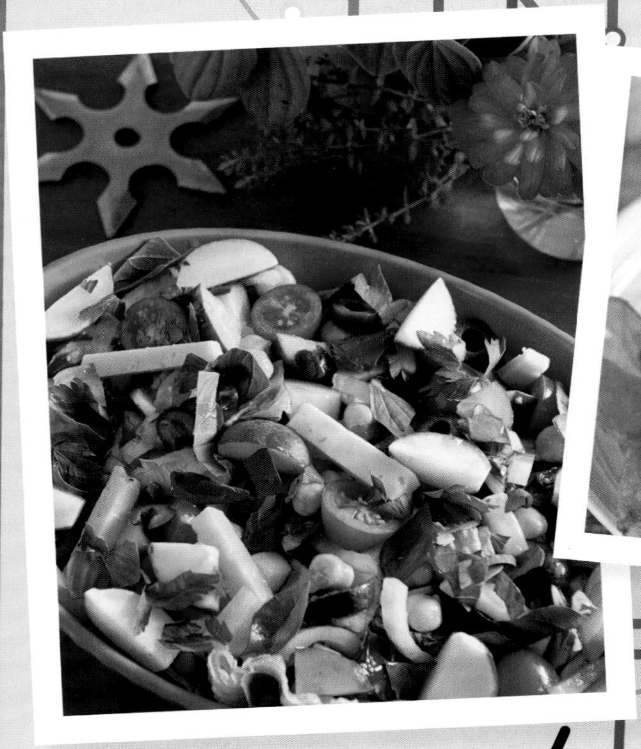

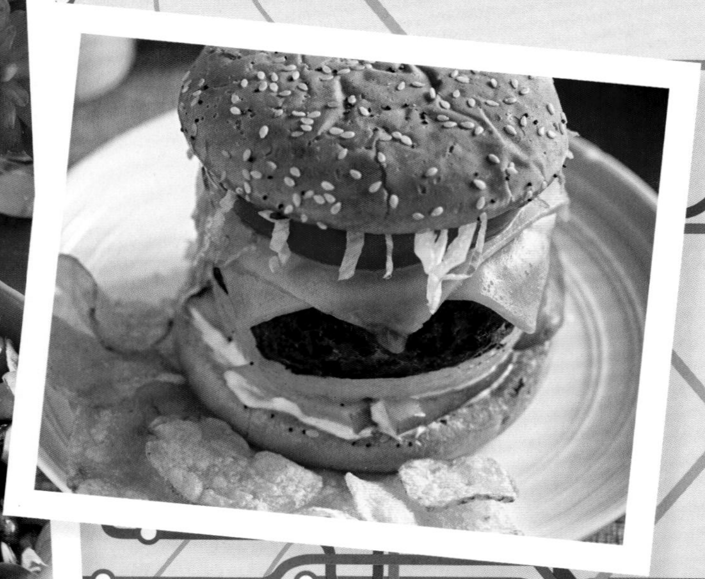

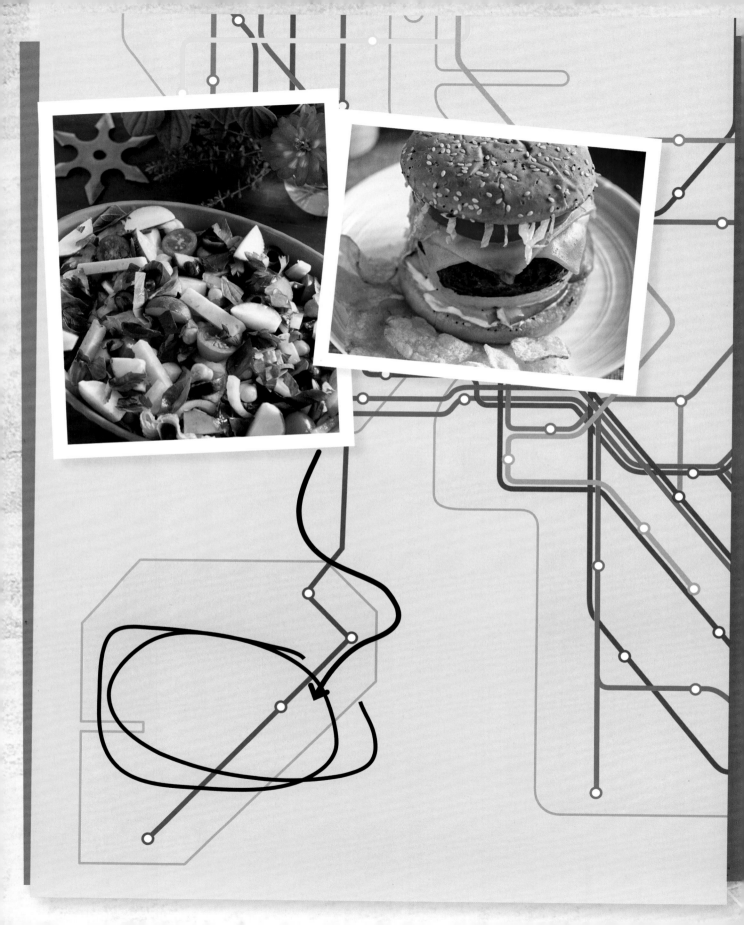

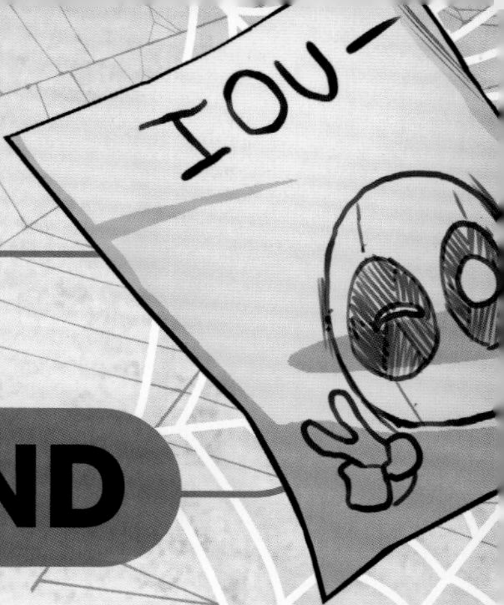
IOU-

4 STATEN ISLAND

Staten Island, the borough where web-swingers go to ride-share. Don't get me wrong, I am a huge fan of all things great and outdoors. But this is the least "city" of the NYC boroughs. The neighborhoods may be friendly around here, but they're also a tad spread out. Main problem is that when your tallest building is only twenty stories high, it takes away my most endearing quality: that I thwip and I quip. It's the top line of my résumé, and it's too late in the game for me to be bitten by a flock of radioactive geese.

Still, I've gotten an invite from everyone's (wait, "everyone" might be a bit too strong) favorite Merc with a Mouth to look around the place. He says I'll be pleasantly surprised, so of course this is going to go horribly wrong, I'm sure of it. We've had our issues in the past (I got him kicked out of the Avengers; he killed my boss). But over time, I've come to respect Wade. Trust, definitely not. But respect? We're getting there. This trip out to Staten Island has also kicked up a hornet's nest worth of memories of this part of town. After we get through with Wade, I'll share some of them with you.

P.S. Will update this section if Deadpool ends up causing trouble.

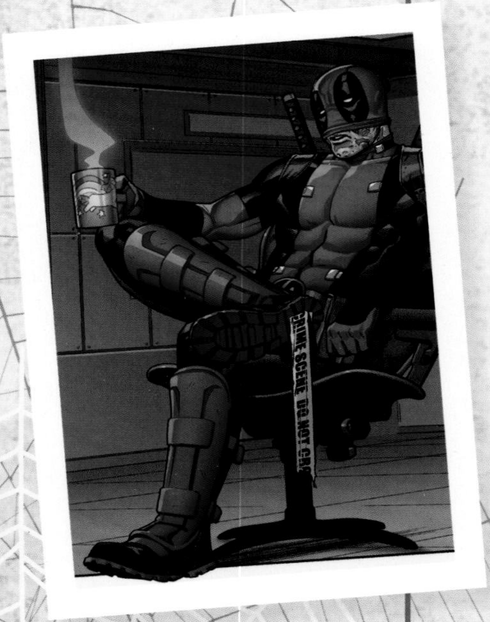

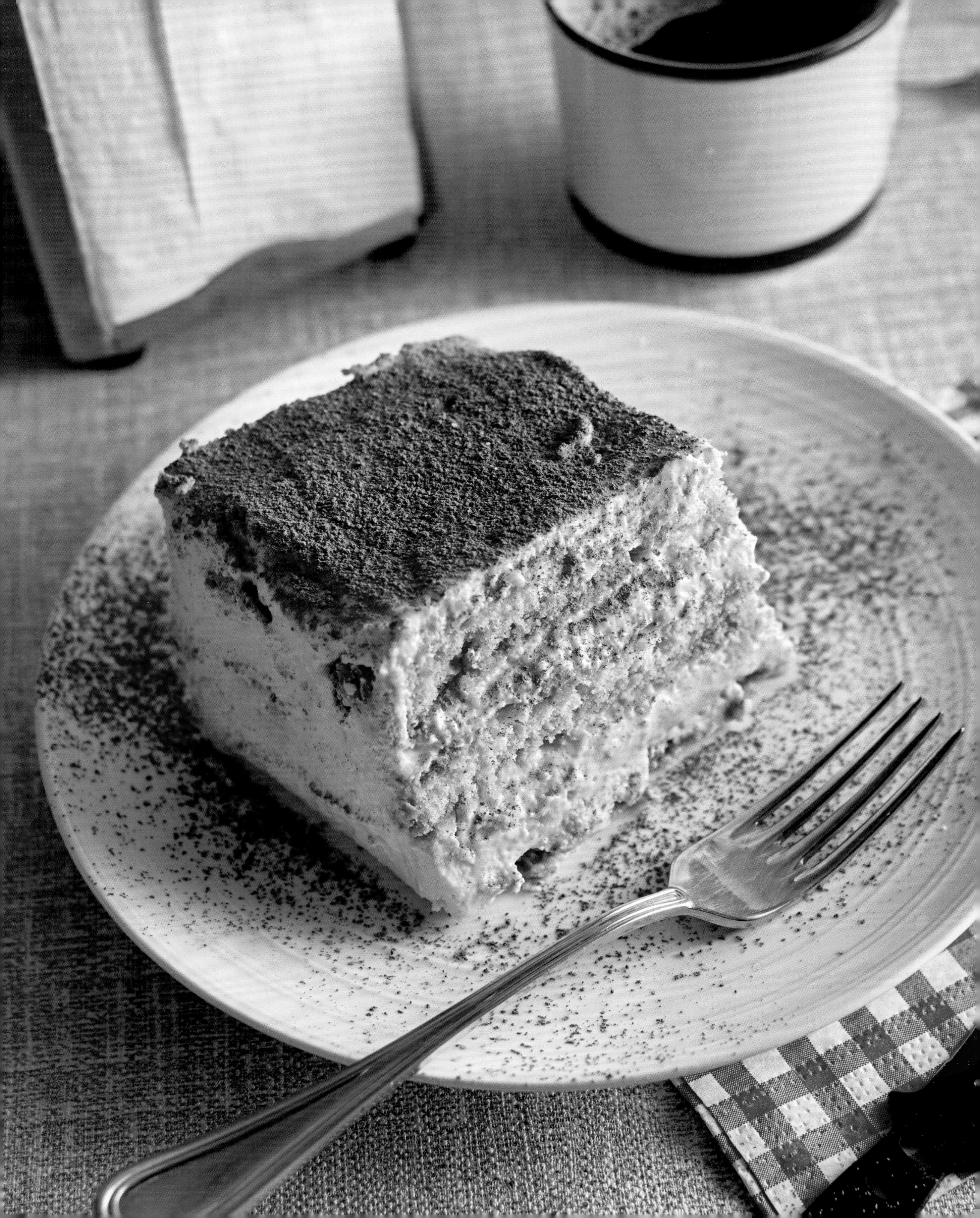

TIRAMISU

GF | V
YIELD: 12 SLICES
PREP TIME: 3 HOURS

DEADPOOL HERE. THANKS FOR MENTIONING ME IN THE INTRO, SPIDEY. UNDERSELLING ME AS ALWAYS, BUT I'VE GOT YOU COVERED. I'M OLD HAT AT THIS COOKBOOK THING—THE PEOPLE LOVE ME. THEY COULDN'T KEEP MINE ON THE SHELVES. I SINGLE-HANDEDLY SAVED BRICK-AND-MORTAR. STICK WITH ME, SPIDEY, I'LL TAKE YOU FAR.

It's not that kind of cookbook. We're not selling this.

SURE IT'S NOT.

Wade!!

OKAY, I'LL PLAY ALONG. <SERIOUS VOICE>: HERE IS A GREAT RECIPE FOR TIRAMISU I GOT FROM A CHEF NAMED NIKKI WHO WORKS UP ON HYLAN BOULEVARD. (NEXT TIME YOU STOP BY, TELL 'EM WADE SENT YOU. SHE'LL PROBABLY THROW SOMETHING SHARP WHEN YOU DO. AND I'LL MEET YOU AT THE NEXT RECIPE LOCATION, IN PORT RICHMOND.)

Wait, how are we even having this conversation? I'm writing this, in a book. *In pen?!?!*

HOW INDEED, SPIDEY . . . HOW INDEED.

That's not an answer, Wade. Ugh!!

- 4 egg yolks
- 1 cup sugar
- 5 tablespoons coffee syrup
- 1½ cups heavy cream
- 1½ cups mascarpone
- 2 cups strong-brewed coffee
- 2 teaspoons vanilla extract
- 3 packs gluten-free ladyfingers
- 2 tablespoons cocoa powder

1. This recipe uses a double boil method, so you'll want to fill a pot with water and set it to simmer. Then, take out a bowl that will be large enough to fit onto the top of your pot without falling in. Make sure that when you do eventually set your bowl on the pot, the water in the pot won't reach the bottom of the bowl.
2. In the bowl, while it's on your counter and away from the heat, add the yolks, sugar and 2 tablespoons of the coffee syrup.
3. Start whisking these together, then place the bowl on top of the simmering pot of water. Keep whisking, moving the bowl on and off the pot to avoid curdling.
4. Continue to heat and whisk off and on the pot until you reach the ribbon stage, after approximately 10 to 12 minutes. This is when you can spoon a ribbon of sauce on top of the rest and it will sit for a moment before sinking in.
5. Once you've reached the ribbon stage, take your bowl off the heat and let the yolk and sugar base sit.

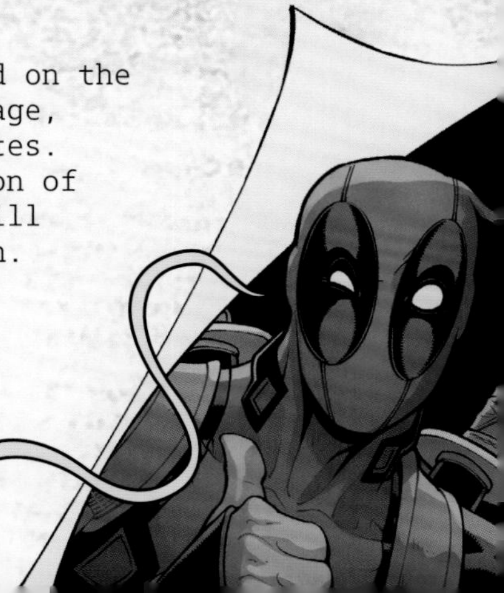

PSST, THIS RECIPE CONTINUES ON THE NEXT PAGE

TOLD YA THE TIRAMISU RECIPE CONTINUED FROM PG 107

6. In your mixer, start whipping the heavy cream until stiff peaks form.

7. Going back to the yolk and sugar base, fold in a third of the mascarpone at a time until fully incorporated. Then do the same with the whipped cream, creating a custard.

8. In a 9-by-9-inch cake pan, smoothly add a few dollops of the custard to create a thin layer at the bottom of the pan.

9. Combine the coffee, the remaining 3 tablespoons of coffee syrup and the vanilla extract in a small bowl and dip the ladyfingers into it one by one. Be sure to fully submerge each cookie. Then set them on top of the custard, creating another layer in the bottom of your cake pan. Break the ladyfingers if you need some smaller piece in order to fully cover the pan.

10. Top with another layer of custard and another layer of coffee-coated ladyfingers. Repeat until the pan is full. Refrigerate for at least 2 hours to chill and set.

11. When you're ready to eat, dust with cocoa powder. Cut and serve.

CHICKEN CUTLET TORTA

YIELD:
1 SANDWICH

PREP TIME:
1 HOUR

It turns out Staten Island has a secret coven of monsters who commingle with the human residents. Some are just out of sight, others a lot less so. I don't know what it says about me that I have no problem uttering, let alone writing those last few lines, or even this next one: Wade is their *king*. A literal *king of monsters*. Like with a throne that's three sizes too big for him and everything. Right off the bat, Wade introduces me to Night Wolf, so named because he's a seven-foot talking wolfman. Still not fazed. He takes me to a place on Travis Avenue that, according to him, makes a chicken torta so good it made him swear off consuming humans . . . for a whole week. Wade, what have you gotten me into?

1 boneless skinless chicken breast, butterflied and pounded

¼ cup refried beans

1 cup all-purpose (AP) flour

2 eggs, beaten

¾ cup breadcrumbs

2 cups canola oil

Salt and pepper

4 tablespoons cotija cheese

1 telera or ciabatta roll

½ avocado

6 tablespoons salsa

2 tablespoons thinly sliced red onion

6 to 8 leaves cilantro

½ cup shredded iceberg lettuce

1. Butterfly the chicken breast by carefully slicing through the thickness of the breast at its center. Stop just before you cut all the way through.

2. Place the chicken breast in the middle of a large, gallon-size ziplock bag and use a meat mallet to gently flatten it to an even thickness. If you don't have a meat mallet, you can use a small saucepot with a flat bottom to pound it out.

3. Warm the refried beans in a small pot on low heat or in the microwave if you have one.

4. Set up your breading station with three containers: one with a cup of flour, one with beaten eggs, and a third with breadcrumbs. Starting with the flour, coat each side of the chicken, then dip in the egg, then coat with the breadcrumbs.

5. Heat the oil in a large frying pan or pot with enough wall height that the oil won't splash out or overflow.

6. Test the oil by dropping a bit of egg mix or breading into it. It should fry up immediately. If ready, gently lay the breaded chicken into the oil. Always lay the slice away from you, so any splashing oil is in the direction away from your hands. Carefully fry chicken on both sides, 3 to 4 minutes per side, until lightly golden. Remove from the oil and set on a paper towel.

7. Season with salt and pepper while chicken is still warm and top with the crumbled cotija cheese.

8. Split the bun in half and spread the warmed refried beans on the bottom. Then top with ½ of an avocado, sliced thin. Season with salt and pepper. Top the avocado with the fried cutlet.

9. Spoon your favorite salsa over the chicken cutlet and top with red onion and cilantro. Finish with the shredded iceberg and the top of the bun.

10. Press down firmly, slice in half with a serrated knife, and dig in.

109

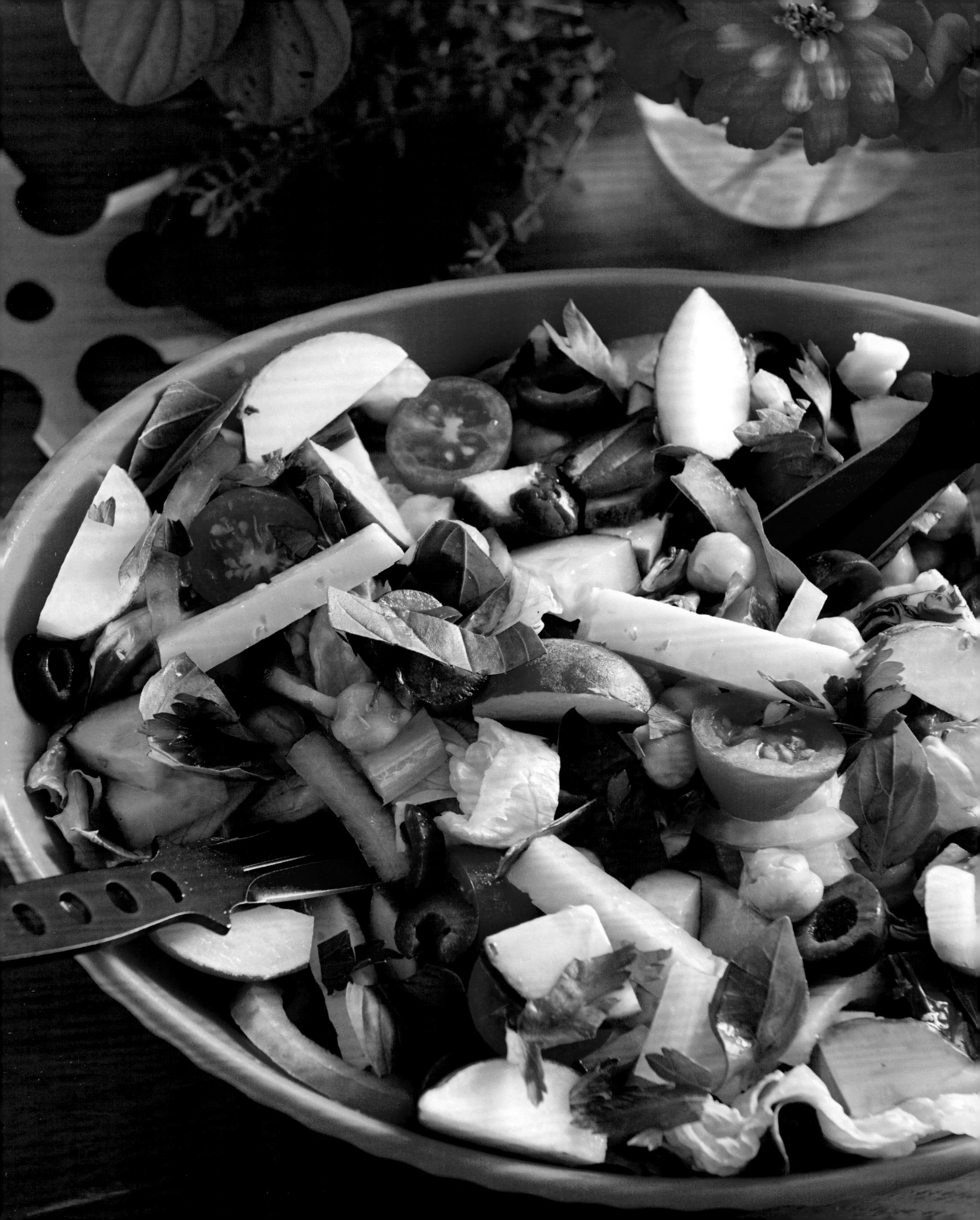

ITALIAN CHOPPED SALAD

YIELD:
4 TO 6
PORTIONS

PREP TIME:
40 MINUTES

His Kingship, Deadpool, finished his tour with a trip to the Botanical Garden on Snug Harbor. He figured it would be a good place for him and his subjects to honor me as a guest, and Wade made the salad. Because of course he did. I would like to note that all the while the fine denizens of Staten Island were, shall we say, nonplussed by the whole thing. I'm not sure if it's a sign I need to come out to SI more often, or less.

FOR THE DRESSING:

½ cup extra virgin olive oil

2 tablespoons red wine vinegar

1 lemon, juiced

2 teaspoons dry oregano (Sicilian, if possible)

1 small clove garlic, grated or microplaned

1 teaspoon kosher salt

1 teaspoon ground black pepper

For the salad:

1 cup cherry tomatoes, cut in half through the equator

2 tablespoons thin-sliced red onions (⅛ inch)

1 cup canned chickpeas

1 cup pitted black olives, sliced ¼ inch thick

1 cup seedless cucumber, cut into ¼-inch dice

1 head iceberg lettuce, chopped in 1-inch by ½-inch strips

1 cup chopped romaine

1 radicchio

1 endive

12 leaves basil, torn

½ cup sliced provolone, ¼ inch thick and 1 inch long

½ cup radishes, cut in quarters

2 tablespoons flat leaf parsley, chopped

OPTIONAL:

½ cup sliced salami, ¼ inch thick and 1 inch long

1. First combine the dressing ingredients in a small bowl, mix well, and set aside.

2. Combine the cherry tomatoes, red onion, chickpeas, black olives, and cucumbers in a bowl. Marinate with 6 tablespoons of the dressing for at least 15 minutes.

3. Gently add the various cut lettuces, basil, and provolone to the marinated vegetables.

4. Spoon the salad onto a large platter and garnish with the radishes and parsley.

5. Season with salt and pepper to taste and serve.

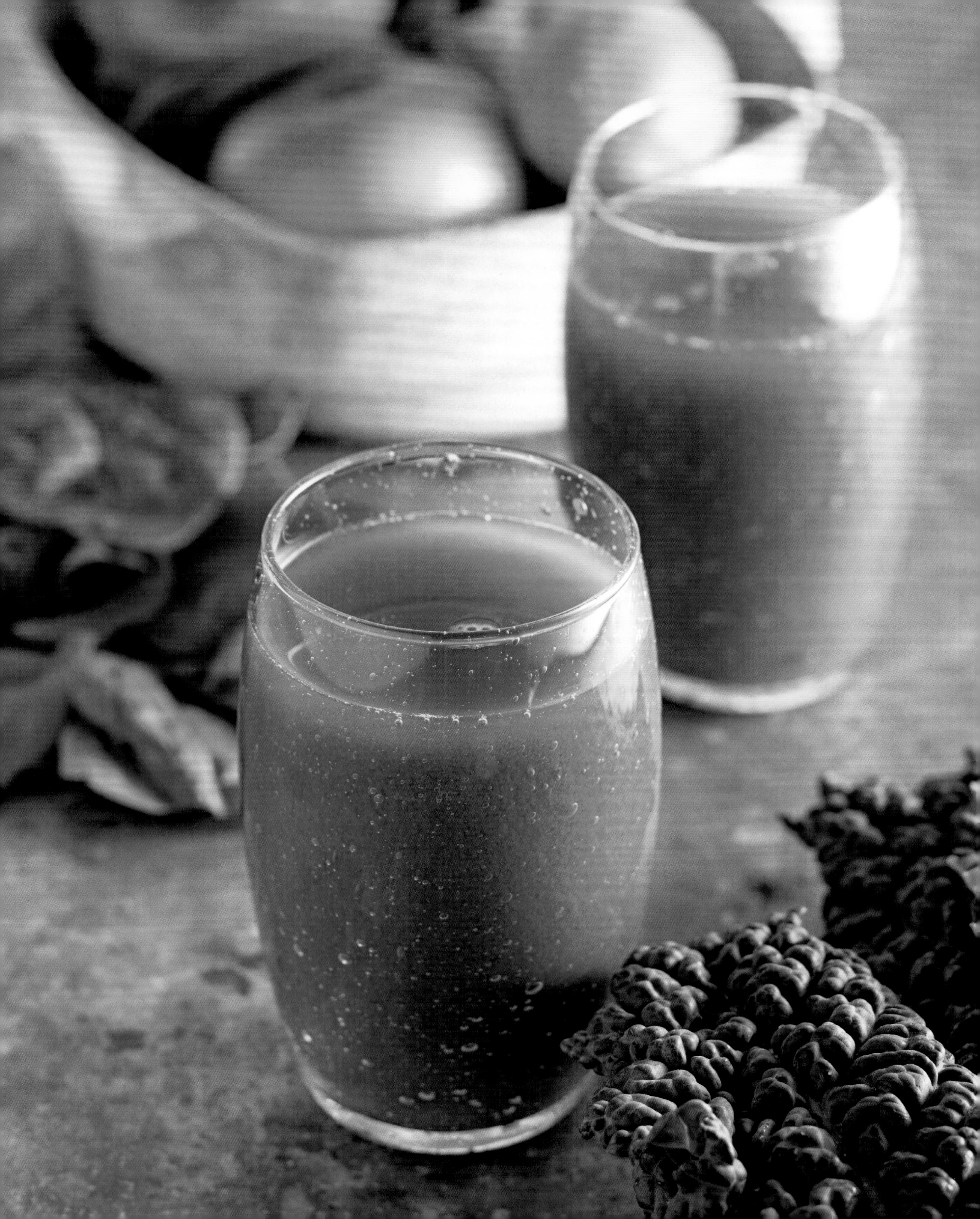

GREEN JUICE

GF | V+
YIELD:
4 CUPS
PREP TIME:
15 MINUTES

Who in their right mind plans a heist on the Staten Island Ferry? The Kangaroo, that's who. He made his presence known by throwing off his trench coat halfway through the 25-minute jaunt from lower Manhattan. I guess he was going for a grand reveal, announcing his presence and all. I wasn't in the mood for a fight, or to hear his elaborate scheme. Instead, I won the day with logic by reminding him that a) he wasn't counting on me being on his ferry, and b) he's known for jumping, not swimming. Defeated, if only emotionally, he shrank back in his seat. I felt bad for him and ended up treating him to a smoothie on the ferry. He went for the Green Juice. Really seemed to perk his ears up. Wouldn't stop gushing about it being the best he'd ever tasted. Well, at least he got something productive out of the day. And I got a recipe to share.

EQUIPMENT:

Juicer

1 bunch kale, washed and chopped

2 cups tightly packed spinach

2 limes, peeled

¼ cup peeled fresh ginger

2 Granny Smith apples, cored

2 to 3 cucumbers, hothouse European variety preferred

1. Prep and load everything into a juicer and juice. It's easier if you mix everything before juicing.

2. Sip, then add more of any ingredient to your taste.

3. Chill and pour into a class to serve.

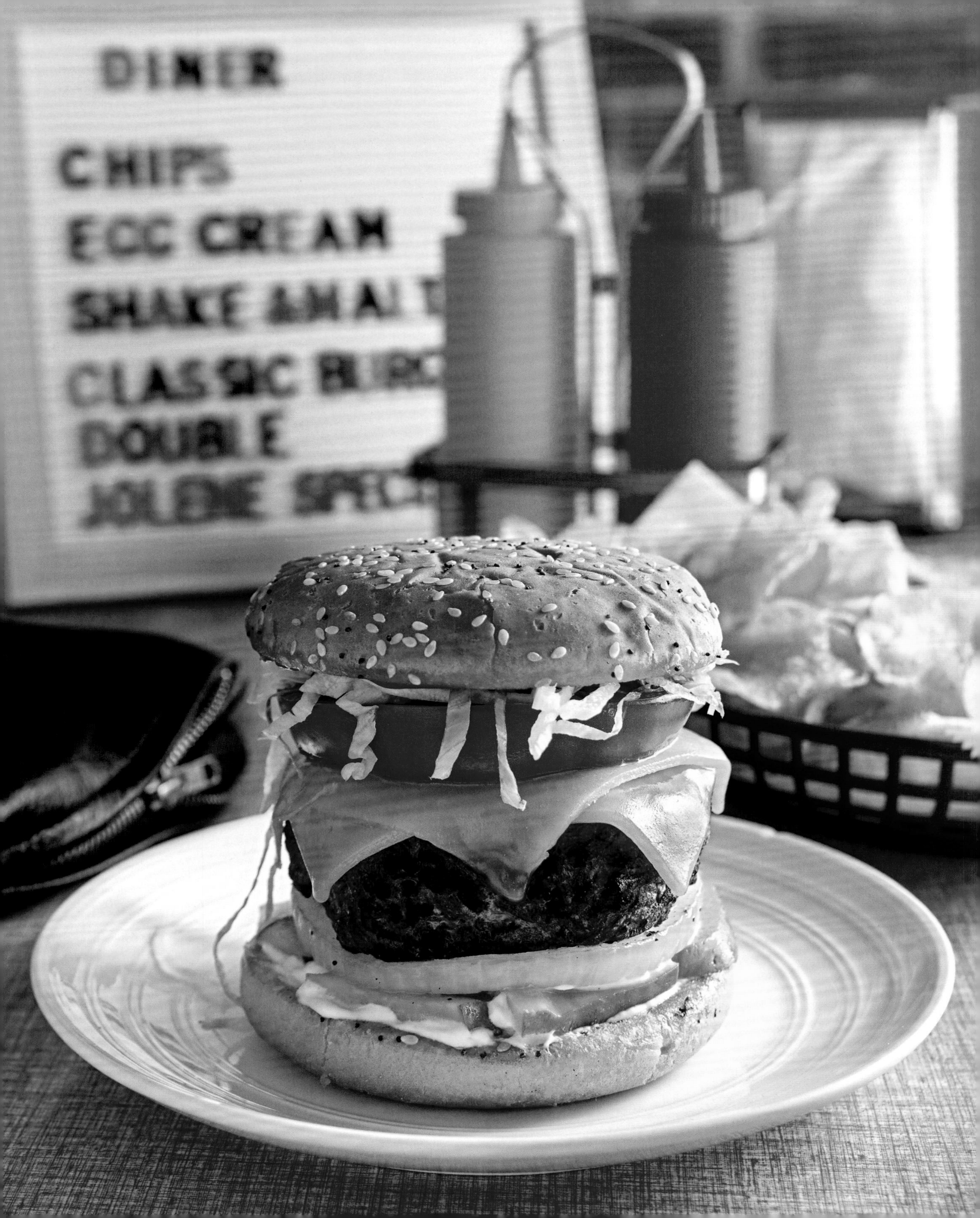
DINER
CHIPS
EGG CREAM
DOUBLE

BELOW-THE-RADAR BURGER

YIELD:
1 BURGER
PREP TIME:
30 MINUTES

Wolverine is the best at what he does. Translation: Logan can get real stabby. We don't hang out much outside of work. He says I'm "too chatty." He's not wrong. And I usually feel lucky if I get a grunt, a glare, and a snarl from him. Imagine my surprise when he invited me out for a burger. Imagine my further surprise when he explained that we had to go to Staten Island for said burger. I will tell you this, he knows his burgers. A secret burger spot, with a classic counter and booths and a waitress named Jolene, all tucked away in the most unassuming building in the least populated borough. It makes perfect sense for a Canuck of few words to prefer a classic burger a full ferry ride away from Manhattan, somewhere quiet that maybe even reminds him of home. Even if it's not the first place you'd expect to find an outstanding burger. Bonus: I think I got, like, eight whole words outta Wolvie while we ate . . . plus the obligatory grunt, glare, and snarl. I think our relationship has turned a corner.

One 8-ounce patty of your preferred burger meat

Salt and pepper

One ½-inch slice of sweet onion

1 tablespoon olive oil

2 slices sharp cheddar

1 seeded or brioche burger bun

Condiments of your choice

4 slices dill pickle

2 slices tomato

½ cup shredded iceberg lettuce

OPTIONAL:

Potato chips

1. Turn on your grill to a high heat. Season the burger with a light snowfall of salt and pepper on both sides. Then season the slice of onion with salt, pepper, and olive oil.

2. Place both the burger and the onion slice on the grill. Lower the lid and cook for about 2 minutes. Then turn the burger 180 degrees and check the onion; you'll want to cook the onion until it's well charred.

3. After about 2 more minutes, flip the burger and onion. Cook, covered, for another 2 minutes. Cover the burger with two slices of cheese and move it on top of the onion. Lower the lid, letting the cheese melt and the juices from the onion and the burger patty meld.

4. When the patty is cooked to your desired level of doneness, remove from the grill. Quickly toast the bun on the grill and begin to build your burger.

5. Spread your desired condiments on either side of the bun and place the pickles on the bottom, then top with the onion, burger patty, tomato, and finally the lettuce. Serve with a side of potato chips!

FRIED EGGS WITH POTATO-PASTRAMI HASH

YIELD:
1 SERVING

PREP TIME:
OVERNIGHT, PLUS 45 MINUTES

Ben Grimm here. And yeah, I know this hunk of hero is more Yancy Street than Hudson River. But sometimes you just want to get away from your regular haunts. Go someplace where the conversation's different. Where the people haven't known you since before a shower of cosmic rays turned you into a large, rocky fellow. You get me? Rose runs a diner in Staten Island that can be found near where the ferry lets off. For those of ya askin', it's a Fantasti-Car-commute for me. I think Aunt Petunia's favorite nephew might start a bit of a ruckus on the ferry, don't ya think? I found Rose's a couple of years ago and keep coming back for the amazing fried egg and hash combo. Plus, it's open all hours. Kinda good when you find yourself returning from a fight with Galactus in deep space or getting back from the Negative Zone (ya end up feeling like a windshield after going up against a dimension fulla bugs). This place covers all my bases, and so does this dish. They were happy to part with the recipe so long as I sent some of you guys their way. Tell 'em Benjy sent ya. They'll treat ya right.

1 Idaho potato

3 tablespoons olive oil

¼ cup diced sweet onion, ¼-inch cubes

¼ cup diced bell pepper, ¼-inch cubes

⅓ cup pastrami, sliced thin or diced

Salt and pepper

1 tablespoon butter

2 eggs

1 tablespoon minced chives

1 tablespoon parsley chiffonade

OPTIONAL:

1 Fresno chile, sliced thin

4 tablespoons red wine vinegar

1. The night before, bake an Idaho potato wrapped in foil in a 350°F oven until fork-tender. Unwrap and place in the fridge until you're ready to use it.

2. Depending on your preference, peel and dice or just dice your potato.

3. Heat a nonstick pan on medium high, then add 2 tablespoons of olive oil, as well as the diced onion and bell pepper. Sauté until fragrant. Add the potatoes and continue to fry for a bit of color, about 5 to 6 minutes. Then add the pastrami and fry until the pastrami starts to render and the hash starts to look golden and delicious, about another 5 minutes. Season with salt and pepper to taste and keep hot.

4. In a small bowl, cover the sliced Fresno chile with red wine vinegar.

5. In a separate pan, or the same one if you've removed the hash and it's clean, add a tablespoon of butter and the remaining tablespoon of oil. Fry two eggs until the doneness of your liking. Season with salt and pepper.

6. Toss the hash with the chives and parsley and place in the bottom of a bowl. Gently lay the fried eggs on top and garnish with the pickled chiles.

NEW YORK BACON, EGG, AND CHEESE

YIELD:
1 SANDWICH
PREP TIME:
15 MINUTES

Morning commutes are the worst, am I right? Whether you're biking, riding, or swinging like yours truly, there's nothing more New York than a Bacon, Egg, and Cheese to start the day right. Consider this a consensus recipe. I'll make no friends choosing just one spot as the best for this combo. And I've got enough enemies, through no fault of my own. So, why here in Staten Island? I've worked a case or two overnight here. It was a breeze to find a great deli just off Amboy Road that makes a go-to Bacon, Egg, and Cheese when I'm out here.

4 slices bacon, cut in half lengthwise

2 tablespoons butter

2 eggs

Salt and pepper

1 to 2 slices American cheese

1 seeded roll

1 tablespoon olive oil

OPTIONAL:

Ketchup, mayonnaise, or hot sauce

1. Cook the bacon until crispy in a nonstick sauté pan on medium heat for about 8 to 10 minutes. Spoon out the bacon grease as it starts to collect at the bottom of the pan, putting it in a bowl for later. Once the bacon is crispy, remove it from the pan and rest it on a paper towel.

2. Wipe out the pan and add 1 tablespoon of butter and 1 tablespoon of the bacon grease. Heat until foamy. Crack the eggs and gently add them to the pan. Season with salt and pepper.

3. As soon as the egg whites are set or solid white, carefully flip the eggs. This should take approximately 2 minutes on each side. Then top the eggs with cheese and cover with a lid for about one minute, or until the cheese has melted.

4. Open the roll and butter the inside walls, then set it inside down on another nonstick pan to toast. Alternatively, feel free to use a toaster oven, if you have one, for your buttered roll.

5. Once the roll is toasted, add ketchup, mayo, and/or hot sauce, if you wish. Then place the bacon on the bottom and top with the eggs. Close it up with the top bun and gently press down.

6. Cut in half with a serrated knife and eat!

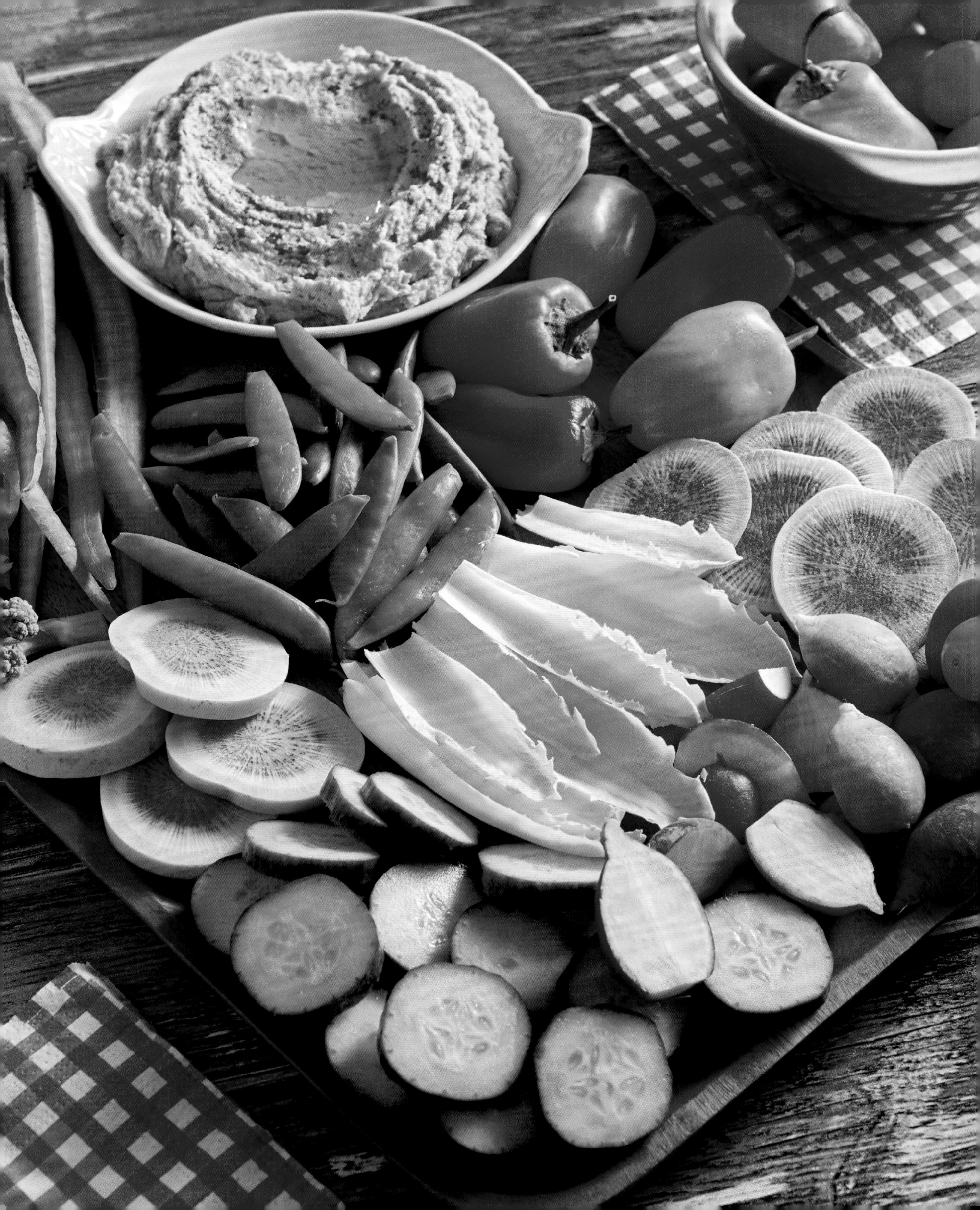

SEASONAL MARKET VEGGIES AND HUMMUS

GF | V+
YIELD:
6 TO 8 SERVINGS
PREP TIME:
45 MINUTES

I'm not without my own cooking skills, you know. When called upon I can put together a mean plate of crudités, especially when I'm invited to a picnic out here at Silver Lake Park, or Willlowbrook Park, or Clove Lakes Park (geez, no wonder they call Staten Island "the borough of parks"). Take note of my culinary genius, I'm not sharing a lot of these. Appreciate this special glimpse into Spidey's kitchen. You can thank me later.

1 small clove garlic, minced

4 tablespoons tahini

1/3 cup extra virgin olive oil, divided, plus 1 tablespoon for plating

4 tablespoons fresh lemon juice

One 15-ounce can chickpeas, drained and rinsed

1 teaspoon kosher salt

1/4 teaspoon ground cumin

1 pinch smoked paprika

1 bunch baby-cut rainbow carrots

2 red or yellow endives

1 bunch radishes, greens still on

1 bunch broccolini

1 pound sugar snap peas

6 baby fennels

1 pint sweet cherry tomatoes

1. In a food processor, combine garlic, tahini, 1/3 cup of the olive oil, and lemon juice. Blend until smooth and airy. You may need to scrape the sides of the bowl a few times.

2. Add the chickpeas and puree, adding water if needed to help smooth it out.

3. When smooth, add salt and cumin, and puree again. Taste and add more salt if needed.

4. Move to a serving bowl and use the back of a spoon to create a divot or well in your hummus to hold the remaining 1 tablespoon of the olive oil. Add a pinch of smoked paprika around the well.

5. Wash, peel, and trim the vegetables, arranging them around a platter randomly to display their colors and shapes. Feel free to make substitutions for seasonality. Serve with the hummus.

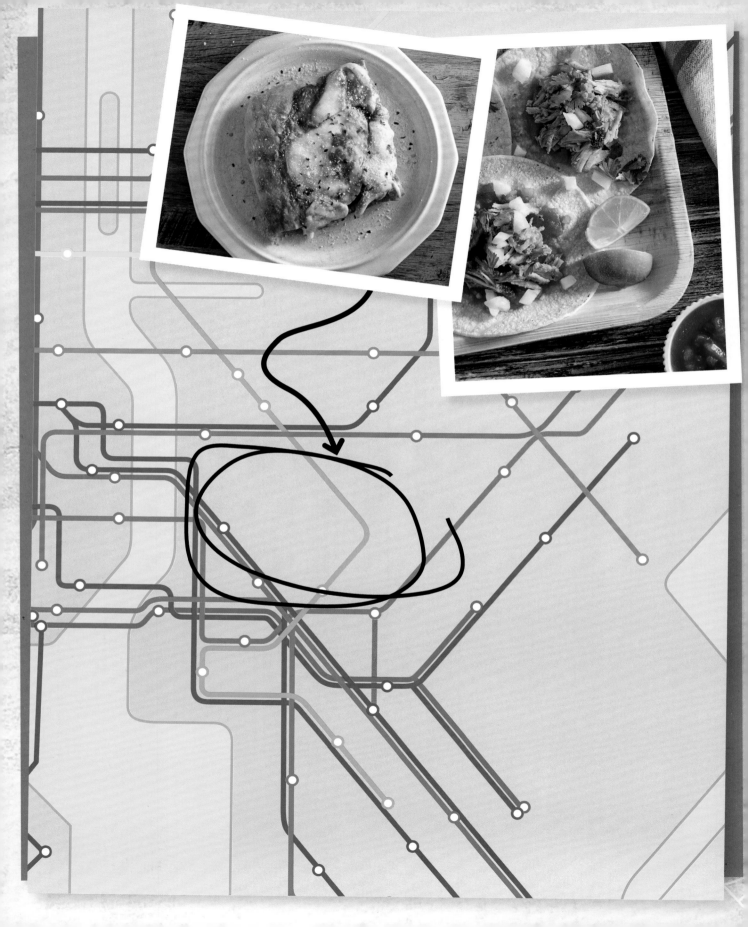

5 BROOKLYN

Welcome to the borough sporting the largest population of any of the five, but the smallest super hero presence. I would gladly relocate to this part of town if not for two things: I don't want to. And have you seen the rents around here?!?!? Geez, I'd need a grant from the Maria Stark Foundation just to afford first and last months.

Just to get back on track, this is an introduction to Brooklyn. According to my intern (you'll hear from him in a bit), that means car-surfing down Flatbush. I guess it saves on webbing. We do what we must to Spider-Man on a budget, and I will only apologize if he has accidentally dented the roof of your car. Anyway, you can't beat the view of the East River from the promenade. Or the West Indian Day Parade on Eastern Parkway to close out the summer. You haven't lived until you've gotten a Spider's-eye view of that thing. All in all, this borough is a veritable web tour packed with culture, museums, people, and food. Here's a quick taste, though it'd be impossible to cover it all.

GRANDMA SLICE

I was underselling the heroes per capita here in Brooklyn. There's a group of archers who call BK home. They're a package deal, so I'll introduce them in a way that by no means reflects their level of importance. There's Hawkeye the younger. She's tough, bright, talented, and will probably be leading the Avengers in a few years if we're not careful. Next is Lucky. A scrappy golden retriever who's been through a lot in his life. He's loyal, smarter than any dog should be, and such a good boy (such a good boy). Third is Hawkeye the older. He's……a work in progress. Elder statesman of this crew, an Avenger with some tenure, and probably would have knocked himself out by now with one of his boxing glove arrows if not for the other two. Side note: Boxing glove arrows defy every known law of physics. I shake my head each time he hits his target with one of those things.

This recipe comes courtesy of Lucky. I'd just finished a team-up with the Hawkeyes, on Thanksgiving no less. Before making my way back uptown, I figured I'd grab something quick and tasty. The Hawkeyes unanimously suggested we let Lucky pick a spot. We followed him to a place in Fort Greene that's apparently his go-to for pizza. Because of course this crew feeds their dog pizza. Say what you will about that, but the dog has outstanding taste. This Grandma Slice is one of his favorites, and I'm inclined to agree with him. (THEY FEED THEIR DOG……PIZZA!!!)

FOR THE DOUGH:

4 cups 00 pizza flour

½ teaspoon instant active dry yeast

1¾ teaspoons kosher salt

1½ teaspoons sugar

1¼ cups water

1½ tablespoons extra virgin olive oil

FOR THE SAUCE:

One 28-ounce can San Marzano tomatoes

½ cup extra virgin olive oil

1 garlic clove, smashed

1 teaspoon kosher salt

1 teaspoon dried oregano

1 pound fresh mozzarella, sliced

½ cup grated Parmesan

1. The night before, make your dough. Start by combining the 00 flour, yeast, salt, and sugar in a mixing bowl. Add the water and 1½ tablespoons of olive oil to the center of the flour mix. Stir to combine.

2. Once all the water and oil has been incorporated, knead the dough with your hands until a shaggy-looking ball forms. Transfer the dough onto a clean surface and knead for another 5 minutes, until the ball begins to smooth out. Oil a clean bowl well and add your dough. Roll it around so it is well oiled, cover tightly with plastic wrap, and store in the refrigerator for at least 12 hours.

3. Pull the dough out two hours before baking. In your oven, move the rack to the bottom rung, preheat to 375°F, and turn on the oven's fan.

4. Drain the tomato water/juice from the can, then add the tomatoes to a food processor with 4 tablespoons of olive oil, plus garlic, salt, and oregano. Puree until smooth. Set aside.

5. Coat a nonstick half sheet tray with the remaining olive oil. Make sure it is very well coated. If more oil is needed, feel free to add.

V

YIELD:
1 HALF-SHEET-TRAY PIZZA, PLUS EXTRA DOUGH FOR MISTAKES

PREP TIME:
1 DAY, PLUS 3 HOURS

6. Gently place your dough on the tray and stretch it evenly to all corners of the sheet tray. Carefully cut excess away with a paring knife. Gently use your fingers to press down all over the dough.
7. Starting from one end, shingle the sliced mozzarella across the dough. You should have just enough to cover the whole pizza.
8. Spoon the pizza sauce sparingly over the gaps between the mozzarella and the dough. Then drizzle it over the mozzarella as well. You should use about 1¼ cup of the sauce. Liberally sprinkle with Parmesan.
9. Place in the oven on the bottom rack and cook for 15 minutes. Turn and cook for another 15 minutes, checking to see if the dough is crisping up. When it's cooked, the dough should start to pull away from the pan easily. At this point, move the pizza to the middle of the oven and continue to cook until the cheese begins to turn golden in patches, around 5 to 10 minutes. Remove and let rest. Cut and serve!

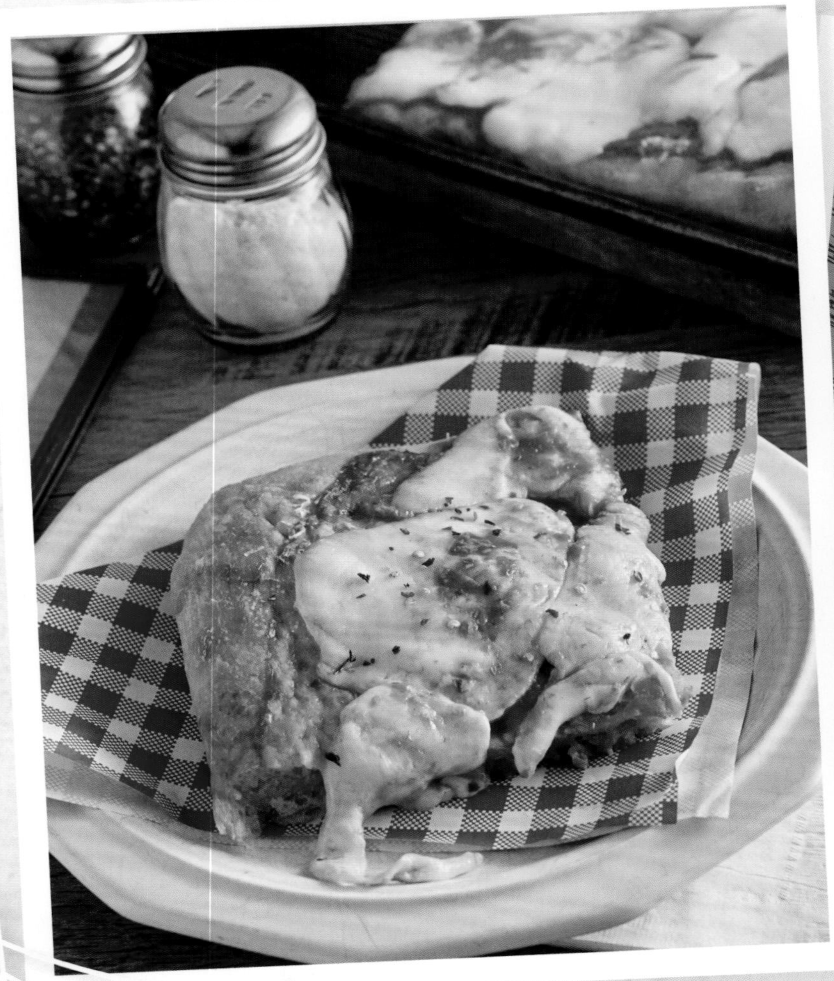

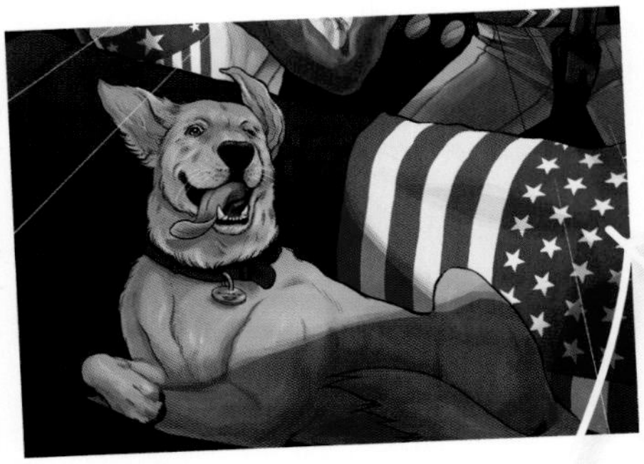

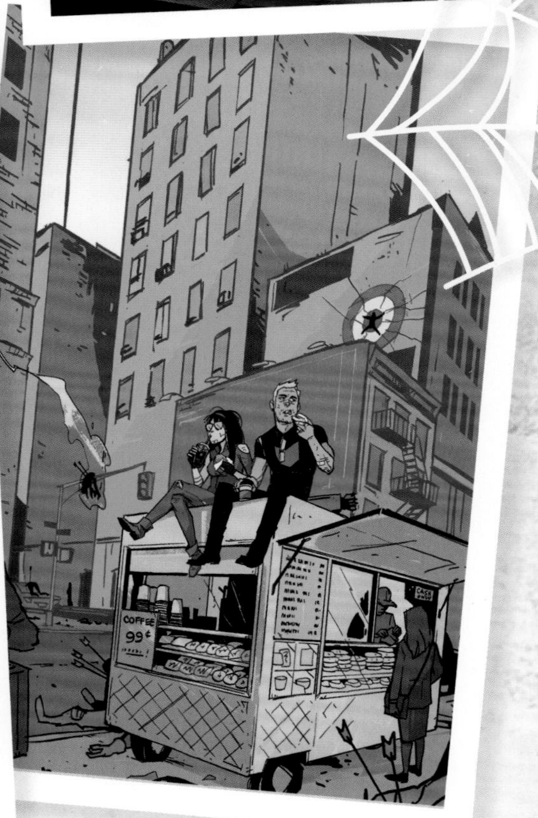
COFFEE
99¢

LAMB SHAWARMA

YIELD:
4 WRAPS

PREP TIME:
OVERNIGHT,
PLUS 30 MINUTES

Did you know I used to own a Spider-Mobile? True story. Sponsorship deal. I stress again: Somebody gave me a car. Like, to drive. And this is even though I told them that I (like more than half of the tri-state area) do not have a license. Details, am I right? Despite my better judgment, I went out on a few missions with my trusty Spider-Mobile, including on my very first, and more than likely last, solo street-level stakeout as I hit the road in Brooklyn looking for the Tarantula (my villains love their themes, don't they?). My meal that night was from a shawarma place that a friend of mine loves. It was the best decision I made. The worst was thinking the Spidey-Mobile, a red and blue onesie, and a lap full of shawarma somehow equaled incognito on the streets of Brooklyn. Need I mention that I didn't capture the Tarantula that evening?

FOR THE LAMB:

2 tablespoons ground cumin

1 tablespoon hot smoked paprika

2 teaspoons ground turmeric

1 teaspoon ground coriander

½ teaspoon ground ginger

¼ teaspoon ground clove

½ teaspoon ground cinnamon

1 teaspoon ground black pepper

1 pound lamb shoulder, sliced thin

4 tablespoons extra virgin olive oil

4 tablespoons lemon juice

1 tablespoon kosher salt

FOR THE WRAP:

½ cup tahini

2 cloves garlic

4 tablespoons water

1 lemon, juiced

1 cup thinly sliced sweet onion

4 shawarma wraps or pitas

1 ripe beefsteak tomato, sliced thin

2 romaine hearts, chopped thin

½ bunch mint, stemmed

½ bunch flat-leaf parsley, stemmed

1. Combine cumin, paprika, turmeric, coriander, ginger, clove, cinnamon, and black pepper and mix well. Reserve half of this spice mix for future recipes.

2. In a 1-gallon ziplock bag or reusable container, combine 2 tablespoons of the spice mix with the thinly sliced lamb, olive oil, lemon juice, and salt. Mix well and refrigerate overnight.

3. In a blender, puree the tahini with the garlic, water, and juice of a lemon. Save for later.

4. When you're ready to cook, heat a large skillet or sauté pan on medium-high heat. Take the lamb slices out of the refrigerator and sauté them with all the marinade until golden and crisping up on both sides. This should take about 12 minutes, depending on your stovetop heat. Remove the lamb to a heatproof bowl.

5. Reuse the now available skillet or sauté pan: Add the onions to the pan with more olive oil if needed, and sauté. As you sauté the onion, scrape off the fond (crusty bits left from sautéing the lamb). When the onions are soft and tender, after about 3 to 4 minutes, mix them with the resting lamb.

6. Warm the pita bread in a toaster until soft and pliable.

7. Add a quarter of the lamb and onion mix to each pita. Top with a couple of slices of tomato and romaine lettuce, dress with two tablespoons of tahini sauce, and garnish with mint and parsley leaves.

8. Wrap your pita and *eat*.

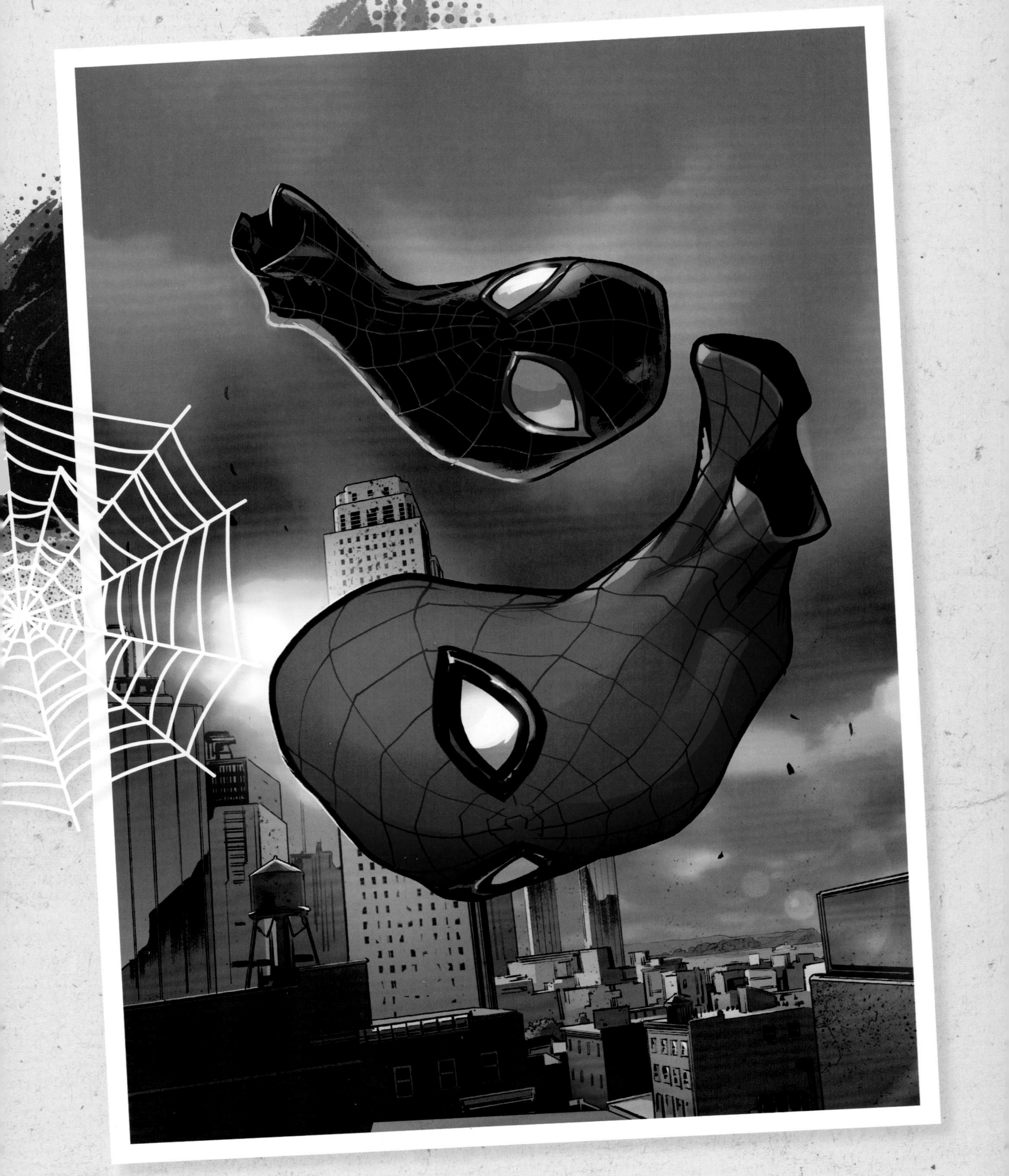

MILES MORALES'S PICKS

While it's not part of my regular crime-fighting beat, Brooklyn is sprawling, with a unique energy and history all its own. I love it so much, I put my intern in charge of things over here. I kid, of course. This guy has taken it upon himself to protect Flatbush, Red Hook, Sheepshead Bay, and Prospect Park. If it's BK, he's on it. He's the real deal. And might have a better handle on this part of town than I do. So he's agreed to provide a few entries in this section. Take it away, Spider-Man.

Hi, everyone. I'm mailing these recipes in and haven't seen the whole book yet. But I'm going to guess I should start like this: I'm not an intern. Last I checked, interns get paid these days. Hint for Spidey: I'd take the occasional refill on web fluid or even just a costume stipend for when my mask rips. What I am is Brooklyn's one and only Spider-Man. Um, I have to admit I'm a little nervous about this. On the plus side, it's kind of like journaling, and I do that a lot at sch—I mean, for my own well-being and self-reflection . . . Sorry, I'm rambling. It's great having Spidey as a mentor, someone who can help me navigate wall-crawling, web-swinging, costume chafing . . . and apparently a mutual gift for oversharing. Sorry again. I hope these recipes make it up to you!

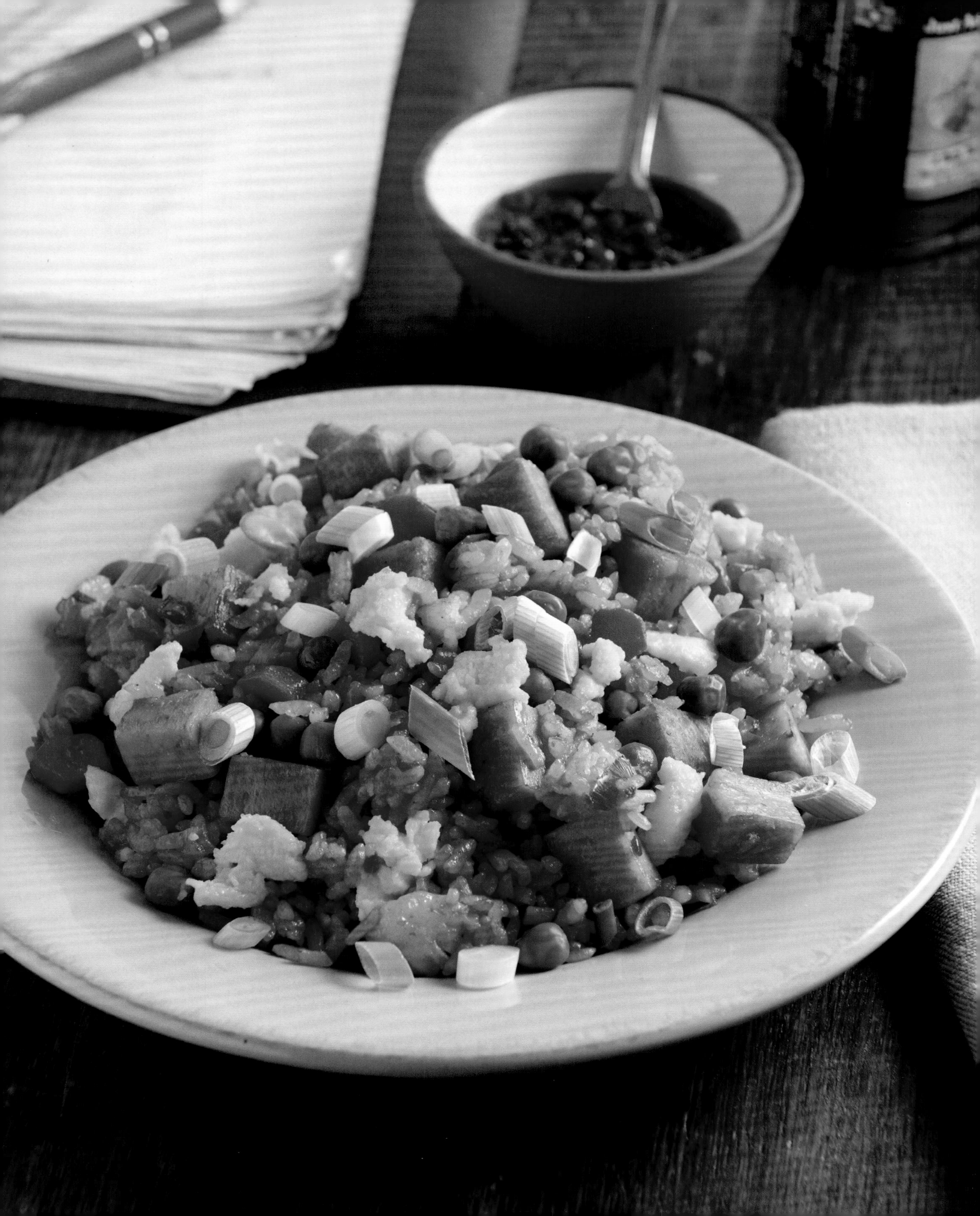

CANNED MEAT FRIED RICE

YIELD:
4 TO 6 SERVINGS
PREP TIME:
25 TO 30
MINUTES

This recipe comes from a nurse I know at a local hospital. She goes by Rio and she's tough. Really, don't mess with her. I'm just saying. Anyway, she told me to mention that this recipe started as a dish from her childhood that she barely remembered how to cook, but it eventually became her son's favorite. It's a tasty dish she could whip up quickly and that her son always appreciated. Because she told me he does. Not because I know her son, or anything like that.

2 tablespoons vegetable oil

2 large eggs

One 12-ounce can processed pork, chopped into small cubes

2 tablespoons sofrito

1 cup finely diced carrot

4 scallions, white and green parts, finely sliced

1 teaspoon sazón

4 cups leftover white rice

1 cup frozen peas, thawed

2 teaspoons soy sauce, plus more to taste

1 tablespoon oyster sauce

1 tablespoon unsalted butter

OPTIONAL:
Chile crisp for garnish

1. Heat 1 tablespoon of vegetable oil over medium-high heat in a large, nonstick wok or pan. Crack eggs into a small bowl and beat lightly, then add to the hot pan. Using a flat spatula, gently move eggs around in oil until just cooked but still very soft. This should take 1 or 2 minutes. Transfer to a deep bowl.

2. Add the processed pork to the still-hot skillet and sauté until the pieces are evenly browned with crisped edges, about 7 to 10 minutes. Using a slotted spoon, transfer to the bowl with the scrambled eggs.

3. Increase heat to high and add the remaining 1 tablespoon of oil. Add the sofrito, diced carrots, and about half of the sliced scallions. Add sazón and sauté for 5 to 7 minutes until the carrots soften, stirring frequently.

4. Add leftover rice (freshly made would be too mushy). Mix well, breaking up any clumps with the spatula. Then add the pork, eggs, and peas. Cook for 1 to 2 more minutes, stirring occasionally until it sizzles and steams.

5. Pour in soy sauce and oyster sauce, and add the butter, stirring vigorously for 1 to 2 more minutes, using the handle to shake the pan to prevent sticking and cook evenly.

6. Transfer the rice to a serving bowl and garnish with the remaining sliced scallions. Season with additional soy sauce or chile crisp if desired. Serve hot.

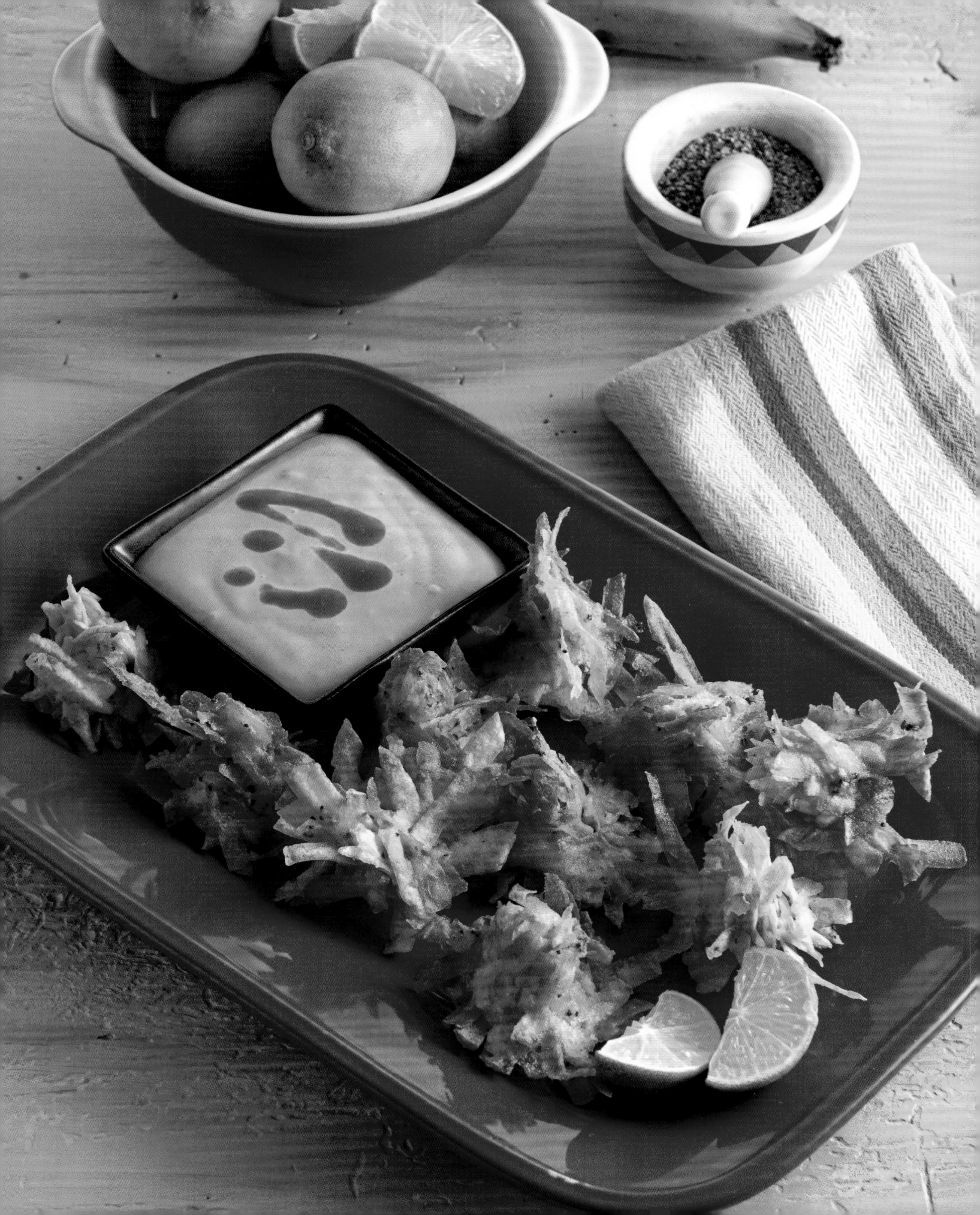

ARAÑITAS

GF | V+
YIELD: 4 SERVINGS
PREP TIME: 20 MINUTES

Rio outdid herself with this second dish. It's fried green plátano, as she'd say: plantains from her native Puerto Rico. They taste so good. I wish she would cook—um, I mean, I wish I could make them for myself every day. The fun part is that the name of this dish translates into "Little Spiders," so she thought it would be cute if she gave me this recipe.

FOR THE ARAÑITAS:

1 teaspoon salt

2 large green plantains (Note that yellow plantains will not work for this recipe)

Vegetable oil

FOR THE DIPPING SAUCE (OPTIONAL):

1/2 cup mayonnaise (vegan versions available, if preferred)

1/3 cup ketchup

1 medium garlic clove, peeled and minced

1/2 teaspoon lime juice, plus more to taste

1 teaspoon kosher salt, plus more to taste

1. Splash of your preferred hot sauce

1. Fill a large bowl with cold water and add 1 teaspoon salt.

2. Peel the plantains by first cutting off both ends, then making three lengthwise slices through the skin. Carefully pull up the peel and remove it, starting at one of the corners with the edge of your fingernail or the tip of your knife if. (Be careful: Plantain skins will stain your hands and clothing.)

3. Transfer whole plantains to the salt water and let sit for 5 to 10 minutes.

4. Pour enough vegetable oil to reach 3 inches in a large, deep skillet. Heat over medium-high heat until oil shimmers and reaches 350° to 375°F. You can test by adding a small piece of plantain; it will sizzle when the oil is hot enough.

5. Meanwhile, prepare mayo ketchup (if using) by combining mayonnaise, ketchup, garlic, lime juice, 1 teaspoon salt, and hot sauce. Mix well with a fork and refrigerate until ready to use.

6. Once oil is hot, remove the plantains from the water and dry very well with paper towels or a clean cloth. Grate the plantains on the large side of the grater, into a deep bowl.

7. Prepare a large plate or cookie sheet with paper towels. Use your fingers to pinch about 1 tablespoon of grated plantain and place into the palm of your hand. Use both hands to press the grated plantain flat; the starches in the plantain will help it stick together, so no need for an additional binder. Repeat until you've used up all the grated plantain.

8. One by one, carefully add grated plantain patties to the hot oil, using a splatter guard as needed to protect from splattering oil, being sure not to crowd the pan. Fry for 3 to 4 minutes total, flipping often to cook evenly.

9. Transfer to a paper towel — lined plate and sprinkle lightly with salt. Let cool for 1 minute (if you can wait that long), and eat immediately, dipping in mayo ketchup.

PIEROGIS

RED & BLACK: I got this recipe off the Rhino during a team-up
I had with him in Red Hook.

RED & BLUE: Excuse me, did you just say the Rhino?

RED & BLACK: Yeah, Aleksei's a sweetheart.

RED & BLUE: Um, sure, when he's not trying to shish kebab yours truly with that horn
of his.

RED & BLACK: C'mon man, he's great. And tells the best stories about his childhood
and how his little old "babushka" would make these amazing pierogis for
him as a treat to make him feel better when he would get in trouble at
school.

RED & BLUE: You keep interesting company, kid. But thanks for your help, I'll handle
the rest of Brooklyn, if you'll take care of jdshfkdshfdkjhaskdjh . . .

Our recording got cut off here, for, reasons . . . But we picked up
long enough for the kid to share the following:

EQUIPMENT:
3-inch-diameter cookie
  cutter

FOR THE DOUGH:
1 cup whole milk

2 tablespoon canola oil

1 egg

3½ cups all-purpose (AP)
  flour

FOR THE FILLING:
2 pounds potatoes

4 tablespoons butter

2 cups small-diced sweet
  onion

1 teaspoon salt

1 teaspoon pepper

½ cup farmer cheese

1 bunch dill, chopped

1 cup sour cream

1 cup apple sauce

1. Peel two pounds of potatoes and cut them into two-inch
   chunks. Cover with cold water in a pot and bring to a
   simmer on high.

2. When cold water comes to a simmer, at about 20 to 30
   minutes, the potatoes will be pretty close to being
   done. To test, see if they just break up with a fork.

3. Drain the potatoes and mash well in a bowl or pot with
   a whisk or potato masher, leaving no lumps. Set aside.

4. To make the dough, mix the milk, canola oil, and egg in
   a bowl. Slowly stream this into a mixer filled with the
   flour.

5. When mixed, remove the dough from the mixer and onto
   a floured surface. Knead for 3 to 5 minutes, until a
   smooth ball is formed. Add more flour or water as you
   go, if necessary. Place in an oiled bowl, cover with
   plastic wrap, and chill in the fridge for 30 minutes.

6. While your dough is chilling, take out a large pan and
   sauté the onions with butter until golden. Season with
   salt and pepper.

7. In a mixing bowl, combine half of the sautéed onions
   with the mashed potatoes and farmer cheese. Mix well
   and season with salt and pepper if needed. Reserve at
   room temperature.

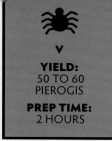

8. Put a large pot of salted water on to boil.

9. Take the pierogi dough from the fridge and roll out on a floured surface, as thin as you can without it tearing. If it's easier, you can do this using part of the dough at a time. Once spread thin, use a 3-inch-diameter cookie cutter to punch out rounds.

10. Fill the dough rounds with about a tablespoon of potato filling each. Seal the dumplings by wetting your fingers with water and pinching the edges.

11. In batches, cook the dumplings in the boiling water. Remove them when they float and the dough is fully cooked, around 2 to 3 minutes per batch. You can keep them hot on a buttered tray until they are all cooked.

12. If you want to take an extra step, sauté them in butter until they start to turn golden.

13. Serve the pierogis on a plate topped with chopped dill and sides of sour cream, apple sauce, and the remaining half of the sautéed onion.

V

YIELD:
50 TO 60 PIEROGIS

PREP TIME:
2 HOURS

SCALLION PANCAKES

V+

YIELD:
6 PANCAKES
PREP TIME:
1 HOUR

Now I've got to mention the Master of Kung Fu, the hero to many and mentor to one well-meaning Spider-Man. The legendary Shang-Chi. I was looking for an edge a while back, as my patented spider-sense was on the fritz. I knew that to refine my skills, I needed to go to a guy who routinely kicked my butt even without powers. Shang-Chi was that guy. With a little patience (actually, a *lot* of patience), Shang-Chi was able to turn yours truly into a master of his own style of kung fu. Afterward, we used to make the trek out to his favorite Chinese restaurant in Brooklyn. I always ordered the scallion pancakes. They were so crunchy, so tasty, so capable of taking my mind off how tough his training was. For the record, it turns out Shang-Chi's a legend in the kitchen, too. When he realized he could motivate me with scallion pancakes, he developed this recipe, which he was happy to share.

½ teaspoon salt

2 cups all-purpose (AP) flour

2 teaspoons canola oil

½ cup boiling water

1½ tablespoons sesame oil

6 scallions, green parts only, sliced thin

FOR FRYING:

4 cups canola oil

OPTIONAL:

4 ounces black vinegar

1. In a mixing bowl, combine salt and 1 cup of the flour. Add 2 teaspoons of canola oil, as well as ½ cup of boiling water. Mix together.

2. In the bowl, or on a floured surface, knead the dough until it becomes a smooth ball. Cover and let it rest for 30 minutes.

3. After resting, roll the dough out into a long snake and cut it into 6 equal pieces. Cover them with a towel.

4. Remove them one by one, leaving the others covered, and roll out each piece of dough into a flat circle, 8 to 10 inches in diameter. Make them as thin as you can go without tearing. Brush liberally with sesame oil and scatter with scallions.

5. Starting on one end of your first flattened circle, roll it over on itself about ¾ inch at a time, until it's a long strip. Press down to seal the edges. Then roll the strip into a wheel and cover. Repeat with the rest, making sure they are all covered. Let sit for 20 minutes.

6. After the pieces have rested again, roll each piece of dough out into a thin circle again, about 6 to 8 inches in diameter, using as much flour as needed. Layer them in parchment with enough flour so they don't stick.

7. In a large sauté pan with high walls, add an inch of canola oil and heat on medium-high.

8. Test the oil for frying temperature by dropping a piece of pancake in. If it floats to the top immediately, you're ready.

9. Use a brush and dust off the excess flour from your first pancake and lay it away from you, into the oil, gently.

10. Using chopsticks, spin the pancake around the oil, gently pushing down so the hot oil hits the top. It should start to puff up and turn golden. Carefully flip with a spatula so that it turns golden on the opposite side. Remove, slowly draining off oil as you do, and place on a tray In a mixing bowl, combine salt and 1 cup of the flour. Add 2 teaspoons of canola oil, as well as $\frac{1}{2}$ cup of boiling water. Mix together.

11. In the bowl, or on a floured surface, knead the dough until it becomes a smooth ball. Cover and let it rest for 30 minutes.

12. After resting, roll the dough out into a long snake and cut it into 6 equal pieces. Cover them with a towel.

13. Remove them one by one, leaving the others covered, and roll out each piece of dough into a flat circle, 8 to 10 inches in diameter. Make them as thin as you can go without tearing. Brush liberally with sesame oil and scatter with scallions.

14. Starting on one end of your first flattened circle, roll it over on itself about $\frac{3}{4}$ inch at a time, until it's a long strip. Press down to seal the edges. Then roll the strip into a wheel and cover. Repeat with the rest, making sure they are all covered. Let sit for 20 minutes.

15. After the pieces have rested again, roll each piece of dough out into a thin circle again, about 6 to 8 inches in diameter, using as much flour as needed. Layer them in parchment with enough flour so they don't stick.

16. In a large sauté pan with high walls, add an inch of canola oil and heat on medium-high.

17. Test the oil for frying temperature by dropping a piece of pancake in. If it floats to the top immediately, you're ready.

18. Use a brush and dust off the excess flour from your first pancake and lay it away from you, into the oil, gently.

19. Using chopsticks, spin the pancake around the oil, gently pushing down so the hot oil hits the top. It should start to puff up and turn golden. Carefully flip with a spatula so that it turns golden on the opposite side. Remove, slowly draining off oil as you do, and place on a tray lined with paper towels. Season with salt to taste right away. It should take about 2 to 3 minutes to cook one pancake start to finish.

20. Repeat with the remaining dough. Watch out for your oil turning foamy. If it does, simply switch out for fresh oil.

21. Cut the pancakes into wedges and serve by themselves or with black vinegar.

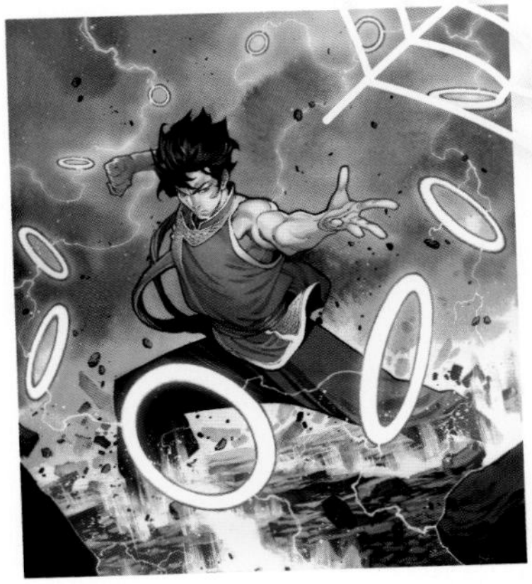

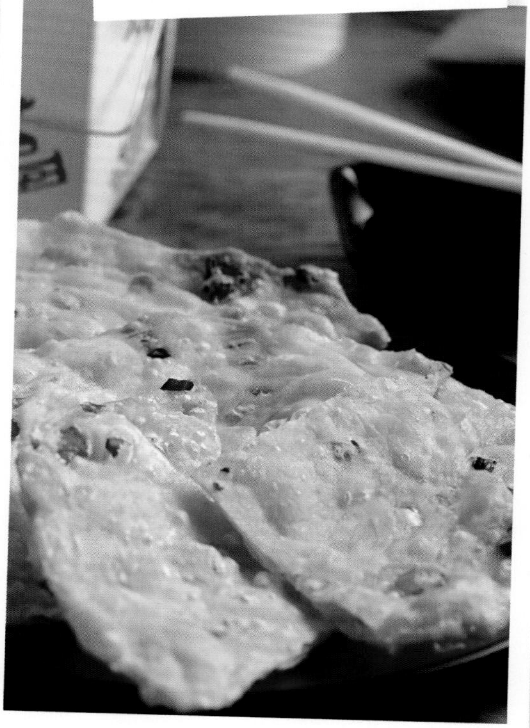

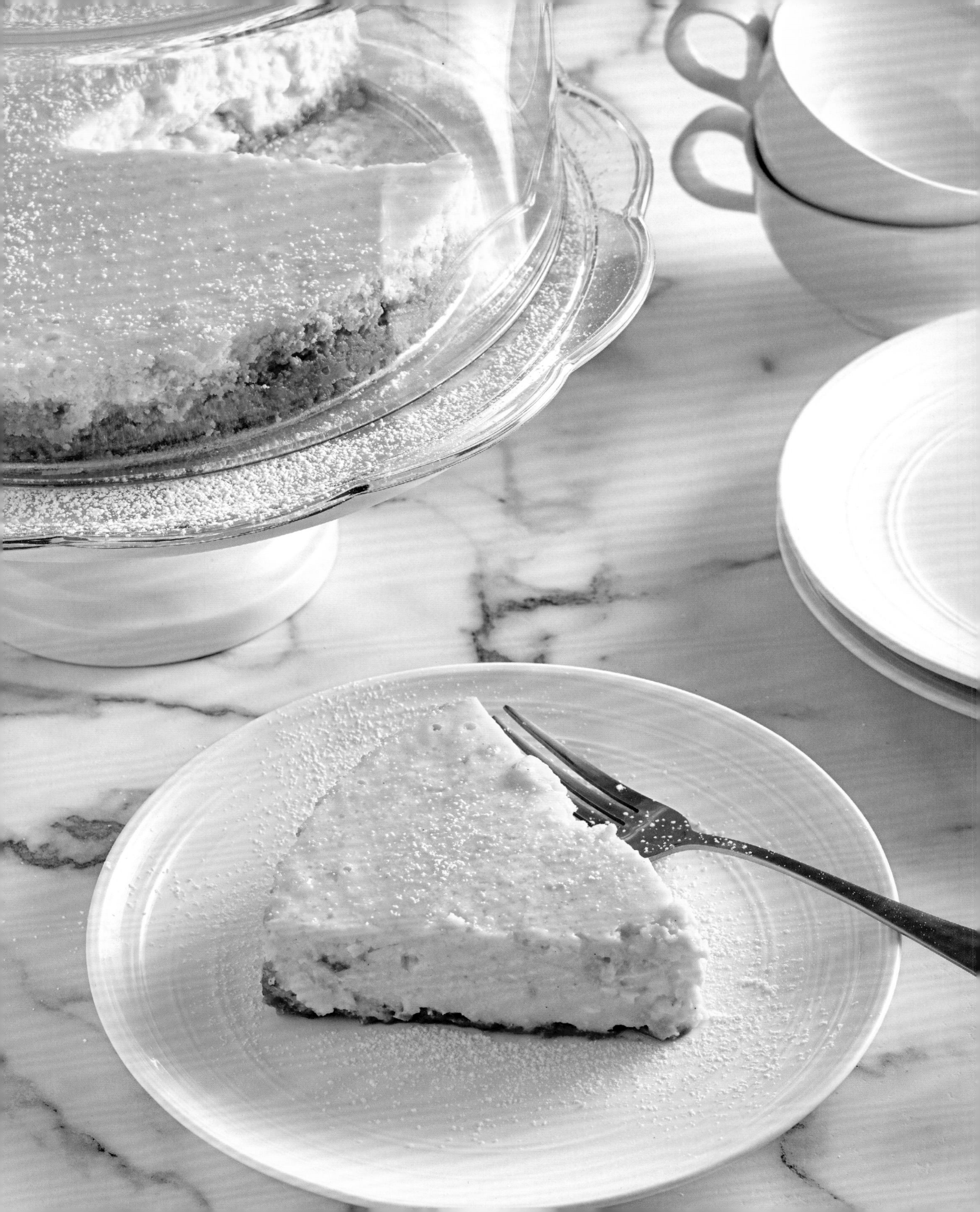

RICOTTA CHEESECAKE

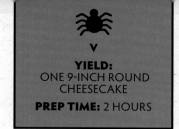

YIELD:
ONE 9-INCH ROUND
CHEESECAKE
PREP TIME: 2 HOURS

Brooklyn's kind of famous for cheesecake in general. But there's a restaurant in the northern most part of downtown, just off the Manhattan Bridge, that makes an amazing, mouth-watering, perfect cheesecake. And I'm not just saying that because a fight I don't remember too well once put me through the window of said restaurant. Said fight might have also blown up their entire cake display. Said owner of said restaurant and a certain wide-eyed wall-crawler might have entered into a gentlemen's agreement for the latter to promote this preeminent pastry any chance he gets. It helps that the cake itself is heavenly.

EQUIPMENT:

9-inch springform cake pan

6 tablespoons butter

1 cup graham cracker crumbs

1 cup and 3 tablespoons of granulated sugar

2½ cups whole milk ricotta cheese

8 ounces cream cheese, room temperature

1 teaspoon kosher salt

4 eggs

1 vanilla bean, scraped

1 orange, zested

3 tablespoons flour

1 tablespoon powdered sugar

1. Melt the butter in on the stove in a small pot or in the microwave and pour over the graham cracker crumbs and three tablespoons of sugar in a bowl. Mix until wet.

2. Preheat your oven to 350°F.

3. Pour the crumb mix evenly into the bottom of a nonstick 9-inch springform cake pan and pack down firmly with the bottom of a flat plastic container.

4. In a mixer, beat the ricotta cheese, cream cheese, salt, and the remaining cup of sugar together until smooth. On a slower speed, add the eggs one at a time.

5. Add the vanilla seeds scraped from the bean and the zest of an orange.

6. When everything looks smooth and well mixed, add the flour slowly and continue mixing until just combined.

7. Gently pour the batter into the cake pan and place on a ½-inch-deep sheet tray and bake in the oven.

8. Bake for approximately 40 minutes, until the top is golden but not cracking and there is a slight jiggle.

9. Let cool on the counter until cheesecake is room temperature, then use a paring knife and free it from the sides of the pan. Once free, unclip the pan and remove the sides.

10. Dust with powdered sugar, cut into wedges, and serve.

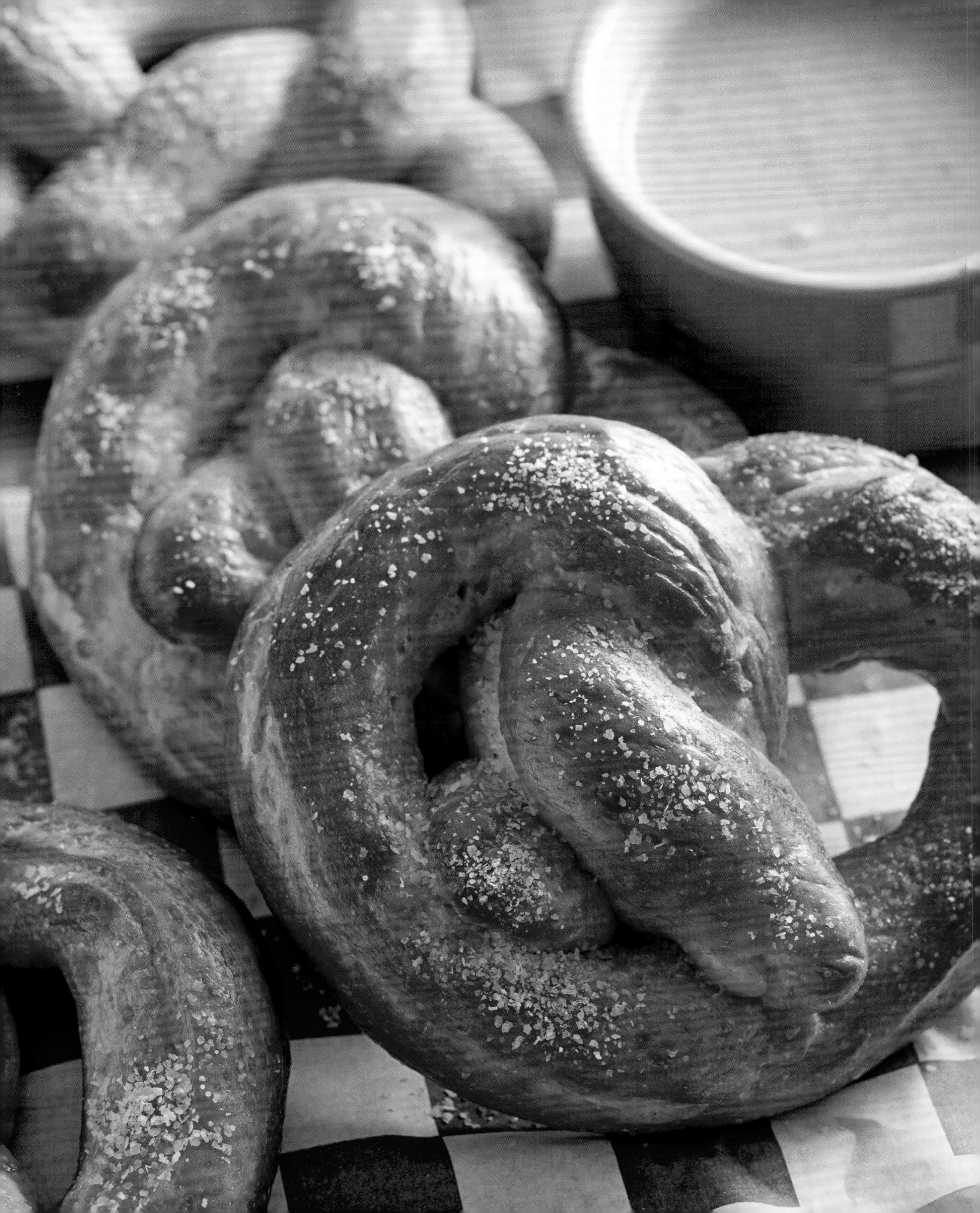

BIERGARTEN SOFT PRETZELS AND SPICY HONEY MUSTARD

V

YIELD:
6 TO 8 PRETZELS

PREP TIME:
2 HOURS

Nightcrawler turned me on to this little German place near Prospect Park that he likes to escape to when being a Krakoan delegate *and* an X-Man gets to be too much. We've been friends ever since we found ourselves in the crosshairs of the Punisher years ago. That's how you all make friends, right? Since then, it's been nice to kick back with a guy almost as agile as I am, just to roof-run and compare notes. (Hi, buddy, let's hang soon.) The important thing here is the pretzel, which is a soft and salty piece of the old country, and I'm thankful to Mr. Wagner for introducing me to it.

FOR THE PRETZELS:

1½ cups warm water
½ tablespoon dry active yeast
2 tablespoons brown sugar
4 cups bread flour
1 teaspoon kosher salt
3 tablespoons melted butter
1 egg
4 tablespoons baking soda
2 tablespoons course sea salt

FOR THE HONEY MUSTARD DIP:

½ cup whole grain mustard
¼ cup spicy brown mustard
½ cup honey
½ cup mayonnaise
1 teaspoon turmeric powder
1 teaspoon chipotle powder

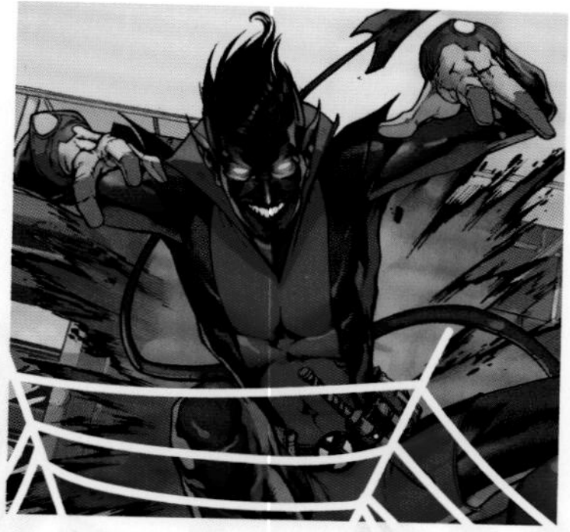

1. Mix together the warm water, active yeast, and sugar until well dissolved and let sit 10 to 15 minutes, or until the solution becomes foamy.
2. In a mixer, combine flour and 1 teaspoon of kosher salt. Slowly mix in the foamy yeast solution, being sure to scrape the bowl and get all the love in.
3. Mix the dough and add in the melted butter. Dough will be messy. Empty onto a floured surface and knead until the dough comes together.
4. Place in a greased bowl and cover. Let rise in a warm place until it's doubled in size, approximately 1½ hours.
5. Preheat your oven to 400°F.
6. Once the dough has doubled, gently portion it into 6 to 8 equal pieces, depending on how big you like your pretzels.
7. Gently roll a portion of dough into a long log about ⅓ inch thick. Lay the log down and fold both ends over to make the pretzel shape. Set aside on an oiled-parchment and repeat.
8. In a separate bowl, mix up one egg.
9. Bring 2 quarts of water and the baking soda to a simmer in a pot large enough to fully submerge a pretzel for blanching.
10. One at a time, dunk the pretzels fully in the water for about 30 to 40 seconds and remove to a toweled surface.
11. Brush the blanched pretzels with the beaten egg and sprinkle on sea salt.
12. Bake in the oven until golden, approximately 12 to 15 minutes. Keep in a warm place till serving.
13. In a small bowl, whisk together the mustards, honey, mayonnaise, turmeric, and chipotle powder. Serve on the side with your pretzels.

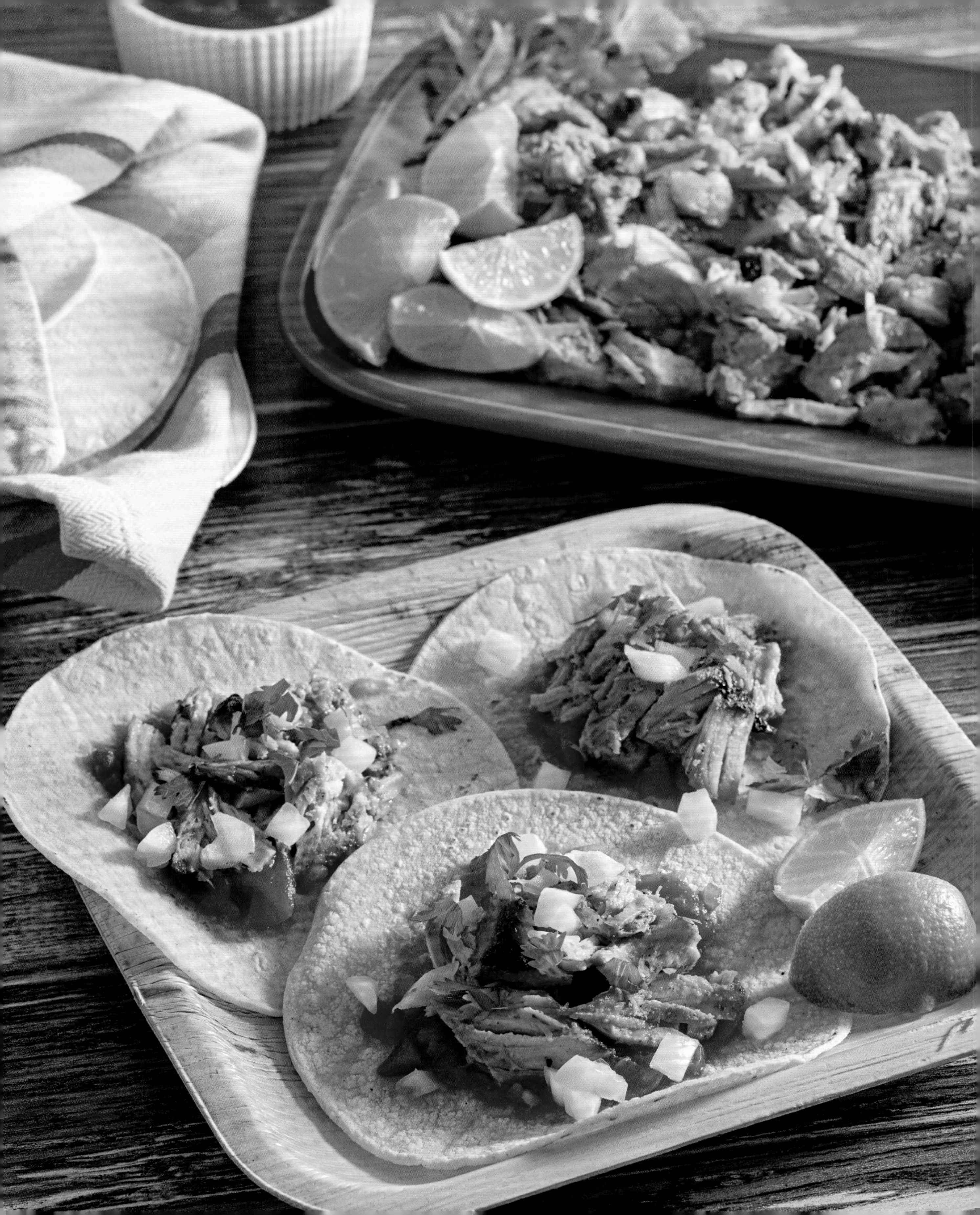

CARNITAS TACOS

YIELD:
6 TO 8 SERVINGS

PREP TIME:
3½ HOURS

I teamed up with another one of my protégées, Araña, to take down a super social influencer by the name of Screwball. It's like her mission was to raise her subscriber count while driving down the neighborhood's property value. Screwball was on a tear through Sunset Park, with her "Random Acts of Awesomeness" almost reducing the neighborhood to rubble. Araña did most of the heavy lifting on the takedown, and the community came out in droves to celebrate one of their own scoring the win and bringing peace to the neighborhood. They also saw yours truly awkwardly hanging along the sidelines. But I'm not one to take away from another hero's moment. They asked, and by that I mean they *insisted*, that we come back for a celebration of our victory. The spread was fabulous, and it came with this killer taco dish.

5 pounds pork shoulder

2 tablespoons kosher salt

1 tablespoon cracked pepper

2 large sweet onions, diced to make about 2 cups

4 cloves garlic, smashed

1 tablespoon ground cumin

1 tablespoon chile powder

1 dried guajillo chile

1 cup pineapple juice

1 cup orange juice

1 quart water

Twenty-four 5-inch corn or flour tortillas

1 bunch cilantro, stemmed

4 limes, cut in wedges

OPTIONAL:

1 jar salsa

1. Preheat oven to 350°F.

2. Cut pork into 2-inch chunks and season with salt and pepper. Place in an oiled pan and sear at high heat, turning until nicely brown on all sides.

3. Combine 1 cup diced onion with garlic, cumin, chili powder, guajillo chile, pineapple juice, orange juice, and water in a mixing bowl. Place everything in a roasting pan, including the seared pork, and cover tightly with plastic wrap and then aluminum foil. Place in the oven.

4. Braise in the oven about 2½ hours, until the meat is fork-tender.

5. Remove the foil and plastic wrap, then set the pork on broil in the oven to caramelize, for approximately 15 to 20 minutes.

6. Warm the tortillas in a nonstick pan one by one, 20 seconds per side, until pliable, and place them on a plate covered with a towel.

7. Serve the meat with warm tortillas and top with fresh picked cilantro, the remaining cup of diced onion, and lime wedges. Add your preferred salsa, if you like.

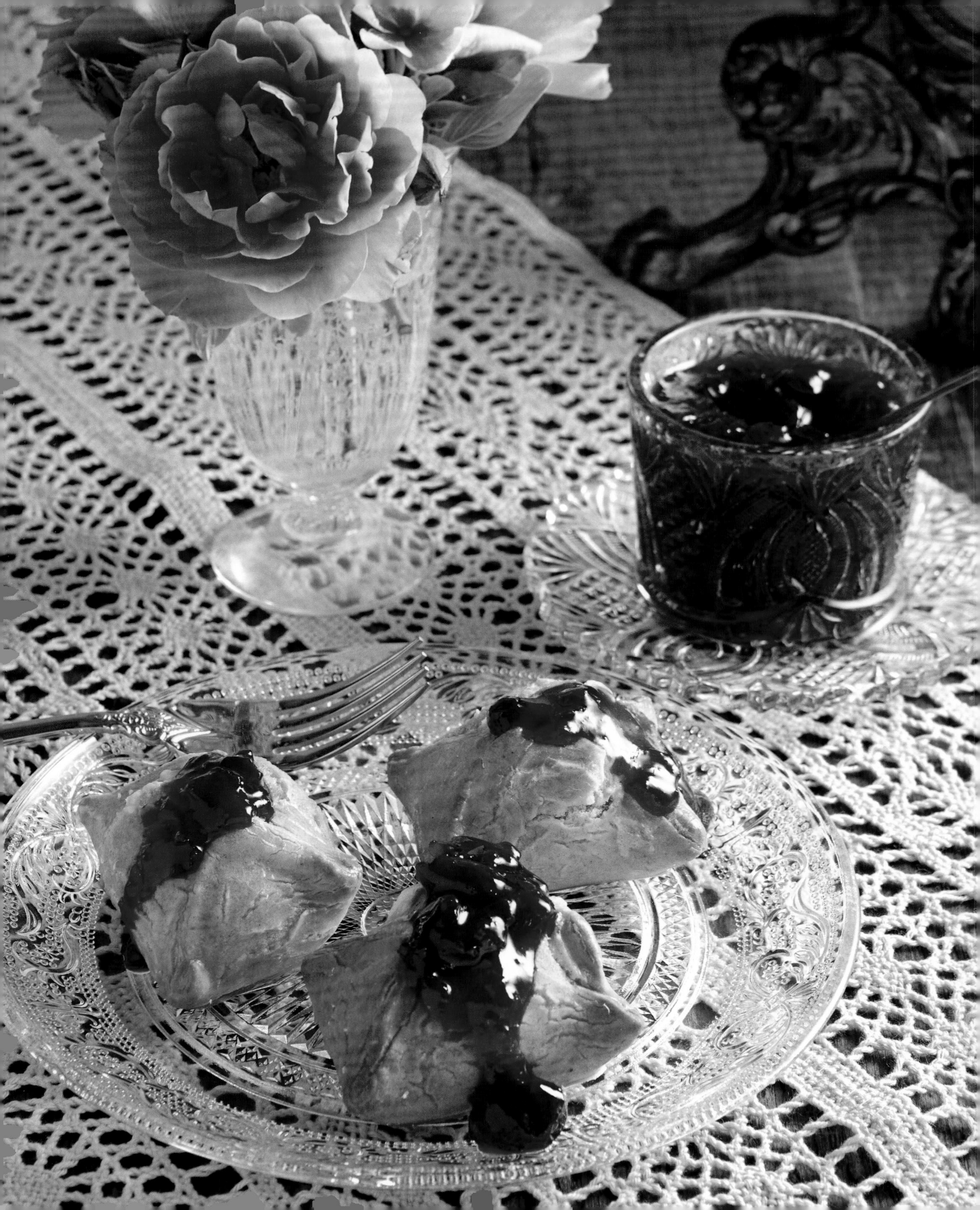

CHEESE KNISHES

YIELD:
20 KNISHES
PREP TIME:
OVERNIGHT, PLUS 2 HOURS

Being a New York–based hero, it's not all laser battles and high-speed chases through Midtown. Sometimes it's as simple and perfect as finding a good perch to take it all in. A good one is at the south end of Borough Park while the sun goes down. From my vantage point, it's the best view in the world. And sometimes that moment of sky-high Zen is complemented by a kind older woman offering you a plate of freshly made potato treats from her windowsill. I really was hanging outside the sixth-story window of Edith's Brooklyn brownstone. I think it says a lot that she offered the strange masked man some food instead of throwing a shoe at me, or a book, or a lamp or a—well, you get the idea. That's the thing about New Yorkers, they're always ready to lend a helping hand. Even if they rarely have a word of small talk to spare. Now that we've gotten to know each other, Edith talks about her kids, her grandkids, and her husband, Jude. I tell her about my day. Now I swing by whenever I can, not just for the food, but for the conversation. She gave me this recipe with her blessing, but on the condition that I stop leaving footprints on her sill. Fair deal.

FOR THE DOUGH:

2 cups all-purpose flour, plus more for dusting

1 teaspoon salt

1 teaspoon baking powder

3 eggs

3 tablespoons canola oil

FOR THE FILLING:

2 cups cottage cheese

½ cup cream cheese

½ cup sugar

1 vanilla bean, scraped

1 lemon, zested

1 egg yolk

2 tablespoons water

TO PLATE:

One 8-ounce jar cherry jam

1. The night before, set a strainer in a bowl and drain the cottage cheese in it. Keep everything in the fridge overnight.

2. To make the dough, combine flour, salt, and baking powder in a mixer.

3. In a separate bowl, whisk eggs and canola oil together, then stream into the flour mix.

4. Remove everything from the mixer and kneed on a flour-covered surface for 5 to 8 minutes, until smooth and elastic. Depending on the moisture, you may need to add flour as you go. Cover with plastic wrap and let rest for 30 minutes in the fridge.

5. Preheat your oven to 375°F.

6. Combine the strained cottage cheese, cream cheese, sugar, scraped vanilla bean seeds, and lemon zest in a clean bowl in the mixer. Set aside.

7. Remove the dough from the fridge and cut it in half. Leaving one half covered in plastic so it doesn't dry out, roll out the other half on a flour-covered surface to about 1/16 of an inch. Cut this into 3-inch squares, and dust them all with flour. Then do the same with the other half of your dough. When finished, set aside covered. The squares will shrink a bit, but you should be able to stretch them back out when you fill them.

8. Taking the first dough square, add one tablespoon of filling to the center and bring the corners of the square up and form a pouch. Seal it shut, wetting your fingers under water if necessary, and place it on a parchment-lined baking tray. Repeat until all the squares are filled and sealed.

9. In a separate bowl, combine the egg yolk with 2 tablespoons of water. Brush this mix onto each knish and then bake them until golden, about 15 to 20 minutes.

10. Serve them warm with a side of cherry jam.

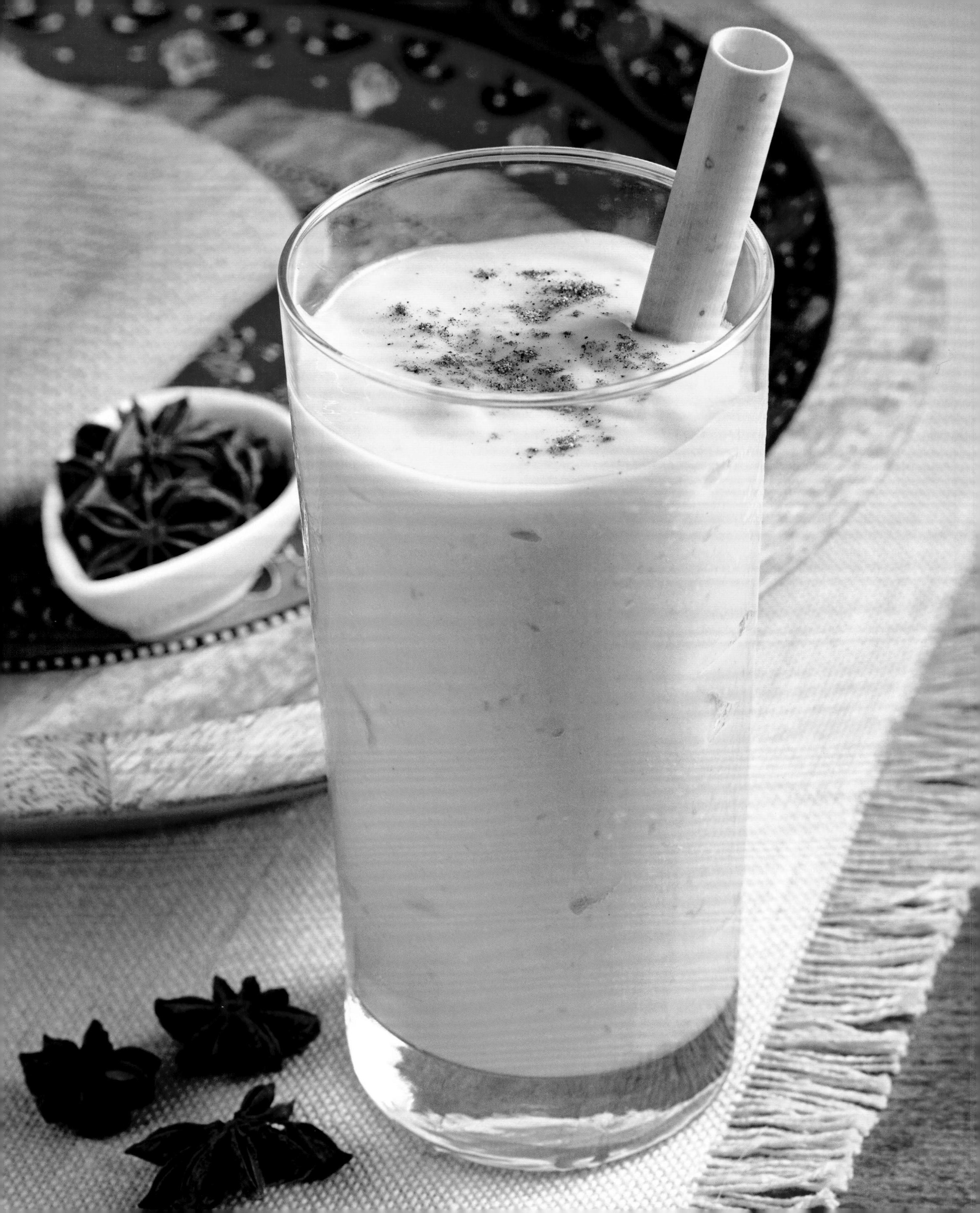

And now, a word from another Multiversal visitor to our shores:

GF | V+
YIELD: 2 GLASSES
PREP TIME: 10 MINUTES

MANGO LASSI

Like a lot of you, I thought I was the only Spider-Man until recently. It was intimidating enough to be responsible for protecting all of Mumbai back on my Earth. And then I was introduced to the multiverse and suddenly "responsibility" was a word with infinite weight. At the same time, it's been nice to find my niche among a group of us who protect the, well, Earths, plural. And I enjoy my time in your version. Especially hanging out with the Spider-Man for your Brooklyn. As a way of saying thanks for his friendship, I introduced him to one of my favorite drinks. While I will not say it's better than the version I get at home, this sweet and sour mix is a winner for me in any dimension. And your Brooklyn Spider-Man seemed to agree with me, so I figured I'd send it in for this book.

1½ cups frozen ripe mango
1 cup coconut yogurt
½ cup coconut milk
2 tablespoons agave
Ice
2 pinches ground cardamom
2 pinches ground star anise

1. Combine mango, yogurt, milk, and agave in a blender. Blend on until smooth. Depending on the mango, you may need to add ice to spin to a consistency you like.
2. Pour into a glass and add a pinch of cardamom and star anise to the top.

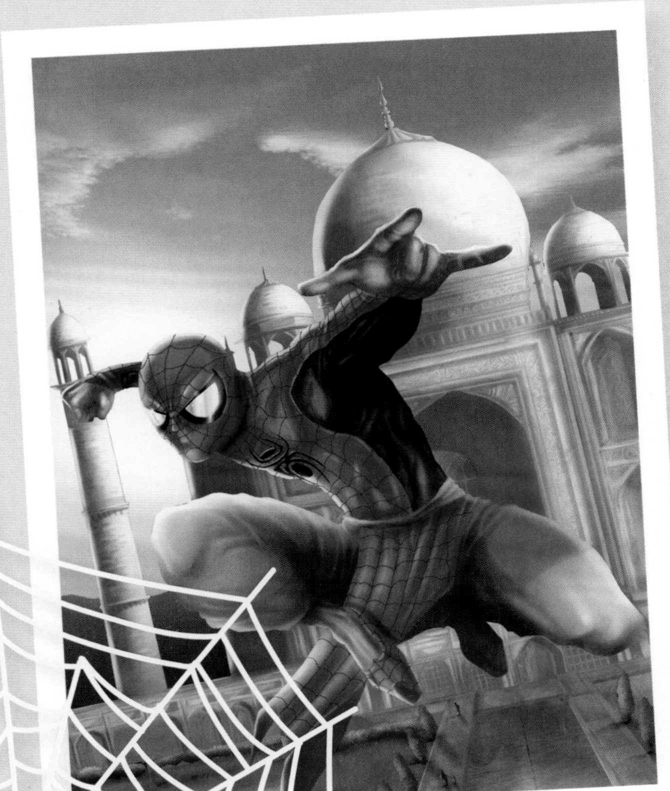

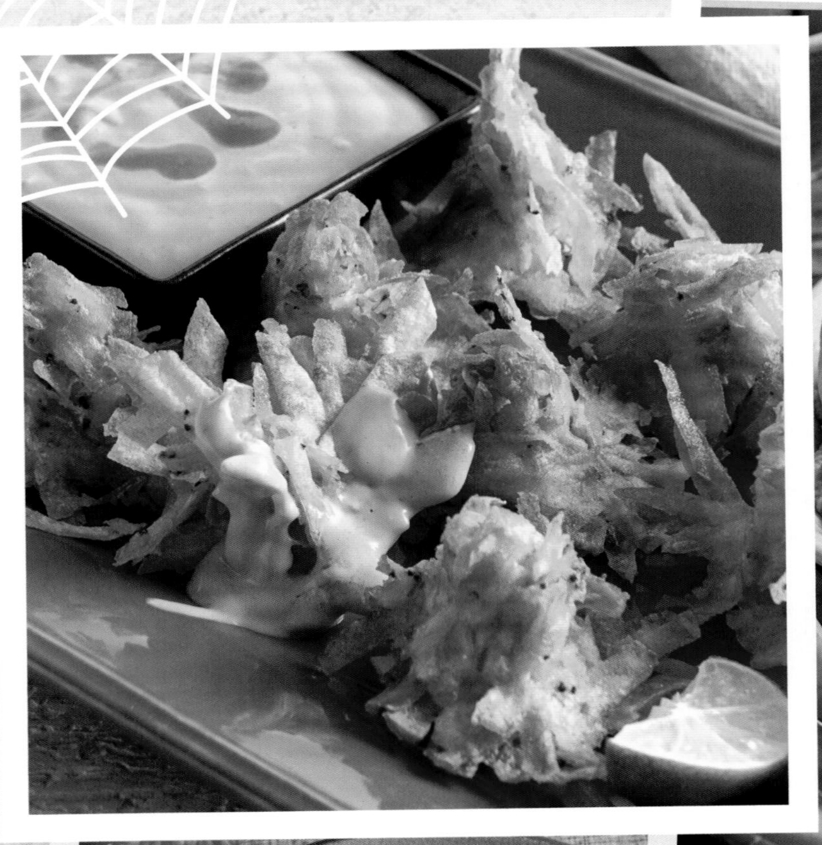
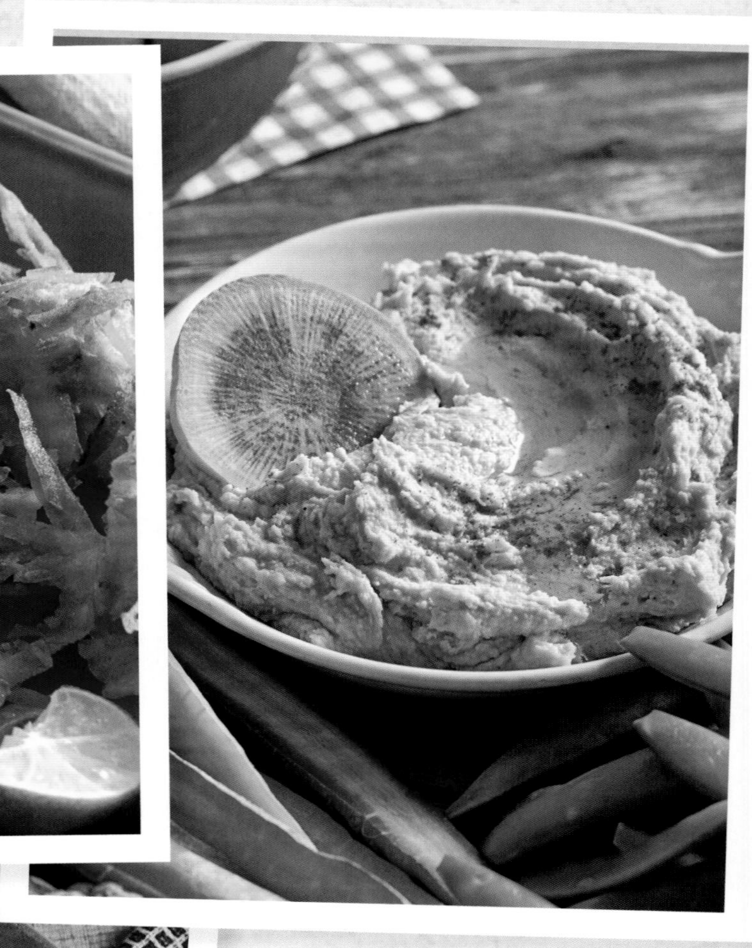
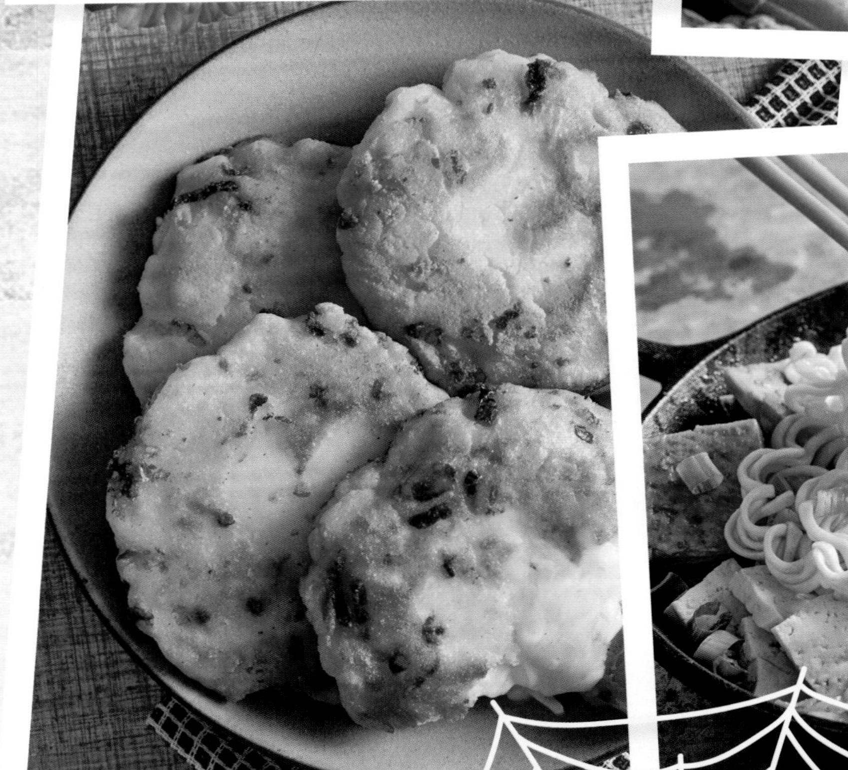
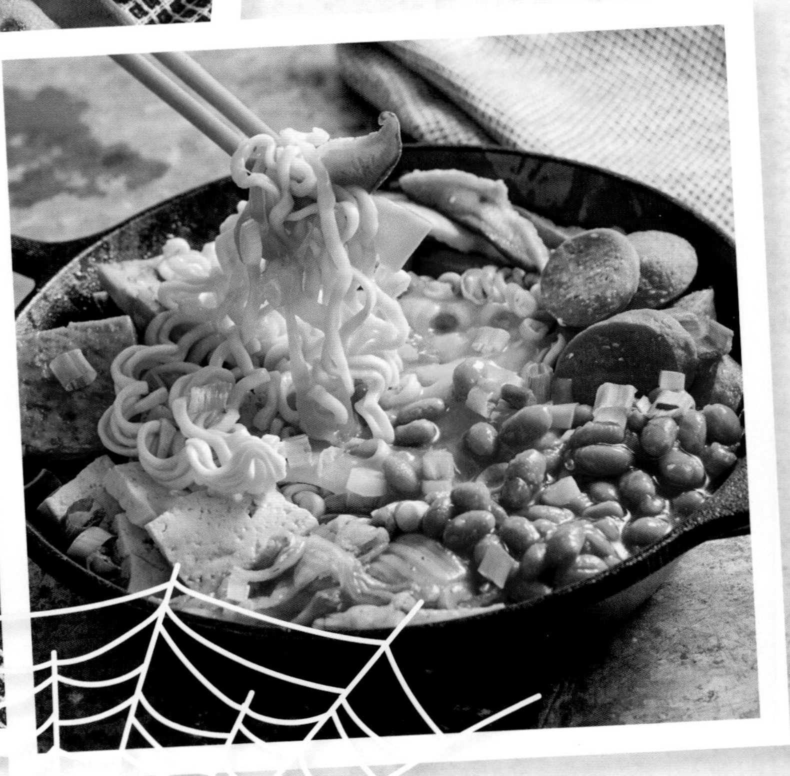

POSTSCRIPT:

Spidey here again, sporting the biggest smile I can muster about how this all came together. (You'll have to take my word for it. Under this mask, smiling from ear to ear.) Especially since by the time you finally get this thing in hand, you'll already have attended the potluck community event we held at F.E.A.S.T. headquarters. I'm a crafty spider when I must be. Though, as you well know, most of the credit for putting the event together goes to May Parker. Yeah, Peter's aunt is a dynamo in her own right and was critical in getting us all together for what turned out to be a day I won't soon forget. We put this book together to celebrate the town we've all come to love and protect. It's my hope that this picture of the day will encourage you to, oh, I dunno, get a little more involved with your community. Or at least bring in your own recipe for the next potluck at [REDACTED]. See ya soon!

DIETARY CONSIDERATIONS

KEY: GF - GLUTEN FREE, V - VEGETARIAN, V+ - VEGAN

CHAPTER 1

QUEENS

Aunt May's Wheatcakes | **V**

Chicken Larb | **GF**

Kraving Veggie Dumplings | **V+**

Jamaican Beef Patty

Italian Hero

Jerk Chicken | **GF**

Falafel | **GF/V+**

Black-and-White Cookies | **V**

Hot and Sour Soup | **V**

Bánh Mì

Cheese Arepas | **GF/V**

Pastrami Sandwich

CHAPTER 2

THE BRONX

Chopped Cheese Sandwich

Pernil Asado | **GF**

Savory Red Lentils | **GF/V+**

Cannoli | **V**

Peruvian Roast Chicken | **GF**

Smoked Salmon Bagel Sando

Prosciutto Mozzarella Sandwich

Multidimensional Eggplant Parmesan | **V**

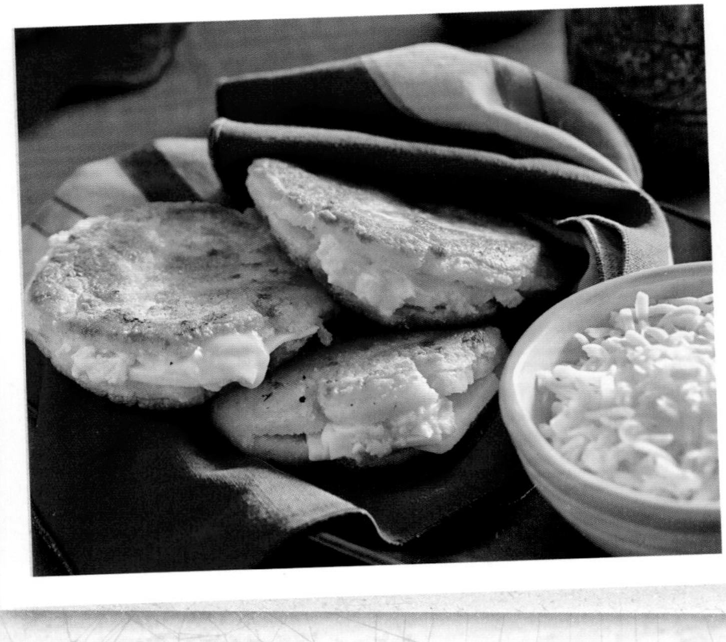

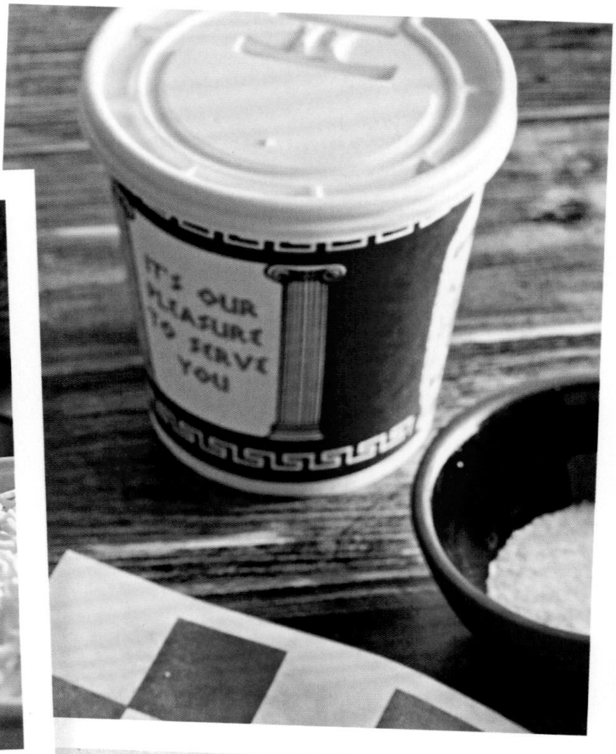
IT'S OUR PLEASURE TO SERVE YOU

CHAPTER 3

MANHATTAN

Vegan Pho | **V+**

Bubble Tea | **GF/V**

Miso Ramen | **V+**

Caesar Salad

Sweet Potato Katsu | **V**

Manhattan Clam Chowder | **GF**

Kebabs | **GF**

Oyakodon

Chai Latte | **GF/V+**

Yakisoba

Dirty Water Dogs

Eggs Benedict | **GF/V**

Chicken Over Rice | **GF**

Spidey's Tasty Tsukune

Army Stew

Korean Fried Chicken

Bulgogi

Sweet and Salty Peanuts | **GF/V+**

Egg Cream | **GF**

Fried Chicken and Waffles

BBQ Salmon and Collards | **GF**

Yule Log | **V**

Ceviche Tigers Milk | **GF**

CHAPTER 4

STATEN ISLAND

Tiramisu | **GF/V**

Chicken Cutlet Torta

Italian Chopped Salad | **V**

Green Juice | **GF/V+**

Below-the-Radar Burger

Fried Eggs with Potato-Pastrami Hash

Seasonal Market Veggies and Hummus | **GF/V+**

New York Bacon, Egg, and Cheese

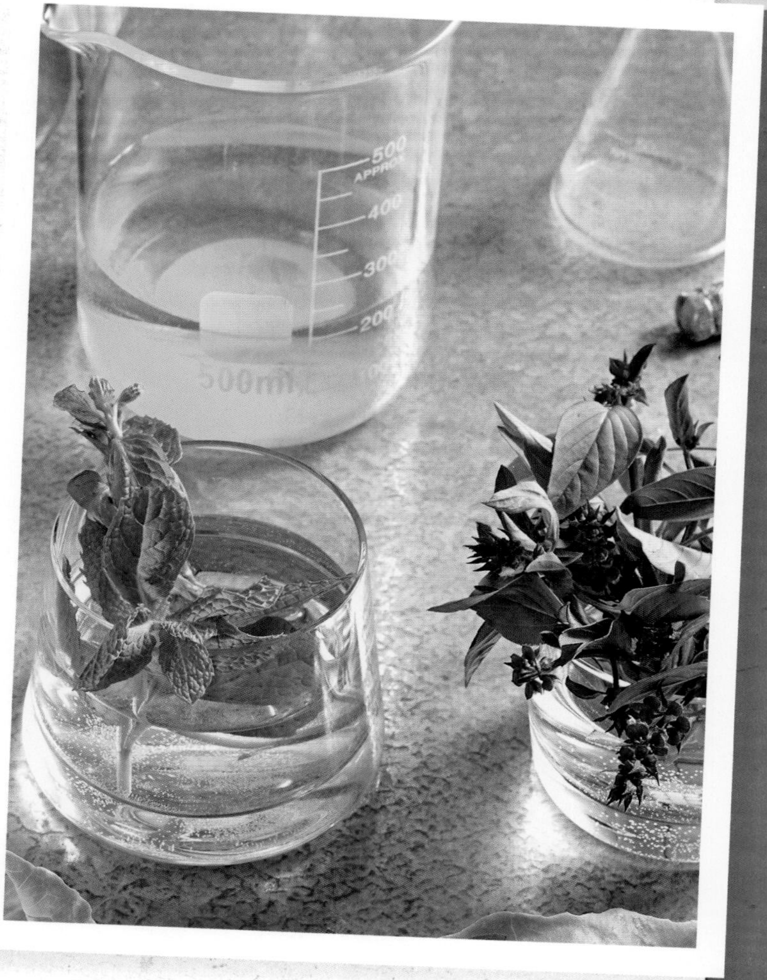

CHAPTER 5

BROOKLYN

Grandma Slice | **V**

Lamb Shawarma

Canned Meat Fried Rice

Arañitas | **GF/V+**

Pierogis | **V**

Ricotta Cheesecake | **V**

Biergarten Soft Pretzels and Spicy Honey Mustard | **V**

Carnitas Tacos

Cheese Knishes | **V**

Scallion Pancakes | **V+**

Mango Lassi | **GF/V+**

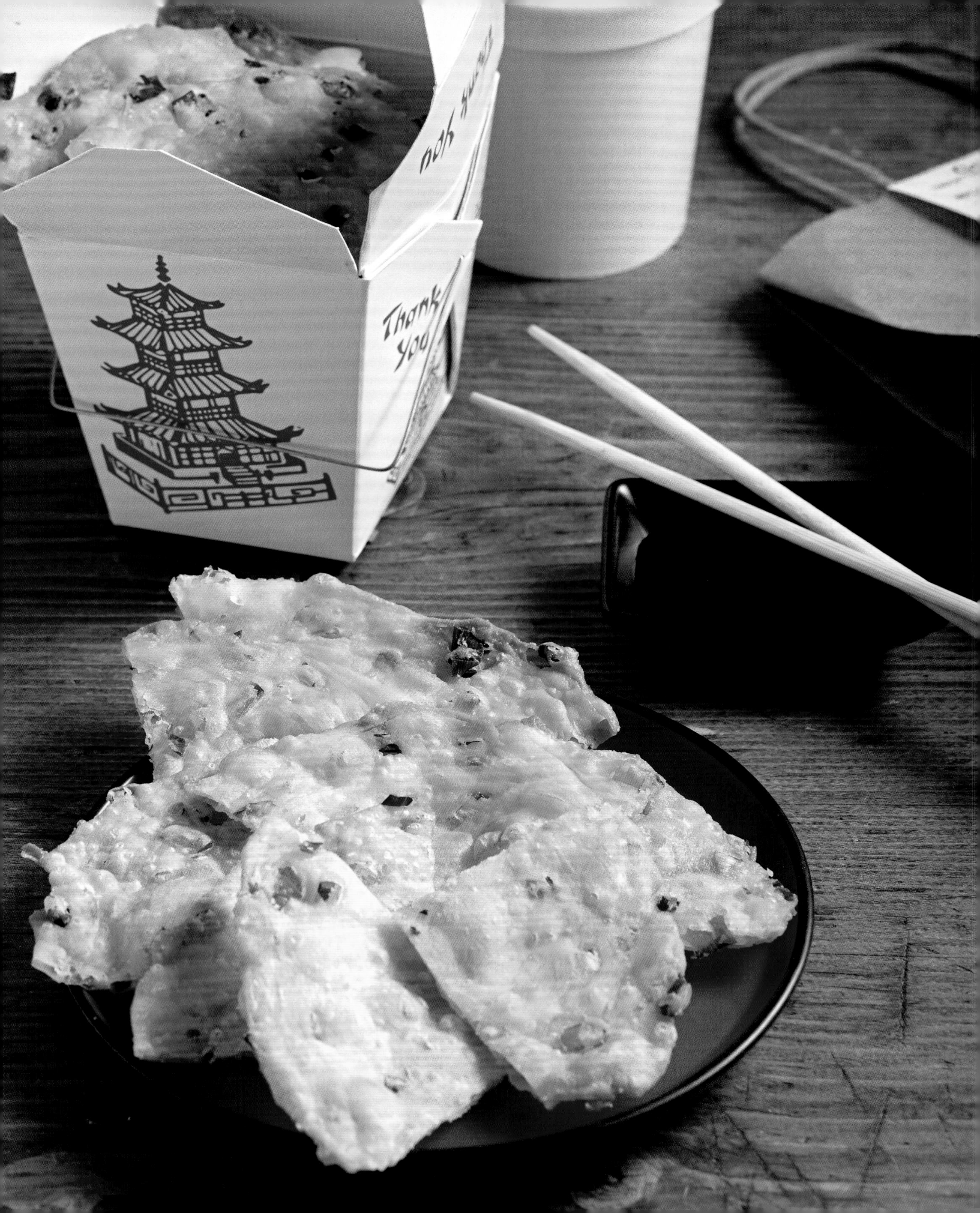
Thank You

MEASUREMENT CONVERSIONS

VOLUME

US	METRIC
½ teaspooon (tsp)	1 ml
1 teaspooon (tsp)	5 ml
1 tablespoon (tbsp)	15 ml
1 fluid ounce (fl. oz)	30 ml
⅕ cup	50 ml
¼ cup	60 ml
⅔ cup	80 ml
3.4 fluid ounces (fl. oz)	100 ml
½ cup	120 ml
⅔ cup	160 ml
¾ cup	180 ml
1 cup	240 ml
1 pint (2 cups)	480 ml
1 quart (4 cups)	.95 liter

TEMPURATURES

Farenheit	Celsius
200°	93.3°
212°	100°
250°	120°
275°	135°
300°	150°
325°	163°
350°	177°
400°	205°
425°	218°
450°	232°
475°	246°

WEIGHT

US	METRIC
0.5 ounce (oz.)	14 grams (g)
1 pound (lb.)	28 grams (g)
¼ pound (lb.)	113 grams (g)
⅓ pound (lb.)	151 grams (g)
½ pound (lb.)	227 grams (g)
1 pound (lb.)	454 grams (g)

GLOSSARY

BÁNH PHO: Vietnamese rice noodles

BLANCH: This is a process of quickly parboiling food and then stopping the cooking process, most commonly used for preparing vegetables or fruits. Water is brought to a boil, the food is added and cooked for a short time, with the exact length depending on the recipe specifics. Then, to stop the food from cooking too much, it is removed from the boiling water and plunged into an ice bath to cool. It is then drained and used in the recipe.

CRIMP: To seal together the edges of two pieces of pastry dough by pressing the dough with the tines of a kitchen fork, the side of a knife, or a pastry crimper. Crimping is a good way to seal together securely the uncooked crusts of a double-crust pie, which may then be fluted if desired.

CHIFFONADE: This French term means "little ribbons." It is the method of taking leaves, such as basil, and stacking them together, rolling them up, and then thinly slicing them to create thin ribbons of garnish.

DEGLAZE: Deglazing is the process of adding liquid—for example, a stock, to a hot pan to release all the caramelized food from the pan. These caramelized bits, called fond, are full of flavor and should not be left behind. Deglazing is often the first step in making a sauce.

EMULSIFY: Combining two liquids that wouldn't naturally dissolve together—for example, oil and vinegar. One way to do this is to slowly add one ingredient to the other while whisking rapidly with a fork.

FRY STATION AND SAFETY: If you're making something that requires deep frying, here are some important tips to prevent you from setting your house (and yourself) on fire:

- If you don't have a dedicated deep fryer, use a Dutch oven or a high-walled sauté pan.

- Never have too much oil in the pan! You don't want hot oil spilling out as soon as you put the food in.

- Use only a suitable cooking oil, like canola, peanut, or vegetable oil.

- Always keep track of the oil temperature with a thermometer. 350° to 375°F should do the trick.

- Never put too much food in the pan at the same time!

- Never put wet food in the pan. It will splatter and may cause burns.

- Always have a lid nearby to cover the pan in case it starts to spill over or catch fire. A properly rated fire extinguisher is also great to have on hand in case of emergencies.

- Never leave the pan unattended and never let children near the pan.

- Never, ever put your face, hand, or any other body part in the hot oil.

JULIENNE: Refers to cutting food, usually vegetables, into long, thin strips, which in turn are called a "julienne." Typically, a julienne is about ⅛-inch wide.

MASAREPA: Precooked cornmeal

MARINATE: This refers to the process of soaking food, often meat or vegetables, in a seasoned liquid before you plan to cook it. Often, the marinade will contain something acidic like vinegar, which can give your food additional flavor and help tenderize meat.

MINCE: A technique for chopping in which you rock the blade of a knife over your ingredient until it is chopped into small, even pieces (finely chopped), or into pieces as fine as possible (minced).

RENDER: A cooking technique where melted fat from diced meat is turned into crisp bits used for garnish. For example, a home chef would render bacon.

RESERVE: This means to temporarily set something aside for use later in the cooking process.

SAUTÉ: Taken from the French verb meaning "to jump," this is the process of cooking quickly in a small amount of fat. Your pan should be preheated with the fat before adding foods so that they sear quickly. There should be plenty of room in the pan so that the food doesn't get crowded and can simmer in its own juices.

SPATCHCOCK: To remove the backbone of poultry, open it up completely, and lay it flat. This process is also referred to as "butteryflying."

STEMMED: To remove the stem from the ingredient, typically a fruit or herb, before cooking.

ZEST: Can be both a noun and a verb. It describes the colorful peel of citrus fruits, as well as the process of scraping a microplane grater across fruit peel as part of your seasoning.

ABOUT THE AUTHORS

JERMAINE MCLAUGHLIN is a London (UK)-born, Brooklyn-based writer, comic historian, and collector of entirely too many action figures. He's a twenty-year veteran of the comic book industry from his time at DC Comics, whose work has been featured on the sites Syfy Wire and The Beat. His work is also featured prominently in the Marvel Comics Library series from Taschen, specifically the collections for *The Avengers*, *The Amazing Spider-Man*, and *The Fantastic Four*.

Jermaine had a blast giving voice to Peter and friends for this book. There's an eight-year-old version of him that still can't believe he got a chance to quip for his favorite wall-crawler.

PAUL ESCHBACH is a Michelin star chef with 25 years of professional culinary experience. He spent almost 10 years living in NYC as a young cook and chef. He's lived in China, Japan, and the West Coast. Currently, he resides on the North Fork of Long Island with his daughter and wife, and dog Kona.

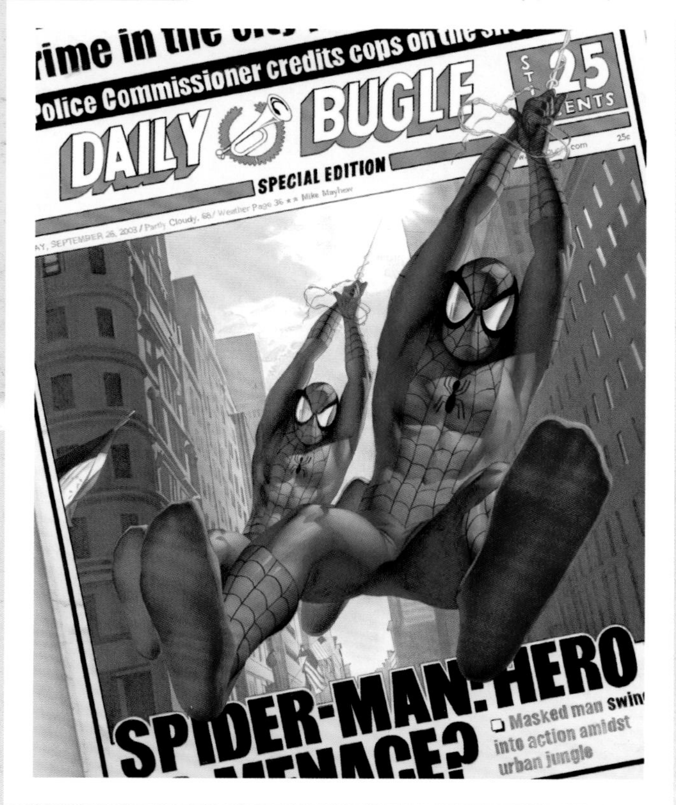
DAILY BUGLE
SPECIAL EDITION
25
into action amidst
urban jungle

VON DIAZ is an Emmy Award-winning documentarian, food historian, and author of *Coconuts & Collards: Recipes and Stories from Puerto Rico to the Deep South* and *Islas: A Celebration of Tropical Cooking*. Her work has been featured in the *New York Times*, *The Washington Post*, NPR, StoryCorps, *Food & Wine Magazine*, and *Bon Appétit*, among many others.

ACKNOWLEDGMENTS

To Sissy, you are amazing, you are my rock. Thank you for always being there.

To Kenton, you're my Miles. Keep taking that leap of faith.

And to Orlando, wish you were here to see this, you would have loved it. Miss you, my friend.

JERMAINE MCLAUGHLIN

To Ella, can't wait to explore this universe with you. IT'S AMAZING.

To Caroline, one more crazy thing to look back on with you. Still lovin' the ride.

To CB, BRO! THANK YOU!

PAUL ESCHBACH

Special thanks to my grandmother, Tata, who taught me everything I know about plantains, and to my favorite taste-testers, Elc and Nina Estrera.

VON DIAZ

NOTES FOR THE NEXT POTLUCK

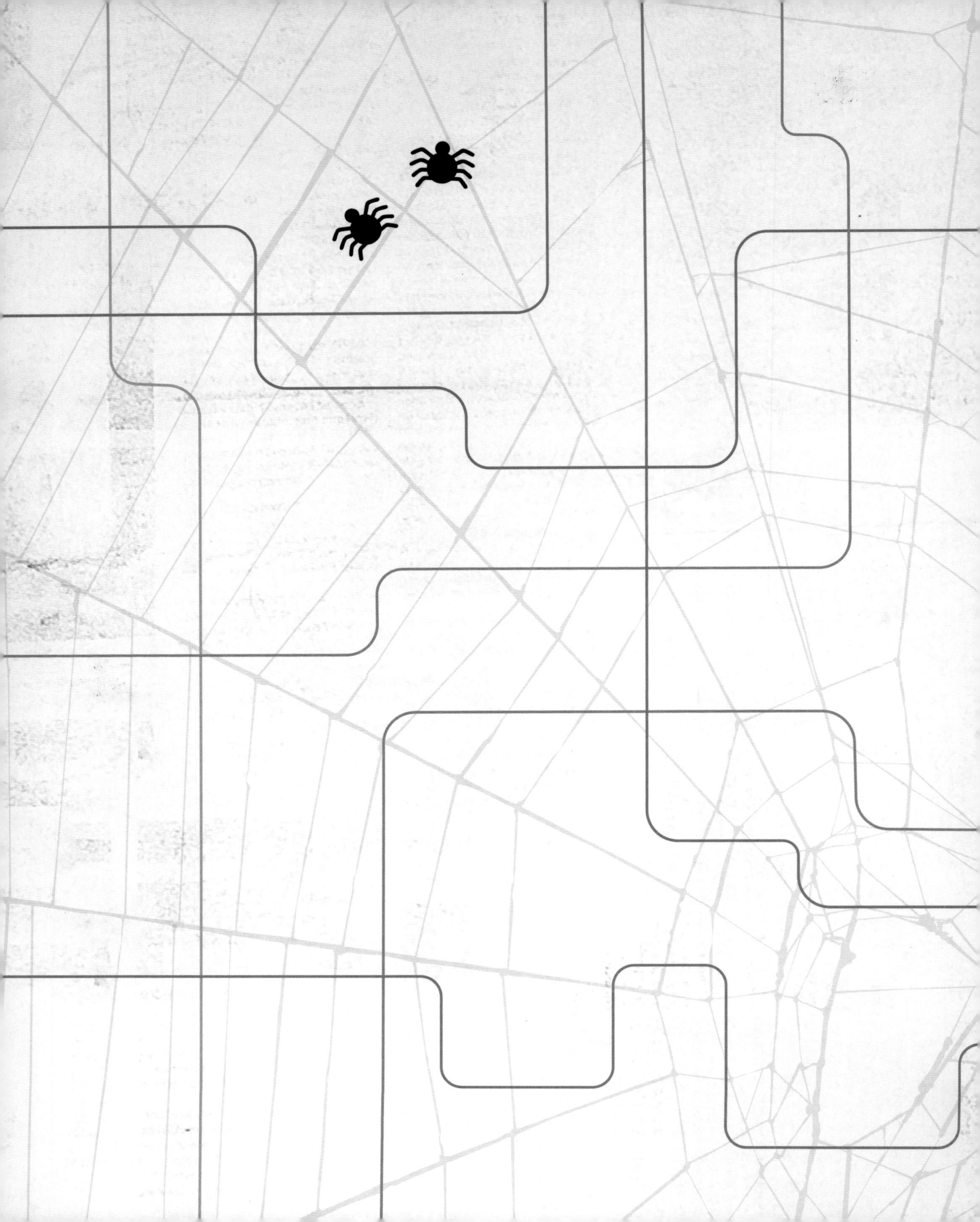